The Home-Based Strategy Dollars

Discover 9+ Profitable Business with Low Investment and Big Rewards. Learn how to Start, Scale Up and Sell Them in a Click

By

Marcus Wayne

monetary loss due to the information herein, either directly or indirectly.

Respective authors own all copyrights not held by the publisher.

The information herein is offered for informational purposes solely and is universal as such. The presentation of the information is without a contract or any guarantee assurance. The trademarks used are without any consent, and the publication of the trademark is without permission or backing by the trademark owner. All trademarks and brands within this book are for clarifying purposes only and are owned by the owners themselves, not affiliated with this document.

Table of Contents

The 9+1 Best Home-Based Business Model of 2021

Private Label Crash Course

Youtube, Tik-Tok and Instagram Made Easy

Short Stays Real Estate with No (or Low) Money Down

The Cryptocurrency Investing | Advanced Guide

Bookkeeping and QuickBooks Made Easy

The 9+1 Best Home-Based Business Model of 2021

Find Out how Millennials Have Built Millionaire Businesses from Home with Soap and Candle Making, Natural Cosmetics and much more

By

Marcus Wayne

Table of Contents

Introduction

Karsanbhai Patel (Patel), the chemist at Mines and Geology Department of the Gujarat Government, produced synthetic powder of detergent phosphate-free in 1969 and began selling this locally. He priced the new yellow powder at 3.50rs per kg. It was at one time when Rs 15 was being charged for Hindustan Lever Limited (HLL) Surf. Soon, in Kishnapur (Gujarat), Patel's hometown, there was a big demand for Nirma. In 10x12 feet space in his home, he began preparing the formula. He had named powder after his daughter's name-Nirupama. On the way to the office by bicycle, about 15 kilometers away, Patel was able to sell around 15-20 packets a day. Thus, the new journey began. Hindustan Lever Limited (HLL) responded in a manner characteristic of many global corporations in the early 1970s, when washing powder Nirma was launched into the market of low-income. "That isn't our business," senior executives said of the new offering. "We don't have to be worried." However very soon, Hindustan Lever Limited (HLL) was persuaded by Nirma's performance in the detergent sector that this wanted to take a closer gaze at the less income market. Low-cost detergents & toilet soaps are almost synonymous with the brand name. Nirma, on the other hand, found that it would've to launch goods targeted at the higher end of the market to maintain the middle-class buyers as they moved up the market. For the luxury market, the firm introduced bathroom soaps. Analysts, on the other hand, claimed Nirma wouldn't be capable of duplicate its performance in the premium market. In the year 2000, the Nirma had a 15 percent share of the toilet soap market and a 30% share of the detergent market. Nirma's revenue for the year ended in March 2000 grew by 17 percent over the previous fiscal year, to 17.17rs. bn, backed by volume development and commissioning of backward integration projects. By 1985, in many areas of the world, washing powder Nirmabecame one of the most common detergent brands. Nirma was a global consumer company by 1999, with a wide variety of soaps, detergents, & personal care items. Nirmahas brought in the latest technologies for the manufacturing facilities in six locations across India, in line with its ideology of delivering premium goods at the best possible costs. The success of Nirma in the intensely competitive market for soaps & detergents was due to its efforts to support the brand, which had been complemented by the sales scope & market penetration. The network of Nirmaspread across the country, with over two million outlets of retail and 400 distributors. Nirma was able to reach out to even the smallest villages due to its vast network. Nirma spread to the markets overseas in 1999 after establishing itself in India. Viaa joint venture called Commerces Overseas Limited, it made its first foray into Bangladesh. Within a year, the company had risen to the top of Bangladesh's detergent market. Other areas such as Middle East, Russia, China, Africa &additional Asian countries were also intended for the entry of the organization. Nirma became a 17 billion Rs company in 3 decades, beginning as a single-product single-man article of clothing in 1969. Under the umbrella name Nirma, the company had several production plants and a large product range. The mission of the organization to have "Better Product, Better Values and Better Living" added much to its growth. Nirma was able to outshine Hindustan Levers Limited (thenHLL) and carve out a niche for oneself in the lower-ends of detergent &market toilet soap. HLL's Surf was the first to be used as a detergent powder in India in 1959. But by the 1970s, merely by making the product available at a reasonable price, Nirma led the demand for detergent powder. Nirma launched its Nirma Beauty soaps to the Indian toilet soap industry in 1990. Nirma had gained a 15% share of 530,000 tons per annum toilet soap industry by 1999, making it India's second-largest producer. Although it was way behind HLL's 65 percent share, the success of Nirma was impressive compared to Godrej, which had an 8 percent share. By 1999-2000, Nirma had already acquired a 38 percent share of India's detergent market of 2.4 million tonnes. For the same period, HLL's market share was 31%. In this book, we will study and analyze the case of Nirma and its rise to the top detergent companies of India. Besides, we will also give profitable ideas and options for starting a lucrative detergent soap,candle making, and natural cosmetics business.

CHAPTER 1: The Nirma Washing Powder's Success Story

The success story of the famous Nirma washing powder began in a small Gujarati farmer's house. We'll tell you about a billionaire father who lost his daughter in a car crash and later discovered a way to get her back to life. When she was alive, only a few people knew of her daughter, but it was the sheer persistence and willpower of this man that made his daughter famous in the world, even though she was no more. This is the story of a man who was born into a poor farming family and turned his daughter's nickname into India's leading detergent, soda ash, and education brand. A man of valor and passion who showed that nothing will hinder you if you have the willpower. Here is the story of **"Sabki Pasand Nirma, Washing Powder Nirma."**

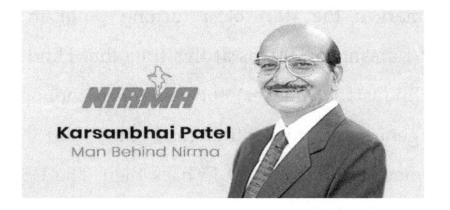

1.1 Invention ofNirma detergent?

Karsanbhai was born in Ruppur, Gujarat, to a farmer's family in 1945. He had earned a bachelor's degree in chemistry by the age of 21. He attempted to do a normal job like his colleagues at first. He served as a lab technician for the Lalbhai Group's New Cotton Mills, which is credited with launching the Indian jeans movement. He also took up a position at the Geology and Mining Department of the Gujarat government after this short stint. The year 1969 marked the start of a turning point in the career trajectory of Karsanbhai. It was at this time that Hindustan Lever Ltd (now Hindustan Unilever) formed a full monopoly on the Indian detergent market under the brand name "Surf." A Surf Pack was sold somewhere from Rs 10-15 back then. The USP was that, unlike normal washing soap bars, it eliminated stains from your clothes and didn't irritate your skin. However, for middle-class families, which had no other choice than to return to the old bar soap, this price point was not affordable. The tycoon in Karsanbhai noticed the issue and devised a plan. A young Karsanbhai will come home from work and dedicate all his time and energy to making a phosphate-free detergent in his yard. He wanted to bear in mind that he needed to produce a detergent with a low manufacturing cost so that everybody could afford it. Karsanbhaiutilized a recipe for a yellow-colored detergent powder that could be marketed for a mere Rs 3 after several trials and failures. He chose to name the invention after Nirupama, his daughter. He finally got the formula right one day, and as an after-work business, he began making detergents in his 100-square-foot backyard. He will cycle around the neighborhoods, selling door-to-door homemade detergent packages. Patel set the price of his detergent at Rs. 3, almost a third less than Hindustan Unilever's well-known brand "Surf." The product's high quality and low price made it a success, and it was well-received by many who saw great benefit in purchasing it. Because of the business's high promise, Karsanbhai quit his government job three years later to pursue it full-time. Karsanbhai was so fond of the commodity that he called it Nirma, after his daughter Nirupama's nickname. To make sure that everybody remembers her, he used her picture (the girl in the white frock) on the pack and in TV advertisements. Such was a father's love for his daughter. While Karsanbhai Patel himself was not an MBA graduate, the techniques he adopted to expand his company left marketers bewildered and amazed. 'Nirma' was not only a game-changer but also a trendsetter for several small companies. Here are a couple of 'Washing Powder Nirma's' management lessons.

1.2 Karsanbhai Patel's sale policy for Nirma detergent

Karsanbhai Patel agreed to start marketing it once the product had a strong formula. On his cycle, he used to go door-to-door and neighborhood-to-neighborhood every day for three years, pitching the detergent. As it was a brand new product, if they found the product poor, he gave his consumers a money-back guarantee. Nirma has been the cheapest detergent in Ahmedabad at the time. As a result, Karsanbhai's product was an immediate hit. He left his government job three years later and set up a store in Ahmedabad to carry out this full-time enterprise. In some areas of Gujarat, his brand was doing very well, but there was a need to expand its scope. At the time, the standard was to offer the product to retailers on credit. This was a huge gamble because if the product didn't sell, Karsanbhai would have had to close down the company. At that time, he chose to try something different. He planned to spend a little money on advertising. These commercials, with their catchy jingles, were directed at housewives. And this bet paid off well. Nirma became a famous household brand and it had to be purchased by people. He did, however, remove 90% of the stock from the market at this time. Potential buyers had asked for the detergent at their local retailers for about a full month but would have to return empty-handed. During this time, retail store owners flocked to Karsanbhai, demanding that the detergent supply be increased. After another month, he eventually decided. Nirma was able to take over the sales and even beat Surf at their own game due to this approach. It went on to become the country's highest-selling detergent. It remained India's largest-selling detergent even after a decade,

1.3 Invest In Research and Development

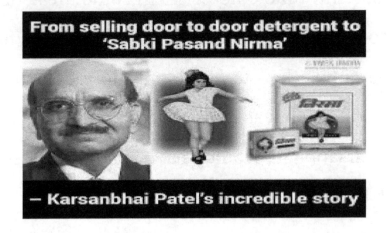

Karsanbhai Patel had little means and was not a man born with a silver spoon in his mouth. Karsanbhai loved experimenting with chemicals after completing a B.Sc. in Chemistry at the age of 21 and then working as a laboratory technician. He noticed that only MNCs in India were selling detergents and there was no economy brand detergent for the country. His excitement about bridging the distance grew, sensing a massive opening, and Karsanbhai began experimenting with chemicals. He quickly succeeded in manufacturing a detergent of high quality at a much cheaper price, which was an immediate success in the industry. Every good product needs a substantial expenditure in time, resources, and commitment in research and development.

1.4 No Higher Costs

Nirma had rewritten the rules of the game within a short time, by delivering high-quality goods at an unprecedentedly low price. Nirma's success was due to its cost-cutting policy. Patel had concentrated from the very beginning on delivering high-value goods at the lowest price possible. The corporation sought to keep improving efficiency while reducing prices. Nirma sought out captive processing plants for raw materials to keep production costs to a minimum. This led to the backward integration initiative, as part of which, at Baroda and Bhavnagar, which became operational in 2000, two state-of-the-art plants were established. This also led to a reduction in raw-material prices. Ahead of time and at a much smaller cost than anticipated, the two new plants were completed. The Baroda plant's second phase was finished 6 months ahead of schedule and at a cost of Rs.2.5 billion compared to the initial projected cost of Rs. 2.8 billion. Compared to the initial projected cost of Rs. 10.36 billion, the Bhavnagar plant was finished in a record period of 2 years at a cost of Rs.9.86 billion. This plant had a workforce of just 500 employees. ConcerningNirma's plant, Tata Chemical's plant, which had around twice the amount, employed ten times the number of workers. Almost 65000 tpa of N-Paraffin was produced by the Baroda plant for Linear Alkyl Benzene (LAB) and Synthetic detergents. Similarly, almost 4.20,000 tpa of soda ash could be produced by the Bhavnagar facility. Akzo Nobel Engineering in Holland produced the Akzo Dry Lime technology used in this factory. The plant had 108 kilometers of salt bunds, which would assist in the potential development of vacuum iodized salt. Patel said, "We have a processing potential of three lakh tons of pure salt. No one in the world had a related plant, but Tata Salt." Nirma had reduced its distribution costs by obviating the need for middlemen. The item went to the dealer straight from the manufacturer. Hiren K Patel (Hiren), CMD, explained to Nirma Customer Care Ltd., "An order is placed and the truck immediately leaves. It's similar to a bank account. We're sending stock, they're sending money." In states like Tamil Nadu, Andhra Pradesh, and southern Karnataka, the company-maintained depots, as it was often difficult to bring stocks to these regions. Stocks were shipped directly from the plants in states like Madhya Pradesh and Uttar Pradesh. In March 2000, Nirma opted for in-house packaging andprinting by obtaining Kisan Factories at Moriya, near Ahmedabad, in a further cost-cutting exercise. Nirma hoped that this would increase the packaging's quality.

1.5 Be Proactive in your approach as it is beneficial for the business

Karsanbhai Patel was the only person who started this business and starting selling Nirma. He was educated and had a government career, but he was never afraid of selling door-to-door detergent. He was diligent in doing something and knew that the company was tiny and bootstrapping, so he had to consider everything and anything about his business that could be fruitful. There is no such thing as a small or large undertaking. And if you are the CEO, you should embrace the obligations that are valuable to the company without guilt.

1.6 Provide Customers with 'Value for Money'

Customers noticed the advantages of purchasing Nirma, and it became an immediate success. They considered the standard to be at par with the giant Surf brand, but to take advantage of the same perks, they just had to pay one-third of the amount. Customers would only appreciate the product if you show them the advantages and give them decent value for their money.

1.7 Define Your Segment

Karsanbhai Patel identified the target segment for his detergent almost as soon as he found the magical formula. He realized that a luxury brand sold in tier 1 cities was the alternative Surf brand, so he concentrated on marketing his brand in tier 2-3 cities. He priced his detergent low and made it a mass brand to get more consumer traction. People from the lower middle class and middle class quickly adopted the product, and it quickly rose in popularity. Where most firms adopted the conventional top-down strategy, i.e., spreading from metro towns to rural cities, Nirma did the reverse and changed the whole game. It is really important to evaluate the competitors for every company and define the most lucrative segment.

1.8 Focus on Building a Brand

It was failing to find vendors outside the city in the early 80s, although the commodity was approved on a small scale in Ahmedabad. Since clients were unaware of its presence, retailers were wary of keeping the detergent in their stores. It resulted in overdue payments, return on inventory, and large business losses. Karsanbhai Patel came up with a good publicity approach to handle the situation and launched a TV advertisement campaign. The popular "Washing powder Nirma, detergent tikiyaNirma" jingle became an anthem for the company and customers began to equate Nirma as a strong brand. The demand for Nirma soon peaked, and with his products, Patel flooded the retail stores. A good brand decreases a buyer's potential risk and increases the company's bargaining power.

1.9 Astutely Manage the Brand Wars

Nirma also had innovative marketing campaigns. Nirma successfully spread the name to other product segments in the mid-nineties, such as premium detergents (Nirma Mega Detergent Cake and Washing Powder), premium toilet soaps, and (Nirma Sandal, NimaPremium, Nirma Lime Fresh). In both the economy and luxury markets, it maintained its initial pricing andmarketing plans. In 2000, with Nirma Beauty Shampoo, NirmaShikakai, and Toothpaste, the firm entered the hair care market. Soaps, unlike detergents, were a private-care commodity. Many consumers had strong emotional attachments with their soap products. Furthermore, HLL segmented the market by price, fragrance appeal, and brand personality. So, against Lifebuoy, Nirma put Nirma Wash, Nirma Beauty Soap against Lux, Nima Rose against

Breeze7, and Nima Lime against Jai Lime. Explaining how Nirma hoped to win this match, playing by the rules of HLL, Hiren said"Worldwide, there are only four or five channels that account for most of the soaps sold: floral, fashion, fitness, freshness." With the relevant scents, Nirma manufactured high-fatty-matter soaps and priced them much lower than other brands. As a result, the 'sub-premium' section was born. The game of controlling the geographical variety of market desires was also perfected by Nirma. The North, for instance, favored pink soaps, and green ones were favored by the South. In the South, sandal soaps were more common. Initially, the company's promotional budget, relative to other FMCG firms, was very poor. In contrast to the usual 6-10 percent, Nirma spent just 1.25-2 percent of its sales on ads. The firm used starlets such as Sangeeta Bijlani, SonaliBendre, and Riya Sen, who were comparatively unknown at the time, to endorse soaps. The promotional messages were both transparent and centered on the product's benefits. Nirma still chose to first put the item on the shelf, get reviews, and then create a lasting ad campaign. Nirma used its tried-and-true tool, price, to introduce toilet soaps and detergents in the premium market. In these divisions, the company intended to rely on quantities as well. However, the margins granted to retailers had shifted. Unlike economic goods, where the cost advantages were passed on to customers, this advantage was passed on to retailers by Nirma. It provided them with massive profit margins. For instance, it offered 52 percent for Nirma premium soap and an incredible margin of 140 percent for Nirma shampoo. In the luxury segment of the soap industry, observers were pessimistic about Nirma's chances of success.

Unlike detergents, the demand for soaps and shampoos was incredibly fragmented. There were only 15-20 brands, and it was hard to get a considerable market share for any soap. This market was also less price sensitive. So, it was hard for any enterprise to support itself on price alone. Analysts thought that shifting the brand value of Nirma would take years. According to a survey conducted by Nirma's marketing agency, Samsika Marketing Consultancy, Nirma was viewed as a low-cost brand. Many people were almost afraid to say they used it. Nirma published corporate advertisements worth Rs 10 bn in India in the late nineties to shed this image. Analysts claim that the fast-growing shampoo market is a safer investment than luxury soaps. Just 30% of the population in India used shampoo, with more than 70% of this group living in urban areas. However, according to some researchers, while the rural market's presumed potential was very high, it was difficult to convince rural folk to use shampoos in actual practice. A further concern faced by Nirma was that of insufficient facilities. While it had a good presence in the smaller towns and villages, it lacked the requisite network for urban centers to penetrate. As a result, Nirma's foray into high-end soaps and shampoos proved to be a flop.

1.10 Diversify the Portfolio

For low-income groups, Nirma began with a low-cost detergent, but later introduced products for higher-income groups, such as Nirma Sandal soap, Nirma Beauty soap, etc.

Not just that, but in 2003, Karsanbhai Patel formed Nirma University to diversify the company's brand portfolio. The brand is currently exploring its options in the cement industry to grow its market. Diversifying the portfolio decreases the company's potential risk of loss while still allowing it to serve a broader variety of consumers.

1.11 Conclusion

While Nirma was best known as a manufacturer of goods for the low-cost economy, it was popular in the middle and upmarket segments. Yet rivalry was also growing at the same time. Although HLL continued to be a major threat, offensive initiatives were also introduced by P&G and Henkel SPIC. In the detergent and washing powder market, participants from the unorganized field were also introduced to the rivalry. Patel was confident of tackling the rivalry, though. "He added, "We keep the price line and the happy customer returns to us normally. Based on its growth strategy, the company has risen in demand and volume in the last three decades: "A buyer is not looking for one-time frills or feel-good variables. The landlord, on the other hand, is searching for a long-term solution to his or her issues." Karsanbhai Patel, who began with a vision of making his daughter famous through his brand and ended up being one of the greatest entrepreneurs of all time, exemplifies the relevance of this quotation. He began with an aim of creating his daughter famous through his brand and ended up becoming one of the greatest entrepreneurs of all time. His name not only gained tremendous respect but also became a trendsetter for many new firms. The brand has taught young entrepreneurs many useful lessons and has proven to be a valuable resource for the region. Karsanbhai Patel has shown that no goal is too lofty if you have the ambition and zeal to achieve it.

1.12 What Karsanbhai Patel and Nirma detergent did for the Indian Economy

Nirma's meteoric growth in prominence culminated in the introduction of a new economic market for detergent powder. It was of good quality and was inexpensive. Plus, contrary to the others, the fact that it was manufactured without phosphates made it the most environmentally-friendly detergent. In comparison, a labor-consuming process was the process of producing the detergent. And thus, Nirma went on to hire more than 14,000 workers and became the country's leading employer.

1.13 Karsanbhai Patel's ventures other than the Nirma detergent

Karsanbhai wanted to grow his FMCG business after Nirma dominated the detergent industry. Nirma launched its line of toilet soaps, beauty soaps, and even shampoos in the premium market. While the latter venture failed, one of their products, edible salt Shudh, is still available and doing well. Overall, Nirma has a 20 percent market share in soap cakes and a 35 percent market share in detergents. That isn't it, however. In 1995, Karsanbhai Patel founded the Nirma Institute of Technology in Ahmedabad. Later, it became one of Gujarat's most prestigious engineering schools. After that, the whole structure was merged under the Nirma University of Science and Technology, which is supervised by the Nirma Education and Research Foundation, and in 2003, the entire structure was unified under the Nirma University of Science and Technology. This is overseen by the Nirma Education and Research Foundation. Since 2004, Karsanbhai's CSR initiative,

Nirmalabs education, has aimed to train and incubate entrepreneurs. Karsanbhai Patel has now turned over the reins of his profitable company to his two sons. Pratibha Patil, the then-President of India, bestowed the Padma Shri on him in 2010. Nirma is now the world's biggest manufacturer of soda ash, and the company has been privately owned since 2012. Karsanbhai Patel invested his huge fortune on a six-seat chopper in 2013, which cost Rs 40 crore. After Gautam Adani (Adani Group) and Pankaj Patel (Zydus Group), he became the third Ahmedabad-based industrialist to purchase a helicopter. Nirma, on the other hand, is still one of India's most popular detergents. And the jingles will live on forever.

CHAPTER 2: Start a Profitable Soap Making Business

As a soap manufacturer, you'll create your recipes for soaps and probably other personal cleaning and beauty products. Ecommerce, farmers markets, arts events, wholesale positioning in spas and boutiques, and even door-to-door sales are all options for selling the goods. You'll test several solutions and see if you can find a steady stream of clients. Learn how to launch a soap-making company of your own.

Steps for starting a soap making business

You've uncovered the ideal market opportunity and are now prepared to take the next step. There's more to launching a company than simply filing papers with the government. We've put together a list of steps to help you get started with your soap-making business. These measures will ensure that the new company is well-planned, legally compliant, and properly registered.

Plan your business

As an entrepreneur, you must have a well-thought-out strategy. It will assist you in figuring out the additional data of your organization and uncovering any unknowns. Given below are some key points to consider:

What are the startup and recurring costs?

Who is the targeted audience?

What is the maximum price you will charge from the customers?

What would you name your company?

What are the costs involved in opening a soap-making business?

You've got a good start if you have a kitchen or workspace as well as a few simple kitchen utensils. Making soap isn't an expensive business to undertake, but you would need to invest in some basic equipment. Ingredients cost at least $200. Lye and fats or oils are used to make soap. That's a good start, but it'll be your special formula that sets you apart. For superior feel, fragrance, and lather, you can use coconut oil, olive oil, almond oil, and several fragrance oils, extracts, and natural additives. To keep materials costs down and simplify production, you could start with only one or two simple recipes. Equipment for producing soap will cost around $300. Your equipment specifications will be determined by the type of soap-making you do. Hot process, cold process, rebatching, and melt and pour are the four basic forms of processing, and each needs different equipment. But, regardless of the route you take, you'll almost definitely need soap molds, packing, and shipping items. You can get your basic ingredients, additives, equipment, and supplies from several online retailers. Marketing software will cost up to $750. A professional-looking website with enticing product images is key to the company's growth. Since your online consumers can't touch or smell your goods, they must be able to judge the good quality of what they see. That means recruiting a graphic designer and web developer to help you make the best out of your logo and online presence is a smart investment. To express your love and dedication to product quality, your visual imagery will be carried through in your labeling and branding. Skilled services will cost up to $200. Is it legal in your state and society for you to run this sort of business from home? Before you put up your shingle, meet with a lawyer for a quick consultation. The Handcrafted Soap & Cosmetics Guild charges a membership fee of $100 per year (HSCG). Small-batch soap makers will benefit from this organization's preparation, funding, and useful networking opportunities. Insurance for general liability and product liability would cost $265-$375 a year. This is also accessible via the HSCG.

What are the ongoing expenses for a soap-making business?

The consumable commodity materials you'll need for ongoing development would be your greatest ongoing expense. Your increasing variable expenses would be more than offset by a rise in revenue if you've priced your offering correctly.

Who is the target market?

While women make up the majority of the demand for homemade soaps, some firms have had success selling male-oriented soap scents. You may approach consumers who admire your product's consistency and luxury, or those who only purchase organic or vegan goods. Customers will note the difference in quality among your soaps and those sold on the shelves of a traditional supermarket.

How does a soap-making business make money?

In the majority of the cases, all of your revenueshall be derived from the products you make or sell.

How much can you charge customers?

Your goods could be sold for $5 or $6 a bar. This is more than your consumers are likely to spend for mass-produced retail soaps, but your product has a high perceived value. Other price points can be met by providing discounts on multiple orders, marketing multi-bar bundles, and extending the product range. Look at local rivals' websites to see what they're costing and how that would impact the pricing. Will you charge more to suggest a higher-end product range, or will you charge less to compensate for the lower per-unit sales margin with higher volume?

How much profit can a soap-making business make?

There are a few well-known soap makers who began their careers in the same way you did. Take, for example, Burt's Bees. Others in your business run it as a side venture, something between a crafts hobby and a modestly profitable business. You will go as far as your dedication, imagination, promotional skills, and hard work can take you, as with many home-based companies.

How can you make your business more profitable?

Many soap makers diversify their product range to include more exotic soaps (goat's milk soap is one example) or complementary goods. Making candles is a natural progression for soap makers who still use a hot process. Others are involved in home fragrances, lip balms, hair care, and even pet products. Focus on what else will cater to the consumer base when speaking about expanding your product mix. Many companies aim to maximize their net income by lowering the cost of goods produced. Growing the earnings by issuing bigger batches at a time is a cost-effective technique.

2.1 What will you name your business?

Choosing the correct name is vital and daunting. If you own a sole proprietorship, you should start using a separate company name from your own. We suggest reviewing the following references before filing a company name:

The state's business records

Federal and state trademark records

Social media sites

Web domain availability

It's important to have your domain name registered before anyone else does.

2.2 Form a legal entity

The sole proprietorship, partnership, limited liability company (LLC), and corporation are the most traditional corporate structures. If your soap manufacturing company is used, creating a legitimate business entity such as an LLC or corporation prevents you from being found legally accountable.

Register for taxes

Before you can start doing business, you'll need to apply for several state and federal taxes. You would need to apply for an EIN to pay for taxation. It's very basic and free.

2.3 Small Business Taxes

Depending on which business arrangement you select, you can have various taxation choices for your corporation. There could be state-specific taxes that apply to your business. In the state sales tax guides, you can read more about state sales taxes and franchise taxes.

2.4 Open a business bank account & credit card

Personal wealth security necessitates the use of dedicated company banking and credit accounts. If your personal and corporate accounts are combined, your personal properties (such as your house, vehicle, and other valuables) are put at risk if your company-issued. This is referred to as piercing the corporate veil in business law. Furthermore, learning how to create company credit will help you receive credit cards and other borrowings under your business's name (rather than your own), lower interest rates, and more credit lines, among other advantages.

2.5 Open a business bank account

This protects your assets from those of your business, which is essential for personal wealth security, as well as making accounting and tax reporting simpler.

2.6 Get a business credit card

It will help you achieve the following benefits:

It builds the company's credit background and will be beneficial for raising capital and profit later on.

It lets you differentiate personal and business expenditures by placing all of your business's costs under one account.

Set up business accounting

Understanding your business's financial results includes keeping track of your different costs and sources of revenue. Maintaining correct and comprehensive reports also makes annual tax filing even simpler.

2.7 Obtain necessary permits and licenses

Failure to obtain required permits and licenses will result in hefty fines or even the closure of your company. If you intend to market homemade soaps, you must first acquire a business license.

2.8 State & Local Business Licensing Requirements

Operating a handmade soap company can necessitate the procurement of some state permits and licenses. Furthermore, several states have varying laws governing the manufacturing of cosmetics and other body care goods. Visit the SBA's guide to state licenses and permits to read more about your state's licensing criteria.

2.9 Labor safety requirements

It is essential to comply with all Occupational Safety and Health Administration protocols.Pertinent requirements include:

Employee injury report

Safety signage

2.10 Certificate of Occupancy

A Certificate of Occupancy is normally required for businesses that operate out of a specific location (CO). All requirements concerning building codes, zoning rules, and local requirements have been followed, according to a CO.If you're thinking about renting a space, keep the following in mind:

Securing a CO is normally the landlord's duty.

Before signing a contract, make sure your landlord has or can get a legitimate CO for a soap-making operation.

A new CO is often needed after a significant renovation. If your company will be renovated before opening, add wording in your lease agreement that specifies that lease payments will not begin before a valid CO is issued.

If you intend to buy or build a place:

You would be responsible for securing a legal CO from a local government body.

Review all building codes and zoning standards for your soap-making business's place to ensure that you'll comply and eligible to get a CO.

2.11 Trademark & Copyright Protection

It is wise to protect your interests by applying for the required trademarks and copyrights if you are creating a new product, idea, brand, or design. The essence of legal standards in distance education is continually evolving, especially when it comes to copyright laws. This is a regularly revised database that can assist you with keeping on top of legal specifications.

2.12 Get business insurance

Insurance, including licenses and permits, are necessary for your company to run safely and legally. In the case of a covered loss, corporate insurance covers your company's financial well-being. There are several insurance schemes tailored for diverse types of companies with various risks. If you're not sure what kinds of risks your company might face, start with General Liability Insurance. This is the most popular form of coverage required by small companies, so it's a good place to start.

2.13 Learn more about General Liability Insurance

Workers' Compensation Insurance is another essential insurance scheme that many companies need. When your company hires staff, your state may mandate you to carry the Workers' Benefits Package.

2.14 Define your brand

Your company's brand is what it stands for, as well as how the general public perceives it. A good name would set the company apart from the market.

How to promote & market a soap making business

Look for areas where you can stand out. Try having a larger-than-usual bar of soap or one that is formulated to last longer. Perhaps you should market a six-pack of sampler soaps in smaller sizes so that your customers can check out your whole product range and pick their preferences. Consider an uncommon fragrance or texture additive for applying to your soaps to make them stand out. When you've found a winning design, publicize it on your website and social media. Also, if you're showing your soaps at an exhibition, bring some unwrapped samples of your entire product line so consumers can touch them, see what they're made of, feel their textures, and experience the various scents.

How to keep customers coming back

bear in mind that you're offering an aesthetic experience. Make sure your logo, labels and packages, and the name of your product line all cater to consumers looking for a low-cost luxury experience. One benefit is that the more your consumers like your stuff, the faster they can consume it and require more. Ensure that you retain contact with your clients and that they are aware of how to contact you. Request email addresses from all of your clients to obtain their approval to send out a monthly e-newsletter or catalog. It's important not to bother someone with so many promotional newsletters, but a monthly newsletter will keep consumers updated on all of the new items you have to sell. You might want to add a toll-free phone number for orders as your company expands.

Establish your web presence

Customers can learn more about your business and the goods or services you deliver by visiting your website. One of the most successful ways to build your web presence is through press releases and social media.

2.15 Soap Making Plan

If you live in the jungle and love your body odor, you would not need soap. It is a regular need and one of the common goods. As a result, soap has a huge demand. There are various varieties of soaps available due to the wide range of skin types. Soaps are manufactured in a multitude of ways to suit the needs of all. One of the most promising FMCGs is soap production. Perhaps this is why so many people are drawn to this sector year after year. Every day, in a country like India, there is a massive demand for soap. However, there are only a few competitors in the business. We have a few ideas for you if you want to launch your own soap company. Let's get this started.

Tips for soap making using the cold process method

Soap making is easy at the most fundamental level. The cold process approach is the most common way to produce soap. It's "cold" because the ingredients aren't heated before being combined. Using the "hot process" technique, you can make soap with heat. We will use the cold process. Soap is made by mixing fats and oils with a lye and water solution in the most basic form. Soap is made from a combination of water, lye, fats, and oils. The fun starts as you change the components and quantities of the various materials. But, to keep things simple, note that soap is essentially a solution of fats and oils, lye, and water. It's as plain as that.

Is making soap without lye possible?

Is it possible to produce soap without lye? Not at all. Soap bases that can be heated and poured into molds can be purchased. You didn't have to use lye to make the base as everyone else did. However, you have no idea what's in those bases. Sodium hydroxide is the lye used to produce bar soap. Soft soaps are made of potassium hydroxide. Leaching lye from wood ashes is an easy way to create it. This form of lye results in a smoother soap.Unless you have access to a chemical supply house, lye is typically difficult to come by locally. It is, however, simple to put an order. Lye is highly caustic, and it can sear the skin and strip color from whatever surface it comes into contact with. If it gets into your eyes, it will blind you. This is a toxic drug and can never be used in a place where children may reach it. Adults, on the other hand, would have no trouble with the lye if they take simple precautions. When dealing with lye, please wear safety goggles. Long sleeves and protective gloves are also recommended. Leave lye or lye mixtures unattended at all times. Uncured soap should be used similarly to lye.

Fats and oils required for making the cold process soap

Another fundamental to producing soap can be found here. To turn oils and fats into soap, different quantities of lye are needed. Every fat that is likely to be used in soap making has a known amount of time it takes to turn oil or fat into soap. Simply look up the amount of lye needed to produce soap from a certain oil in a table. The volume of lye used in each recipe is then determined based on the oils used. Using a little less lye than is needed to transform all of the oils into soap. This is achieved as a precautionary step to ensure that all of the lye is absorbed during the process. The lye discount is the volume of lye used that is reduced. It's normal to use around 5% less lye than is needed to completely transform the oils into soap. Coconut, palm, and olive oils are the most common oils used in soap making. If you just use those three oils to make soap, you will make amazing results. Each of these oils has its collection of characteristics that make it useful as a soaping oil. You can produce a soap with only one of the oils, but the results won't be as strong as if you used all three. This is why. If you want a lot of bubbles in your soap, coconut oil is the way to go. It's the root of a slew of big, light bubbles. However, soap made entirely of coconut oil cleans so well that it extracts much of the oil from the skin, leaving it dry. This is why it can only account for about 30% of the soap oils. Palm oil is important for hard, long-lasting bars, but it isn't as clean or bubbly as coconut oil.

This fat is often referred to as "vegetable tallow," but it is similar to beef tallow in any way. If you don't want to eat meat fats, use them instead of beef fat. Then you should ask about olive oil. Just olive oil is used to produce castile soap conventionally. If you've ever used this form of soap, you know how good it is as a skin conditioner. It's amazing. However, if olive oil is the only oil used in the soap, the effect is tiny little bubbles and bars that fade away quicker than you'd like. As a result, this type of oil is only used to make up about 40% of the oils in a recipe. Granted, soap can be made from almost any form of fat or oil, and there are several alternatives.

Adding ingredients for premium luxury results

If you choose to use other oils, just apply a small amount during the final stages of the soap-making process. you'll find that you can use almond oil in your example recipe. Simply raise the amount of olive oil in the formula and leave out the almond oil. It was chosen because it brings a little more to the bar's feel and quality. Soap can be used for a lot more than just producing pure soap. All of the additives are what make soap production so exciting. Clays, natural oils, medicinal products, colors, patterns, and a slew of other alternatives are available as additives. The first step to perfect soap is to get the fundamentals correctly, which can be achieved fast and effectively. After learning the fundamentals of soap manufacturing, the soap manufacturer progresses to using a range of exotic ingredients.

How to make soap?

We'll go into the fundamentals of how the soap is made. Bear in mind that this is just the first step. Following that, you may need additional materials and a special recipe to distinguish the product from competitors.

Ingredients

Given below are the following ingredients that would be required for preparing soap:

Take 2/3 cup of coconut oil (that will create lather) and the same amount of olive oil. Moreover, 2/3 cup almond, safflower oil,or grape seed will also be needed.

Then you'll need a quarter cup of lye, which is sodium hydroxide in its purest form. Finally, you'll require 3/4 cup of cool water that is distilled or pure.

You'll also need oatmeal, aloe vera gel, cornmeal, clay, salt, and any other items you choose to use.

Instructions

Listed below are the step-by-step directions that you must follow in the preparation of soap:

Put on your gloves and pour lye and water into a canning jar. Allow them to sit for a few minutes after they've been stirred gently and the water has begun to clear.

Now pour in the oil from the pint jar. Then Stir well, then put the jar in a warm pan of the water that is bubbling (and/or you maymicrowave it, when you do, place temperature to one hundred and twenty degrees F).

Remove the lye after that is finished. Allow the lye to cool. Remove pint jar & allow your oil to cool as well. Both can achieve a temperature of 95 to 105 degrees Fahrenheit. If the temperature drops below 95 degrees F, the soap will begin to crumble.

Pour them into a mixing bowl until they've hit the ideal temperature and whisk until fully combined. After stirring for five minutes, mix it with an immersion blender.

Then, to make the soap special, apply herbs, essential oils, & any other things that go with it. They can be thoroughly combined so they appear coarse. Place them in molds & cover with a towel.

After a day check the soap and let it stay for an additional 12 to 24 hours if it's either warm or soft.

When the soaps are fully cured, wrap them in the paper wax & lock them in an airtight jar for a week. Since this soap contains oil on its own, we'll need an airtight jar. As a consequence, interaction with air will cause it to pick up debris and dust.

Soap making machine and price

 fiber covered mixing machine will cost you at least about US$ 1000. This price includes a fiber-covered mixing machine capable of producing 200 kilograms of detergent powder.

Where to get soap making machine?

Online, you can buy a soap-manufacturing machine. Soap manufacturing machines are available from several online retailers. These websites sell the requisite appliances, including the microwave, blender, wrapper, mold, and labeler, also the main device. A soap-making unit, for example, can be bought for the US

$ 5000. This item can be used to produce toilet soaps and detergent cakes. If you're searching for something less costly, say under the US $ 1500 apiece, you can easily find it on the market. It can be used to produce soap for bathing purposes. There are also other products of varying price points. However, the budget may start at one dollar an item. You'll get a good detergent maker for this amount.

Soap making raw material and price

The Soap-making ingredients may be bought for a very cheap price. It is much less costly if you buy them in bulk. If you may get the price correct upfront, the rest of the company will be a breeze later on. As a consequence, we prefer bulk raw materials. Alkali and fat are the two main raw materials used to produce soap. the raw material which is most commonly used in soap manufacture is sodium hydroxide. Potassium hydroxide, on the other hand, maybe used. The latter makes a soap that is more soluble in water. As a result, potassium hydroxide creates "warm soap." Locally, raw products are available at a reduced quality. You can discoverraw materials for manufacturing soaps online or in your neighborhood with a fast Google search. People typically buy this locally so it cuts the price even further. Rest assured that rates can differ depending on your needs. It depends solely on how much you're making & how much of the raw material you'll need. Caustic soda costs about US $ 150-250 permetric ton on the market. The price of 1000 grams of laundry soap ranges between US$1 and $1.25.

Soap making formulae

legitimate chemical formulae for the soap's $C_{17}H_{35}COONa$. Its chemical name is thus sodium stearate. However,it is important to note that it's for the common soapthat is used for personal purposes only. For the detergents, there arenormally long chains of carboxylic acid as well as sulfonate salts or ammonium salt.

2.16 Soap selling process

Let us now go through the packaging, distribution, marketing, and promotion processes.

Colorful wrappings

Choose a bright & eye-catching label that will guarantee that the product is noticed. To set it apart from the competition, style it & use the proper design.

Branding

Make the most of this opportunity to build your brand through packaging. Choose a design that you think best reflects your business.

Go simple

Today's entrepreneurs aim for simplicity. Examine the performance of POP displays as well. If they don't live up to your standards, it's time to make a change.

Soap marketing strategy

You can use the following strategies for marketing soap:

Email marketing

And the ones who also sign up for your offer are truly interested in the soaps, email marketing is the perfect way to market. It's also becoming highly customizable and cost-efficient these days.

Blogging

The next logical move is to start blogging. You'll need to hunt down some prominent bloggers who may help you spread the word about the business. You may even invite them to write a review on their blog about a sample of the product.

Social media

Due to availability of the social media, it is now easier to create a brand. Furthermore, guess what? It's the shortest and least expensive alternative. The secret is to make something go viral. this could be the merchandise, online presence, or your ads.

2.17 Soap making supplies

To make it function properly, you'll need some modernized tools equipment, as well as a lot of the space. You will need to find rental space to make the soap. Some of the typical things you'll need to get started include cyclone, mixing vessels, perfumers, blowers, reactors, furnaces, weighing scales, and blenders.

2.18 Marketing area for soap

The marketing region you select will be decided by the audience you're targeting. You would be able to segment your customers depending on age and demographic in social media marketing. Your marketing field can be decided by the type of soap you sell. If you're selling detergent cakes, for example, they're mainly aimed at homemakers of different ages. As a consequence, you will show the commercial depending on age & gender. Marketing is successful on a variety of measures. It simply depends upon whether you've online or a physical company. In any case, it's better to entrust this to a practitioner.

2.19 Total investment

The Investment isn't based on raw materials. Just As mentioned above, different raw materials are used for personal and detergent soaps. Therefore investment will be different for each category.

You must take into consideration the size and place of the business for starting the business. SoYou need minimum money of US $ 20,000to purchase the machinery along withprimary raw materials –if you decide to start with little.

Raw materials shall cost the US $ 2500 per month. Moreover, making unit rentalswouldcharge not less than the US $ 1000 per month. In addition to the above-mentioned costs, the salary of the plant manager is expected to be aroundthe US $ 500. Equipment shall cost around the US $ 10,000 or more.

In addition to the above prices, you need the US $ 500 for license & registration. Moreover, you will need another US $ 800 to cover the accidental coverage. the Marketing might cost you approximatelyUS $ 500 per month.

2.20 Selling price

Supply, materials, brand, packaging, and other factors impact soap pricing. When you're only starting, keep the rates comparable to those of your rivals.

Prices are determined by several factors. A lower-cost soap is generally assumed to be of lower quality. As a result, we won't keep prices very low about market prices.

Additionally, too high prices could decrease overall demand. As a consequence, we will arrive at the golden middle & retain it just marginally, so at all, below current levels.

2.21 Profit margin

Measure profit margins through factoring in your annual manufacturing expenses. You must also remember manpower, raw materials, utilities, and maintenance costs.

This business has a high-profit margin, but it also has a lot of competition from well-known brands. As a result, profit margins would be dictated by the price of the goods.

Know more about your rivals' prices and, as a result, determine which would give the greatest return – find the "golden value point" for the sales.

2.22 Precaution

It is important to obtain insurance. it is why, in addition to other necessities, insurance must still be part of the investment.

Another crucial step's to understand the company's legal framework. Obtain both the "consent to establish" and "consent to operate."

2.23 Risk

In the soap industry, the risk is not creating a large enough brand to compete with the rivals. There are a lot of competitors in the business, so making a name for your company can be challenging.

Another danger is that the company will collapse due to a lack of consumer awareness. To run a good soap company, you must first select the right market.

2.24 Conclusion

Soap production, as satisfying as this is, necessitates thorough study and measured risk-taking. Seeking your niche and launching a company are just simple activities. However, careful preparation and intervention are necessary to make this a success. Make sure you don't undersell yourself & that you also stand out.

2.25 Advantage of starting a soap making business at home

Soap making requires little investment to start with

The supplies needed to make soap can be easily acquired

Equipment required can also be easily acquired

It is comparatively much easier to learn the making of soap

There is already good demand for handmade soap and people are willing to purchase handmade soap,

You can easily specialize in your particular field

It's rather easier to make soap that is both distinctive and different from the existing ones

You can create other products that can gel in with your existing products

You can generate handsome profits by selling soap

It is very easy to locate a market for the soaps

2.26 How Much Money Can You Make Making Soap?

That's a tough question to answer because so much depends on you. And, just to be clear, producing soap is not lucrative. Of course, the money is in the soap sales. To make money selling a product, much as with any other business endeavor takes a lot of time and commitment.

CHAPTER 3: Start a Profitable Candle Making Business

Candlemakers are extremely professional artisans who pay particular attention to the sensory aesthetics of their products and experienced business people who know how to entice consumers with innovative marketing tactics. Learn how to launch a candle-making company of your own.

3.1 Steps for starting a candle making business

You've uncovered the ideal market opportunity and are now prepared to take the next step. There's more to launching a company than simply filing papers with the government. We've put together a list of steps to help you get started with your candle-making business. These measures will ensure that the new company is well-planned, legally compliant, and properly registered.

Plan your business

As an entrepreneur, you must have a well-thought-out strategy. It will assist you in figuring out the additional data of your organization and uncovering any unknowns. Given below are some key points to consider:

What are the startup and recurring costs?

Who is the targeted audience?

What is the maximum price you will charge from the customers?

What would you name your company?

What are the costs involved in opening a candle-making business?

You will be able to start your business at home, based on local zoning rules, making use of your kitchen heat source as well as utensils. Many online retailers, including Candle Science and CandleChem, offer a starter kit of items. To start, your candle materials shouldn't cost more than a few hundred dollars. This includes:

Paraffin, gel, soy, beeswax, or other wax

Wicks

Jars, tins, or other containers (though bear in mind that if you're just selling pillar candles, you won't need containers)

Fragrance oils

Coloring agents

Packaging materials

Transportation costs of raw goods in and finished products out

Web growth, which can cost anywhere from nothing to a few hundred dollars based on the expertise in the industry and at least properly contributes to some other start-up costs. A booth will cost $100 per day if you intend to showcase your goods at different exhibits and festivals, plus you'll have to pay for fuel and other travel expenses. You can also contact an insurance provider first. Since there is a chance of a fire accident, you can ensure that your company is fire-proofed and that you have a fire extinguisher onboard. You can also have an initial consultation with a lawyer to decide what licenses or permits are required in your region.

What are the ongoing expenses for a candle-making business?

The majority of the business revolves around different varieties of wax, your containers, and paint and scent additives. You can purchase these goods in bulk at lower per-unit prices once you've established your business model is viable. Wax, for example, can be ordered in 25-pound sizes for as little as a dollar per pound. Wicks are sold in 100-foot spools. Bulk amounts of containers, such as glass pots, mason jars, and tins, are also available.

Who is the target market?

Anyone who needs candles is your end customer. Some may have specific concerns, such as lights in the case of a power outage, and others are searching for a more sensory experience. Churches that use candles to decorate prayer offerings or stores that wish to bring a dramatic effect to their showrooms are often fantastic consumers. You may also approach resellers that can order the goods in vast quantities. Shop owners from the neighborhood and beyond will be among them. Customers like these are usually seen at arts and crafts shows. Try renting stalls at arts and crafts shows, flea markets, festivals and fairs, and other similar venues if you love seeing your customers face to face in an atmosphere where they can truly appreciate the aesthetics of your goods.

How does a candle-making business make money?

Candlemakers market candles to customers directly or indirectly through resellers such as boutiques, gift stores, and other arts and crafts shopping outlets. Since candle making is such a wide field, differentiate yourself by the types of candles you sell (pillar, floating, votive, tea, etc.) or the quality of your offering. Experiment with scents, textures, and molds to come up with something unique that is worth premium pricing. Furthermore, for optimum profit margins on your sales, you can still be on the lookout for low-cost raw material suppliers. To widen your target audience, think of related products or candle styles.

3.2 How much can you charge customers?

Your goods could sell for as little as a few bucks or as much as $20 or more per unit. Pricing will be dictated by the nature and reach of your product line, as well as your target market, marketing plan, and competitiveness. If you want to be the lowest vendor, make sure you're buying your raw materials at a discount and that you're still aware of what your rivals are charging. To save the most cost per unit, you'll want to buy wax, wicks, coloring agents, scents, and other products in bulk. If your goal is to market a higher-end product line, price is less important as long as your goods are visually pleasing. If you find a retail reseller that can move a lot of your product, you might want to consider giving deep discounts on prices.

How much profit can a candle-making business make?

Profit margins of 50% or more are not out of the question. While the cost of materials is not especially high, make sure you have the resources to devote to making your company profitable.

How can you make your business more profitable?

Consider expanding the product offerings once you've perfected the principles of candle-making. For example, learning how to mold or carve candles into any shape will improve the cost and revenue potential. Alternatively, you might start selling fancy oil lamps made from liquid candles. Find scented soaps and incense as well as other sensory items. You might be able to learn how to make these additions to your expanding product line, or you might be able to figure out where to purchase them for resale. Consider offering candle-making lessons if you have the requisite space in your workshop. You might contact the local community center or community college in this effort and see if they'd be involved in adding your class to their program. Finally, is the company prosperous enough that you might consider franchising it? You have to give this important factor a thorough consideration if you want to enhance your profits.

What will you name your business?

Choosing the correct name is vital and daunting. If you own a sole proprietorship, you should start using a separate company name from your own. We suggest reviewing the following references before filing a company name:

The state's business records

Federal and state trademark records

Social media sites

Web domain availability

It's important to get your domain name registered before anyone else. After registering a domain name, you should consider setting upa professional email account (@yourcompany.com).

Form a legal entity

The sole proprietorship, partnership, limited liability company (LLC), and corporation are the most traditional corporate structures. If your candle manufacturing company is used, creating a legitimate business entity such as an LLC or corporation prevents you from being found legally accountable.

Register for taxes

Before you can start doing business, you'll need to apply for several state and federal taxes. You would need to apply for an EIN to pay for taxation. It's very basic and free.

Small Business Taxes

Depending on which business arrangement you select, you can have various taxation choices for your corporation. There could be state-specific taxes that apply to your business. In the state sales tax guides, you can read more about state sales taxes and franchise taxes.

Open a business bank account & credit card

Personal wealth security necessitates the use of dedicated company banking and credit accounts. If your personal and corporate accounts are combined, your personal properties (such as your house, vehicle, and other valuables) are put at risk if your company-issued. This is referred to as piercing the corporate veil in business law. Furthermore, learning how to create company credit will help you receive credit cards and another borrowing under your business's name (rather than your own), lower interest rates, and more credit lines, among other advantages.

Open a business bank account

This protects your assets from those of your business, which is essential for personal wealth security, as well as making accounting and tax reporting simpler.

Get a business credit card

It will help you achieve the following benefits:

It builds the company's credit background and will be beneficial for raising capital and profit later on.

It lets you differentiate personal and business expenditures by placing all of your business's costs under one account.

Set up business accounting

Understanding your business's financial results includes keeping track of your different costs and sources of revenue. Maintaining correct and comprehensive reports also makes annual tax filing even simpler.

Labor safety requirements

It is essential to comply with all Occupational Safety and Health Administration protocols. Pertinent requirements include:

Employee injury report

Safety signage

Certificate of Occupancy

A Certificate of Occupancy is normally required for businesses that operate out of a specific location (CO). All requirements concerning building codes, zoning rules, and local requirements have been followed, according to a CO. If you're thinking about renting a space, keep the following in mind:

Securing a CO is normally the landlord's duty.

Before signing a contract, make sure your landlord has or can get a legitimate CO for a soap-making operation.

A new CO is often needed after a significant renovation. If your company will be renovated before opening, add wording in your lease agreement that specifies that lease payments will not begin before a valid CO is issued.

If you intend to buy or build a place:

You would be responsible for securing a legal CO from a local government body.

Review all building codes and zoning standards for your candle-making business's place to ensure that you'll comply and eligible to get a CO.

Trademark & Copyright Protection

It is wise to protect your interests by applying for the required trademarks and copyrights if you are creating a new product, idea, brand, or design. The essence of legal standards in distance education is continually evolving, especially when it comes to copyright laws. This is a regularly revised database that can assist you with keeping on top of legal specifications.

Get business insurance

Insurance, including licenses and permits, are necessary for your company to run safely and legally. In the case of a covered loss, corporate insurance covers your company's financial well-being. There are several insurance schemes tailored for diverse types of companies with various risks. If you're not sure what kinds of risks your company might face, start with General Liability Insurance.

This is the most popular form of coverage required by small companies, so it's a good place to start.

Define your brand

Your company's brand is what it stands for, as well as how the general public perceives it. A good name would set the company apart from the market.

How to promote & market a candle making business

The first and most crucial step is to decide who you intend to reach. Is your average customer a cost-conscious shopper, or is she more concerned with the sensory experience? If your target market is the former, you should be able to deliver fair prices. If it's the latter, make sure your product range is well-presented and that your color and scent options are pleasing. Try building an online presence on sites including eBay, Amazon, and Etsy. Since these platforms have a lot of competition, keep the costs as low as possible. There is a slew of other arts and crafts marketplaces, but they aren't as well-known as Etsy (and therefore potentially less populated with competitors). Among them are ArtFire, Big Cartel, and Craft Is Art, to name a few.

How to keep customers coming back

You aim to not only retain buyers but to keep them coming back. Since candles are consumable goods that must be replaced daily, the current consumer partnerships may become profitable over time. As a result, make sure you fulfill their needs so that they appreciate the quality of your goods and know-how to reach you if stocks run out. As a consequence, any order must provide easy-to-find contact information, such as your website, email address, or phone number (or all three). As part of the packaging, you could add a business card or sticker with this detail. Make sure shoppers and passers-by alike get your business card when approaching clients in people, such as at art shows or flea markets. Often, get their names and permission to connect them to an email list you give out, maybe before peak candle-buying seasons like the holidays or Mother's Day.

Establish your web presence

Customers can learn more about your business and the goods or services you deliver by visiting your website. One of the most successful ways to build your online presence is through press releases and social media.

Top of Form

Bottom of Form

Is this Business Right For You?

The perfect candle maker is passionate about the craft and has experience in sales and promotion. Candlemakers may start small, with a minimal budget and inventory, in the kitchen and storage room of their home or apartment. Since candles are always thought of as commodity products, you must continually search for ways to brand your line to set yourself apart from the competition. Excellent image photography, a solid web presence, and savvy sales expertise can help you highlight your product line attractively.

What are some skills and experiences that will help you build a successful candle-making business?

The bulk of people get into this business as hobby candle builders. You should appreciate the aesthetics of making candles and related products and have a clear understanding of how to mark your business. You should be familiar with the principles of eCommerce and how to build an online presence. If you sell from a booth at a fair, your display presentation skills are relevant both online (in the quality of your images and written product descriptions) and in physical displays. If you plan to market your product line in person, either to consumers personally or to resellers, personal sales skill is important. You must trust in the goods and be able to convince people to do so as well.

What is the growth potential for a candle-making business?

A good full-time candle maker could earn between $25,000 and $50,000 per year. However, if you sell to a big reseller, you might make more money. Consider franchising your organization once it has become popular enough for others to choose to follow in your footsteps. Candle making is an easy business to launch on your own. However, your ambition likely is to become so well-known that you'll need assistance with crafting, selling, and/or shipping your merchandise. Begin by enlisting the support of friends or family members if required, such as to match seasonal revenue spikes. Don't recruit permanent full-time support once you've been through ample revenue periods to realize that you'll be able to easily reach payroll over the year. Also, contact the accountant to hear about all the hidden expenses.

Candles Pricing

From a business standpoint, you'll need to find out how much you need/want to receive every hour and how many candles you can make in that time. Divide the hourly wage by the number of units (candles) generated to get a figure to add to the basic cost of the supplies used to manufacture each candle until you have these two numbers. Consider the following scenario: You pay $50 on ingredients (not equipment) and can make 20 candles from them. For the supplies, you paid $2.50 per candle. Making candles is a way for you to earn $20 per hour. Since the 20 candles you made took two hours to make, the overall cost is two times $20, or $40. Then you divide $40 by 20 to get a $2 per candle labor rate. When you apply the $2 labor cost to the $2.50 content cost, you get $4.50 per candle. This isn't a great example because you'll need to pay for other expenses like the additional utilities needed to produce the candles and the expense of importing supplies like boilers, pots, and jugs.

How much should you charge for candles?

This is based on the sort of brand you choose to be affiliated with. If you intend to sell bulk candles at a low price, you should expect your company to turn out a huge amount of low-cost candles with a slight but steady profit per candle. Votive candles are cheap and can be ordered for as little as $0.50 each. This approach can be very successful, particularly when several cheap candles are purchased in bulk, resulting in several sales for each customer. The drawback is that you would have to bring in a lot of money to make a big profit. You'll almost definitely need to expand, recruiting someone to help you achieve your broad production goals. Another choice is to create your brand. This means catering to a more discerning public able to pay a premium price for a candle. Some high-end artisanal candles will cost upwards of $200 each. For a brand, you'd have to worry about the packaging theme and what you're encouraging your clients to do with their candles.

3.3 Benefits of candle making business

If you've ever visited a big shopping center, you've probably seen a variety of candle shops. There are whole areas devoted to candles in several major department stores. To give you an example of how strong the candle business is, over 1 million pounds of wax are used to produce candles for the US market alone every year. The candle industry is worth around $2.3 billion a year without additional products such as candlesticks, ceramic pots, and so on. Who makes the most candle purchases? Seasonal holidays account for just 35% of overall sales, making them an outstanding all-year-round investment. Outside of these days, candles are purchased for 65 percent of the year. The most popular motives for buying a candle as a present include a seasonal gift, a housewarming gift, a dinner party gift, a thank you gift, and adult birthday presents. People nowadays believe fragrance to be the most important consideration when buying a candle. Make sure the candles you're thinking of selling have high-quality scents since this can be the difference between success and failure in the candle industry.

Conclusion

In 1969, in a period when India's domestic detergent industry had very few competitors, predominantly multi-national firms, which targeted the affluent of India, Karsanbhai launched Nirma. The detergents were not affordable for most middle-class and poor citizens. Karsanbhai began producing detergent powder in the backyard of his home in Khokra, near Ahmedabad and selling it door to door for Rs 3 per kg, while other brands were charging Rs 13 per kg. Business Standard reported how Karsanbhai came up with a genius idea during the early 1980s, when theNirma was still struggling with the sales, for drying out market of the goods collecting all the due credits. This was accompanied by a huge ad campaign featuring his daughter singing the iconic Nirma jingle in a white frock. Customers were flocking to markets, only to return empty-handed. Karsanbhai flooded the industry with his goods as the demand for Nirma peaked, leading to huge sales. Nirma's sales peaked that year, making it the most successful detergent, well outselling its closest competitor, Hindustan Unilever's Surf. As Karsanbhai purchased the cement firm LafargeHolcim for 1.4 billion dollars that year, he showed once again that thebusinessappetite is away from over. Mint reported how the deal in Rajasthan and the surrounding area would help Nirma achieve a stronger grip. While a media-shy guy, Karsanbhai, an entrepreneur in the truest sense, has a sharp eye for nation-building. In 1995, he founded the Nirma Institute of Technology, which was followed by the Nirma University of Science and Technology, which was founded in 2003 and is supervised by the Nirma Education and Research Foundation. He initiated the education project Nirmalabs in 2004, aimed at educating and incubating entrepreneurs in India. Karsanbhai Patel received the Padma Shri award in 2010. Just like Nirma, you can also transform your soap and candle-making business into large corporate businesses with the help of your ingenious marketing and creative skills, dedication, perseverance, and unfearfulness of new and challenging situations.

Private Label Crash Course

Build Your First 6-Figure Business Supported by a Collection of 9+1 Profitable Strategies. Find the Best Products, Build an Enlighten Team and Start Your Personal Brand

By

Marcus Wayne

Table of Contents

Introduction

A private label is where a person or corporation paying another business to make a commodity without its name, emblem, etc. The person or business then applies to the packaging their name and design. So, what sorts of items should be labeled privately? From skincare and dietary treatments and infant essentials, pet products, and kitchen utensils, pretty much all under the sun. The benefit of private labeling is that nothing innovative needs to be produced or developed by you. You can add your mark on it as long as it's not a proprietary commodity and label it yours. For the last ten years, private labels have risen by at least double the number of popular household products. In reality, there is a lot of conversation about the rise of private labels or retail brands around the world these days. Or we need to claim private brands, maybe since they are indeed labels by the end of each day. Opportunities to have ever-better-value offerings for both of us as consumers. Possibilities for everyone to push the main factors transforming the world of today and tomorrow. Yes, it's not the Private Label curse. It could well, in truth, be a present. A blessing that pushes us all to question the status quo again. A gift that pushes one to step positively with some of the main big forces that form the world of today to collaborate together more successfully and collaboratively. A blessing that is increasingly important to all of us, whether in the United Kingdom, the United States, China, or Scandinavia. If we like it or not, Private Label will soon have a single category of quick products in the country. In the last ten years, private labels have risen at least double the amount of popular consumer packaged goods brands. How did the Private Label expand at the above remarkable pace, and what lessons does it give players in the more narrowly established markets of fast-moving consumer goods? We like to think of it as a food event, but it's increasingly a complete experience of consumption. Flavors' globalization, marketers, and individuals have made Private Label a global fact. More and more, Private Label is the face of today's retailer. Comprehend it. This isn't going to go away. Act about it. Perhaps we should name them PRIVATE Companies from now on. Perhaps we might create very different tactics to survive if we began naming them brands instead of labels. Brands are concerned about combating their closest competing brand. Will they behave as though their closest advertised rival is the Private Label? Maybe they could, because maybe if they did, they might behave very differently in reality. The commodity has gone on. In turn, as Private Label has become a brand power in its own right, it has become privatized. It cannot be ignored as a single mark anymore. It's something a ton more. While taken out of context, Private Label is turning controversial for this cause, maybe more than any other, placing owners on the backhand side and retail section on the offensive. Neither group appears especially keen to publicly address it or cooperate on something outside development. Products have brought copycatting stores to court, and dealers have de-listed popular brands from their racks. There's a tiny concession space. It increasingly distorts agreed shopping habits and usage trends in order to exacerbate problems more. It is a brand that can often account for two out of three physical transactions made by your consumer. A brand that is gradually seen as an alternate product and value of parity. A company that will out-weigh and out-image any typical brand by exploiting the retailer's corporate strength and spending. A brand that can drive producers into a vicious cycle of loss in the market. A trillion-dollar market that, as you realize its sheer scale and future effects, must be the least evaluated and poorly understood industry around. An industry that in the years to come is going to get a lot larger. There would theoretically be billions of dollars of sales redirected by brand owners to this power. Are you confident your plans are ready? The remedies? But, as the solution, what do people recommend? Lower costs, increase efficiency, and be more imaginative. This is not just a remedy that you can pursue as a standard component of your business growth. It is simply not sufficient. This is an opportunity that requires the unusual and the unconventional. Or else rise to the challenge. The Private Label is a wake-up call from a brand creator. Wake up to the truth in the company. Wake up in search of a shopper. Wake up to what you might theoretically do for your company. Wake up to proactivity for real. Wake up to a chance to get the rest of the planet back into communication with your company. Private label has arisen from the conventionally held assumption that firms will benefit and conquer the competition by providing either higher value at a higher cost for their consumers (or shoppers) or fair value at a cheaper cost (retailer brands). In other terms, it's a preference between distinction (or innovation) and low cost, and it's safe to assume that only then have retailers fallen into the former to offer the latter to the shopper reliably in spades. As Coke (and Tesco) can also inform you, it pays dividends to see the brand on any street corner. However, as some of our research highlights would demonstrate, there is still a significant perception difference between Private Label and existing manufacturer labels in terms of quality/value. As long as the shopper is concerned, at least, without the other, one will not thrive, and broadly speaking, maker labels are better positioned to offer sound 'innovation' and 'value' to retailers. Just 16% of shoppers in all regions sincerely agree that a supermarket of retailer-owned goods can only be expected in the future. So, we think there is a potential for brands to constantly reinvent themselves through shopper intuition, deeper brand commitment, and creativity. The potential for retailers to continuously add value is there. The potential exists for producers to maximize their manufacturing ability and for interactions to be reinvented by agencies. But most critically, the potential is there to constantly impress and entertain the shopper, far beyond all their hopes. The other alternative frequently provided is to get yourself into making a private label. However, you may be compelled by Private Label to analyze the very simple essence of the company in which you are and to doubt whether it is strong enough to move you further. Ask for your goods. Ask how and to whom you are offering. Ask if you still are tuning into the agents of transition. Your corporate purpose issues. Ask if you have the best staff and processes to meet this crucial problem. Finally, Private Label is a concern for manufacturers alike. Knowing how to profitably manage it without undermining the very essence of the organization you are with. And the manufacturers that you work with. Yes, you may assume that you can survive without them. Yet we're advising, be very, very patient. If you want to be a genuinely successful marketing tool in terms of bringing to the shopper, you need one another. In comparison, we exist in an age in which the newspapers are building up major global supermarket chains as the latest businesses to despise. Why are you stopping this? As the messenger, you use Private Label, a messenger that not only reveals that you deliver excellent value and costs but also indicates that you think for your consumer and their long-term social needs. And you are really doing what you can to support them. Now, even more on this. The private label is, to a great degree, a hidden force. The conservative nature of the subject-matter literature tends to downplay its actual place in the world, a function far from conservative in fact, and a role in which Private Label is undeniably the single greatest influence on our businesses and goods today. Brands, engagement professionals, and scholars have consistently ignored or underestimated this. That's got to change.

Chapter 1: Getting Started-Private Label

A private label is where a person or corporation paying another business to make a commodity without its name, emblem, etc. The person or business then applies to the packaging their name and design. So, what sorts of items should be labeled privately? From skincare and dietary treatments and infant essentials, pet products, and kitchen utensils, pretty much all under the sun. The benefit of private labeling is that nothing innovative needs to be produced or developed by you. You can add your mark on it as long as it's not a proprietary commodity and label it yours. A private label product is made and marketed under a retailer's brand name through a contract or third-party maker. You specify all about the commodity as the distributor-what goes into it, how everything is packaged, what the logo looks like-you pay to get it manufactured and shipped to your shop. This is in relation to purchasing goods with their corporate logos on them from other businesses. A successful brand identity can be the crucial base for building loyal customers, customer growth, and a competitive edge. Care of your corporate name as your company's face is how you are viewed by the audience. Without a detailed, excellently defined brand identity, the consumer might not realize who you are. In the end, you need to create a personal link. The potential exists for producers to maximize their manufacturing ability and for interactions to be reinvented by agencies. But most critically, the potential is there to constantly impress and entertain the shopper, far beyond all their hopes. The other alternative frequently provided is to get yourself into making a private label. However, you may be compelled by Private Label to analyze the very simple essence of the company in which you are and to doubt whether it is strong enough to move you further.

1.1 What is Private Label?

A private label product is made and marketed under a retailer's brand name through a contract or third-party maker. You specify all about the commodity as the distributor-what goes into it, how everything is packaged, what the logo looks like-you pay to get it manufactured and shipped to your shop. This is in relation to purchasing goods with their corporate logos on them from other businesses.

1.2 Private Label Categories

Almost every consumer product category has both branded and private label offerings, including:

- Condiments and salad dressings

- Cosmetics

- Personal care

- Frozen foods

- Dairy items

- Beverages

- Household cleaners

- Paper products

1.3 Different types of Private Label as profitable strategies

Generic Private Label

Generic private-label goods are one of the conventional private label tactics used to provide the price-conscious consumer with a low-price alternative. The brand doesn't matter to these consumers. With limited advertising and no marketing, the goods are inexpensive, undifferentiated, poor inconsistency. In commoditized and low-involvement goods, these private labels are primarily present. For both discount stores in Western nations, this technique is widespread.

Copycat Brands

In order to draw buyers, manufacturers play on the price point, retaining the packaging identical to a national brand that offers a sense of the product's similar consistency. These goods are reverse engineered, utilizing factories of identical technologies from national brand products. In wide categories that have a clear market champion, certain private labels are mostly present. In the detergent group, Massive Corporation blindly embraces the copycat brand approach. Detergents against rival products with identical packaging have been launched, albeit at a cheaper price.

Premium store brands

Retailers now have started utilizing private labels, rather than just as a pricing strategy, as a store point of difference. Premium store brands are valued higher and are also high in performance than the national brands. Here, the customer proposal is to be the greatest brand that money will purchase. In the retailer's shop, these products get influential eye-catching locations. In the advertising, the manufacturer insists on the excellent consistency of the goods.

Value innovators

Retailers manufacture goods that have all the value-adding characteristics and eliminate the non-value-adding characteristics in order to reduce costs, one point ahead of the copycat approach, and thus provide the customer with the best value deal. The danger of being imitated also rests in these labels. As it produces furniture under a modern market paradigm that involves self-service, assembling, and transporting yourself, Ikea is renowned for its better goods.

1.4 White Label vs. Private Label Dropshipping?

You can select between white label and private label dropshipping if you want to launch an online store. Both words define goods that have been branded by a reseller, but the two definitions very distinctly. Particularly to beginners, they may seem quite complicated, so let's go through each one and explain their relative benefits.

Private Labeling

Private marking is where a company selectively makes a commodity for a store that offers it under its own name. Costco utilizes private marking, for instance, by marketing its own "Kirkland" brand that no other store can offer. As a consequence, goods with private labels are typically less pricey than national brands. Plus, they can be very lucrative if they're promoted properly. Dropshipping is a convenient method for private-label goods to be distributed. You will find a dropshipping provider if you are an online shop owner who can offer items directly to you and incorporate your branding. Dropshipping is an e-commerce market concept in which no inventory is held by the manufacturer. The retailer, instead, manages the packaging, packing, and delivery of goods to the end customer. In other terms, for dropshipping, the goods are delivered directly to consumers, and they are never used by stores.

White Labeling

A white-label product is a manufactured product that a company makes but is rebranded by marketers to make it look as though it had been produced. Each dealer is authorized to resell the item under its own title and labeling. Unlike private labels, several retailers may market a white-label commodity. For e.g., you can have your own branding and labels on the goods that are delivered if you wish to market a product under your brand name utilizing the dropshipping business strategy. It is often safer to search at something that already has a market when it comes to items with a white mark. It's dangerous to produce goods with white marks that consumers are not comfortable with. It's safer to go for existing brands that people regularly use. As with private labels, dropshipping makes it simple to market online white-label goods. Again, the items are delivered directly from the producers to customers, and the commodities are seldom seen by dealers.

Advantages & Disadvantages of White Labeling

You won't have to go through the complicated logistics of making a commodity in one of these two e-commerce market models. You can save a lot of time and money without significant expenditure of time and energy in product design and production. In essence, you will concentrate on selling the commodity to the target group and branding it. In order to expand your company, you won't spread yourself thin and can concentrate on other areas of expertise. So, let's go through the common advantages and disadvantages of each business model:

Advantages of White Labeling

There are some real benefits of the white labeling market model, including:

- **It saves time and money.**

It's just cheaper to white mark an established commodity instead of wasting resources on developing a product from scratch.

- **Gain a large profit**

In general, white label goods are exclusively marketed by suppliers and may be bought at cheap market rates.

Disadvantages of White Labeling

There are, on the other side, some risks of white marking, including:

- **Limited options for branding**

Because it will be the producer or retailer who makes the white label product's bottle, label, and packaging, depending on the concept, you can just decide what it will deliver for you.

- **Limited choices of products**

Just the goods that the maker produces will be preferred, and you will not be allowed to produce anything special to the market.

- **Competition is tough**

It is challenging to stand out from the other online vendors that, white-label or not, sell the same items.

1.5 Dropshipping Private Label

We have addressed that different dropshipping products are among the simplest methods for private or white label items to be distributed. So, let's go about how private or white label items can be dropshipped.

Finding a supplier

In order to achieve the sustainability of online shops, having a successful dropshipping supplier is utterly crucial. In quest of finding a directory of dropshipping vendors who sell private label facilities, you should look at business websites or just do a search on Google. Seeking a niche will allow you and your business to stand out from other retail vendors. Make sure that you conduct consumer analysis to figure out what sort of thing you would prefer to rebrand or distribute.

Establishing the identity with the brand

A successful brand identity can be the crucial base for building loyal customers, customer growth, and a competitive edge. Care of your corporate name as your company's face is how you are viewed by the audience. Without a detailed, excellently defined brand identity, the consumer might not realize who you are. In the end, you need to create a personal link. Brand awareness must be expressed in the products, slogan, website, and packaging. It can offer a' derived from human attributes' to your brand. Brands with a very well-established personality make the brand intimately relatable, connecting consumers at a relational level and having to have the commodity in their lives. This is relevant for dropshipping products, including the private and white labels.

Increase awareness about your label and brand

Growing your brand recognition is another important move towards building a profitable brand. If the product is fresh, then identifying your target customers and discovering ways to draw consumers to your shop is the very first thing you'll want to achieve. This is so if it's the private label dropshipping goods. Here are some forms that brand recognition can be improved without any expense:

- Build content on your website with the addition of a blog

- Developing your social network online identity

- To engage and network with more clients and get product feedback.

- To maximize your keyword scores, perform SEO.

1.6 Deciding What to Private Label

You might be wondering about what's a competitive commodity to private label. The secret to this phase and probably the most crucial step in beginning a private label company is researching and putting efforts into finding a good product. You ought to figure out which products/services are in the market to ensure if your product would sell. To see what people, look for on the internet and get ideas about what you can offer from there, you can use programs available online. If you intend to launch your private label company on online marketplaces, you'll want to use a testing method that actually monitors what individuals are searching for on that platform. For this, popular programs include

Helium 10 and Jungle Scout. They both provide several resources to help you continue your market path with your private label.

What Makes A Good Private Label Product?

The biggest point to hold in mind when applying for a private label for a commodity is to find one that:

It is in strong market demand and has limited competition from sellers.

This can help you stop being trapped with things that you will not offer.

Has a strong margin for benefit

Taking into consideration how much the item would cost you vs. how much you will market it for. If the item is held in a warehouse, plus the expenses involved with sale online, don't neglect to take into account the delivery costs from your source to you and from you to your client, packing and storage fees.

If you can manage the expenses

If you have a $1,000 or $10,000 startup investment budget, you need to take into consideration how many units you will need/want to buy and how much of the budget you will spend.

How to Find Suppliers

It's time to search for a producer or trade firm that provides private label service once you have a commodity in mind that you would like to private label. You can select anywhere in the world to make your goods. And several times, the type of service/product you select would rely on where you choose to get your product made. For e.g., China might be worth considering if you are trying to sell toys or gadgets because they seem to produce a ton of these types of items at very low prices. Consider looking for Alibaba or AliExpress if you want to go on this path. Both of these platforms are bulk markets where the goods are identified by suppliers and trade houses, where you can find almost everything. Because with all our federal rules, it's a great choice to source in the U.S. whether you want to offer food, dietary foods, cosmetic goods, or something else you bring in or on your body. Check on Google for items sourced domestically. Say you're searching for vegan deodorant source, just type in Google "vegan perfume private label

U.K." to get a list of companies that can use vegan deodorants for private label.

What to Ask Private Label Suppliers

Once you've drawn up a list of possible vendors, calling each one and posing some questions is a smart idea.

Pricing Per Unit

The price would usually already be accessible for you to see on the website for each item. However, depending on how many units you order, most manufacturers give a discount. Knowing this data would also assist you in estimating the gross margin.

MOQ

In the private label/wholesale environment, this is a generic word used because it stands for "minimum order" or the minimum number of units you will order at a time. On their website/product listing, most vendors will mention their MOQ, although you will only have to inquire for some. The MOQ of a producer can be as few as five units, although it can be 1,000 and beyond for some. Although this may be negotiable often, asking this upfront is a smart move so that you can prepare and budget appropriately.

Customization

It is nice to know what the factory is and will not do in advance so that you can stop trying to swap vendors later unless you are seeking to apply your branding to the package, customize packages, or make modifications to the product.

Production Time

It is helpful to know how long it would take your provider to meet orders when your private label company continues to expand, and you continue to prepare for potential orders. Typically, the norm is around 15 days (depending on the commodity and order size), so it can go up from there.

Response Time

Take notice of how long it takes for the supplier to get back to you, bearing in mind that you are initiating a long-term future trading partnership. You would want to make sure that your communication individual is trustworthy, prompt, and specifically addresses your questions. If your provider is based in another country, take into consideration that they are in a separate time zone and that you will not automatically obtain a reply. During their business hours, being present will allow the operation easier.

Samples

Ask for prototypes such that the consistency and particular requirements can be measured. Many vendors can submit a sample free of charge, while others may start charging a small fee. Anyway, it's certainly not something you'd skimp on, especially if you're trying to give the highest service to your customers.

Customizing Your Product

In how your product can market, customizing your product will play a huge role. Question yourself, "What's going to set my version apart from the competition?" The response to this is key in having a prospective customer select your product over the product of a more known, well-reviewed business. Perhaps it's as quick as providing color combinations or getting fancy packaging, or it might be easier to enhance a function that you want more in-depth. Such customizations, such as packaging upgrades, are likely to be achieved by your supplier, and some can be accomplished through yourself or by your suppliers, such as custom marking with product specifics and a logo. Customizing the goods in any form is the main message here. Stand out by having it different (and better) than the rivals '. By basically slapping the mark on it, you don't want to sell the same exact thing as another brand.

You are selling your Private Label product.

You may pick anywhere to market your private-label line of items. Here's an extensive list of online sales places or suggestions on how to get into shops.

A Personal Online Store

Such customizations, such as packaging upgrades, are likely to be achieved by your supplier, and some can be accomplished through yourself or by your suppliers, such as custom marking with product specifics and a logo. Customizing the goods in any form is the main message here. Stand out by having it different (and better) than the rivals '. By simply yanking your tag on it, you wouldn't want to give the same product as yet another brand.

Brick-And-Mortar

Sitting the goods on the shelf of a physical shop offers consumers the ability to see your product that they would never have dreamed of it otherwise. In other words, customers have to practically "search" for services or products they want to buy online. But if they don't think about it, they're not going to search and probably won't find it unless you pay serious bucks promoting it. If shoppers are still in a shop and happen to see it, it builds brand/product recognition at least. Fees and requirements for getting shelf-space vary by store, but it can be a decent place to start from local, family-owned stores. Read more regarding boutique collaborations or having your own storefront.

Markets

Markers and art fairs for producers are on the increase. Consumers love to shop locally and want to help their community's artisans. They're a perfect way to get instant input from customers, too. Find out how to start trading and find craft markets at farmer's markets.

Don't limit yourself.

Start with a variety of channels, in-person shops, and websites. You would be able to see over a span of time how many sales you create from each one, how much money each produces, etc. You should just stick doing what's profitable, then. It is certainly a road to launch your private label company, and it will be months until you can bring the goods on the market. But the trip can be well worth it if you do your product testing, pick the best source, separate the product from the market, and price it right.

Chapter 2: Profitable Strategies in Building Six-Figure Business

For private-label products, manufacturers may raise gross margins by managing the whole supply chain from manufacture to distribution. Clothing traders have been pushing different private-label options for years. Costco has the Kirkland private-label name. Nordstrom's got Caslon. And Kohl's has Sonoma as its in-house, billion-dollar brand. Although online stores have supplied other industries with private label labels, basic products for tangible products focused on low-cost hardware and office equipment, the move to clothes implies a brazen policy expansion. Any volume seller is looking at the advantages of growing private-label brand's goods in order to drive sustainability and connect with a more aware and conscious millennial generation who are known for not being very brand loyal.

2.1 Private Label for Profitability

Profits are powered by private labels. A private-labeled commodity or product with parity in operation and consistency with major labels will cost manufacturers 40 to 50 percent less to develop and sell to consumers. In order to negotiate with online marketplace empires and other online suppliers who offer low-cost products without caring about reducing margins, merchants will then switch around to provide greater discounts. Online, where customers have 100 percent pricing transparency, this is especially essential. This functions on both luxury and commodity items. Building and maintaining a private label often enables manufacturers to develop exclusive goods for higher prices or to manufacture commodity products below brands at a sustainable price. To boost their inventory rotation, manufacturers are now using private-label tactics. Retail stores with services from private labels could also have more than four seasons a year. An innovative team in private label, such as the JCPenney team of 250 designers working in-house or the internal production and procurement departments of Nordstrom, will contend on an equal footing with fast-trending fashion stores like H&M.

Factors to be Considered

It may be dangerous to hop into this business without carefully thinking it over. Before investing and dedicating time to a privately-label approach, here are some factors to be considered:

- **Identifying low cost and high-quality manufacturer**

A colossal advantage is strong production suppliers, while poor manufacturers or suppliers are a horrific liability. Spend the effort to do it correctly. There are hundreds or thousands of suppliers capable of producing stuff that you would need. Find the producer that fits all the requirements for price and consistency; often, identifying the markets that are relevant. You may also want to learn from Portugal or Vietnam for clothing. Vietnam, South Korea, and China have manufacturing expertise in electronics. Take note that costs for suppliers differ greatly depending on the order's size.

- **Strengthen the Skills in Design and Procurement**

The private label includes relationships with producers of agricultural and consumer goods, component retailers, multinational warehouses, and distribution suppliers.Will you broaden the current partnerships between suppliers? If not, determine whether to consult the staff or purchase the expertise that will render the retail company a key competency of the strategy regarding the private label. Consider a completely dedicated bet on vertical trading, too.

- **Using brand pricing and external signs as guiding principles for pricing policy**

Research your rival brands closely while designing your own products under the banner of a private label. Retailers ought to make up their mind whether to generate the product as a luxury product and expend marketing expenses or to position it as an alternate brand by selling below national labels. If product attributes can be readily contrasted and placed as a substitute brand, it is important to consider the price point of comparable goods to position them correctly against competitors' national brand/products label brands. In other situations, were comparing features is not something very straightforward. Retailers can use a number of internal market pointers for pricing, such as site traffic, ratings, consumer feedback, and retailers can recognize the popularity of the product. Today, if a commodity is popular/interest-generating, but the converging performance is low, this can cause a price reduction/promotion intervention.

- **Acknowledge the differences in categories and manage them smartly**

Consumers can browse for functionality within a particular perceived cost sub-set for white and hard goods. Buyers searching for features are opting for a dryer or washing machine.Potential customers are looking for other qualities, such as cloth, shape, trendiness, for soft items like clothing. Those features deter similarities.

- **Decide Efficient Customized Label Blend**

The best combination of private label and branded items has to be determined by retailers. Are buyers looking for a feature in a certain product category or range on the website? Collecting web search data can help marketers make a choice. They have to remember the client base as well. If the consumer pool is predominantly 28- to 51-year-old buyers, private label goods can be more value aware and prefer small-scale proliferation.

- **Implement Algorithmic, Data-Driving Pricing Methods**

With constantly evolving customer preferences, at every given level in time, you should be able to recognize demand levels and continually seek the optimum price value. Factor in leveraging algorithms based on technology systems to easily evaluate price levels and strategies; when priced carefully with supporting data, private-label brands also deliver unexpected revenues. For e.g., the commodity was priced well below the national brand by a generic manufacturer of merchandise with a very well private label refrigerator brand, just to experience a drop in revenue.The store began checking multiple price ranges, steadily pushing up the segment. Sales started to fall with the first $200 onwards. And, magically, revenue and traffic boomed until the price reached a hidden barrier. This sounds counterintuitive, but the private-label company has already been put in a competitive area with national labels in the view of the consumer. Instead of seeing it as a lower quality commodity, clients began to see it as domestic brands.

They were prepared to move since the price levels were always cheaper than domestic brands. In a considerably more profitable buyer zone, it was repositioned by moving the idea up the continuum. If consumers interpret things the same way with analytic pricing, the same SKU will gain double the profits. These are some of the most important elements in successfully initiating your private label initiative at any major retailer. Going over these basics will strip the efforts of the bulk of danger.

2.2 9+1 Pricing Strategies

Want to maximize profit on your product sales?

Aside from other publicity and business tactics, a strong pricing policy is indeed something you need to concentrate on. When setting the price for your goods or services, what considerations do you consider? When determining the prices for your goods or services, there are a number of considerations, including:

- Production cost

- positioning strategies

- competitor's products

- Distribution cost

- Target consumer base

When buying a commodity, price is a very important consideration for a buyer. A productive pricing system can also have a profound influence on the company's performance. And often, it decides whether or not the organization can succeed. So, what are those tactics you should suggest in order to improve the revenue and be more profitable?

Premium Pricing

Marketers put rates higher than their competitors or rivals for this promotional policy. However, it is used where there is a major competitive edge, and a relatively cheaper price is safe for the marketer or the organization to charge. For small businesses that offer exclusive services or products, high pricing is perfect. A corporation, however, can check that the packaging of the goods, its promotional campaigns, and the décor or luxury facilities of the store all fit to maintain the fixed price.

- **Example of Premium Pricing**

Let's take the example of luxury specialty retail stores that charge you a little extra but sell you exclusive styles and tailored clothing.

Penetration Pricing

To try to draw buyers? Ok, this technique is going to help you with the purpose.Lower rates are given on utilities or goods under this strategy. Although this technique is used by many emerging firms, it does appear to lead to an initial reduction of profits for the business. Over time, though, the growth of product or service recognition will drive revenues and allow small businesses to stand out. In the long run, as a business succeeds in entering the sector, its costs always end up growing to represent the condition of its role in the sector.

Economy Pricing

The advertisement expense of a service or commodity is held at a low in this strategy. The technique is used during a certain period where the organization does not invest much in promoting the service or product.

Example of Economy Pricing

The first few budget airlines, for instance, are offered at low rates in discount airlines to fill in the jet. A broad variety of businesses, from discount stores and generic grocery manufacturers, use Economy Pricing. The technique, though, maybe dangerous for small firms when they lack the market scale of larger corporations. Small companies can fail to make a sufficient profit with low rates, but strategically tailoring price-cuts to your most loyal customers or consumers may be a successful way to guarantee their loyalty for years to come.

Price Skimming

This technique is meant to assist enterprises in focusing on the sale of innovative services or goods. During the preliminary process, this strategy means setting high prices. The rates are then reduced steadily when the competitor's goods or services arrive on the market. When the product is first released in the marketplace, this price approach produces an image of exclusivity and good quality.

Psychology Pricing

This method of pricing deals with a client's psychology. For e.g., setting the price of a ring at $99 is likely to draw more clients than setting prices at $100. But the concern is, in terms of a very limited gap, why are consumers more drawn to a product's former price? Psychology suggests that on a price tag, customers prefer to give greater attention to the first digits. When stores apply $0.99 on product tags of $1.99 or $2.99, you can find identical promotional strategies. The purpose of this approach, therefore, is to build an image of greater value for the consumer.

Bundle Pricing

How often have you been persuaded to purchase a multipack of 6 packets for $2.99 instead of purchasing one packet for $0.65? Or an SMS kit instead of texting on the individual rates?Without sacrificing efficiency, we all enjoy commodities that cost us less. This is why package selling is a success for both the vendor and the consumer and is profitable. The vendor gets to sell more of their inventory, and for less cost, the consumer gets to purchase the product in bulk. For instance, if bundle package of chips is for $1.30 and 3 multipacks for2.50$. The probability of purchasing three packs is more than purchasing only one. Bundle pricing enhances the worth sense when you are actually offering your consumers anything for free.

Value Pricing

This technique is used when external forces such as increased rivalry or unemployment cause corporations to offer valuable promotional offerings or goods, e.g., combo offers or value meals at KFC and other restaurants, to sustain sales. Quality pricing lets a buyer know like for the same price, they are receiving a ton of product. In several respects, profit pricing is analogous to economic pricing. So, let's make this very clear that there is added benefit with regard to service or product in value pricing. Generally speaking, price cuts should not rise in value.

Promotional Pricing

Promotional pricing is a really common method for sales and can be used in different department stores and restaurants, etc. Part of this promotional policy are methods such as money off coupons, Buy One Get One Free, and promotions.

Cost-based Pricing

This method entails determining cost-based rates for the commodity to be made, shipped, and sold. In addition, a fair rate of profit is usually added by the corporation or sector to compensate for the risks as well as initiatives.Businesses such as Walmart and Ryanair are seeking to become low-cost suppliers. These businesses may set lower rates by constantly lowering costs whenever feasible. This undoubtedly contributes to lower profits but better profits and revenues. Companies with higher costs can, therefore, often rely on this approach to pricing. Yet, in general, in order to demand greater profits and rates, these businesses purposely generate higher costs. The aforementioned techniques are the most widely adopted strategies used by corporations to increase profit from sales of their product or service. In its own unique way, any pricing strategy is effective. Therefore, consider your marketplace and other conditions before selecting a pricing plan for your good or service to bring the most out of the strategy used. Therefore, becoming mindful of the competitive place when setting a price is important. What the clients or buyers anticipate in terms of the price should be considered in the marketing mix.

2.3 Best Practices in Private Label Branding

Can you recall when generic or non-national branded items with large black lettering and bad product consistency indicated simple white or yellow packing materials? After the unmemorable early days of supermarket labels, stores have clearly come a long way. In fact, many private label labels today are practically indistinguishable from their producer-branded equivalents on the shelves.

Align with and support the master (retail) brand

It is certainly no accident that some of the best private label company portfolios are those that tend to be in tune with the supermarket master brand's positioning and strategic purpose. Preferably, their positioning is strongly complementary to the supermarket master brand, enhancing the latter's equity and beneficial relationships.

Bring differentiation to the category; fulfill unmet customer needs.

When their products are additive to the supermarket, or better still, the overall competition, private label labels are maybe at their strongest. One way to achieve this is to bring the category to something completely differentiated. Another similar approach is to resolve consumer expectations that are not fulfilled by the big national labels.Importantly, this difference can be more than just a cheaper price than the brands of the manufacturer. In the good or service offering itself, private label labels can often be exclusive. Safeway is a perfect illustration of introducing distinction to the market and thereby addressing an increasingly unmet desire of the customer. Finally, creativity is another form in which private label labels may offer category and consumer distinction.

Establish clear boundaries for private label brands

There is also a temptation to expand it everywhere and anywhere in the shop once retailers effectively establish a good private label brand. This extends horizontally across types of goods and vertically across ranges of price/value. However, the tendency to over-extend or dilute the private label brand properties is resisted by better practice retailers.

Define brands based on emotional attributes

Since they feel an intrinsic bond to them, customers prefer to gravitate towards (and stay faithful to) products. There is no more for products with private labels than for brands with national suppliers. For private label labels, it is important that they stand for something more than just price/value and much more than a commodity attribute. They need to have an emotional advantage to which customers may connect. This essential nuance is understood by marketers that have become popular with exclusive labels and find ways to distill emotional equity through their private label brands.

Distinguish brands with a distinct identity and appropriate brand linkages

Finally, a distinctive and highly identifiable visual identity is established by leading label labels and embraces a clear messaging approach. They still maintain clear rules specifying the degree to which the private label mark may and should be identifiably affiliated with the supermarket master brand. An attractive visual presence and strategically advantageous brand design are undeniably part of what makes private label companies popular or leads to their downfall if overlooked.

2.4 Positives and Negatives of Private Label

Advantages

There is a legitimate explanation for retailers that are involved in flooding their stores with items with their brand name. Many of the main benefits of goods with private labeling include:

- **Handling Production**

Third-party suppliers operate at the behest of the supplier, providing full influence over the ingredients and consistency of the goods.

- **Control overpricing**

Retailers may also assess sales cost and efficient selling due to leverage over the product.

- **Adaptability**

In reaction to growing consumer demand for a new feature, smaller stores have the opportunity to move rapidly to bring a private label product into development, whereas larger firms might not be involved in a product or niche category.

- **Managing branding Decisions**

The company name and package concept produced by the manufacturer carry private label items.

- **Managing profitability**

Retailers monitor the amount of profitability their goods offer due to control over manufacturing expenses and pricing.

- ## Increased margins

Private labels enable manufacturers to sell and raise the profit margin more competitively on their goods. Compared to producing brands, several manufacturers gain 25-30 percent higher profit profits on private labels.

- ## Customer loyalty

Nowadays, consumers want goods manufactured locally, and they would like more if they enjoy the private label products. You would be the only outlet who would be willing to supply them with such goods. It is challenging to win the trust of individuals in the retail sector.

Disadvantages

As much as you have the financial capital to spend in creating such a commodity, the risks of introducing a private label brand are few. Primary drawbacks include:

- ## Manufacturer dependency

Since the manufacturing of your product range is in possession of a third-party vendor, working with accomplished businesses is critical. Otherwise, if the manufacturer gets into challenges, you might lose out on opportunities.

- **Difficulty building loyalty**

In a number of retail stores, existing household brands have the upper hand and can always be found. Only in your shops can your goods be sold, restricting consumer access to it. Restricted supply, of note, may also be an asset, providing clients an incentive to come back and purchase from you. Although private label goods are usually offered at a lower price point than their brothers of the corporate name, certain private label brands are also branded as luxury products, with a higher price tag to show it.

2.5 Keys to Private Label Greatness

As of late, we are doing a lot of innovative work in the Private Label sector, and here is a good refresher of The Core Values that we believe in for developing our own labels that are strategically convincing. We also see that there are particular fundamental stories in their creation throughout all great store brand cases, but there are seven values that they must abide by to be genuinely strategically convincing.

Principles of Equity and Environment

From a branding and design point of view, there has never been more interest in the grocery store and how we connect, affect purchasing decisions, and even construct theatre inside it. This is real in every part of the world. Of course, there is a reverence we all have to have for the cultural uniqueness of the grocery store, from country to country, since some customers are in the store just once a week, to other food and market experience where customers connect every day. Even with these diverse regional variations in frequency, familiarity, and satisfaction inside the retail shop, there is a common emphasis on making the store brand function more credibly and more convincingly with consumers in general.

The equity connection

Immersing oneself in the retailer's overarching goal, its perception and equity distinction as it is now, and what is achievable in the future is important. To achieve this, the right branding collaborators coordinate with the senior brass of the distributors with which they operate, as well as the organization's top merchants and store name specialists. They take into account all the main targets for which a merchant is fishing and then see how to enhance store brands as being one of the key tools to accomplish their task. Store products strengthen the retailer's total equity and vice-versa, and they struggle because they do not.

Environmental support

A kit can only do too many. Your store brand will get overloaded if it does not have the off-shelf environmental help in the vast stream of 40,000+ items that many of the largest supermarkets carry today. Beyond the box, give it existence and speech. To help your brand, use the theatre in the shop.

Be preferential

For supermarket brands, own products, exclusive brands, and the like, there are loads of common nomenclatures. "But whatever the language, don't treat your store brands to the larger national brands as weaker "stepchildren. Don't be afraid to handle your supermarket labels preferentially in the store, beyond the incisive box template for your company. In their importance, in their distribution of space, in their positioning of shelves, and in their show and cross-merchandising all throughout the shop. No need to apologize to the CPGs or succumb to the study of planograms.

Don't blindly follow.

For years, there has been a "follow the herd" attitude of store labels, and today it still persists. Because of what Walmart has achieved with Such Prices, many retailers we talk to now are terrified of "white" packaging. So often, individuals are hyper-attentive to the competition and norms and what's going around the market of store labels. The bottom line is that you can build your own vision in a very creative and special way. Do not blindly obey the naming conventions, color conventions, or typically mundane price-centered store brands set by broad categories and how they have traditionally behaved in order to reconsider anything intelligently.

Three layers have to work together.

Make sure you are not concerned with visual language alone with the positioning of the store labels and how they are to be fully distinguished for the future. This is the responsibility of a number of production agencies, who feel they are only employed to rewrite the store brand's aesthetic vocabulary. If we want to encourage these products to be produced differently, we need to understand how the graphic language is created, indeed, but also how it is structurally packaged and the language we use to orally convey the item. Graphic, systemic, and verbal languages all cohesively operate together.

Steve Jobs never asked the consumer.

Apple is one of the world's most creative and well-thought-out, profitable enterprises. When questioned what Steve Jobs felt about research in a New York Times report and how Apple uses it to direct new product creation, he replied, "None... it's not the job of consumers to know what they want." There are so many retailers that use research to store products in their innovative development phase, and this is a mistake. Customers will still turn to the protection and what is comfortable with them, but if they are the only sounding board, you will not have the most creative performance.

On the brand's positioning

In using the name of the shop on the individual store brand packaging, there are no universal guidelines, just as there are no generalizations to create about how large the store brand should stretch. Both of these brands had a very definitive strategic positioning when producing Greenway, Hartford Reserve, and Via Roma for A&P, and this relationship that established the role of the company was a very significant part of the process. Clearly describe it, know that you want to distinguish the brand rather than sheer costs, own it thoroughly in the consumer's head, and correctly reiterate it. In the development of an ambitious store brand platform, these ideals would suit you well because they are standards that the best supermarket brands live by with true conviction. The name brand industry continues to be guided by continuing innovative creativity, a true steel hand in spreading out from the single "price" veil, and to be persuasive in their own right. And store brands need to be promoted with vigor, motivation, and media support.

Chapter 3: Finding the Products & Starting Your Personal Brand

You should concentrate on creating a reputation before you start your company, one that is recognizable and valued, and a private label benefits both you and the retailer or supplier you select. The first move with your organization is importing the goods you choose to market, products that do not crack easily, which have satisfaction for the customer. The second and most significant move is to make your brand known to current and future clients. The more customers remember your brand, the higher it is possible that your revenue rate will be. Through selecting producers or suppliers who will submit your goods via Private Label, you will help this along. This operates by encouraging the consumer to position their orders with you, then deliver them to the retailer and directly dispatching the product. The return home address would be that of the company in most situations, but for Private Label, this will be yours. This ensures that whether they have any concerns or queries, the consumer would assume that the service/product has come from you, and they will only contact you. This helps you build up a brand reputation, but using trustworthy vendors, depends on you, and you deliver top-quality customer support. In general, manufacturers are willing to use private labels since it suggests that they do not have to be interested in any consumer problems.To sum up, while you are looking to get your brand out and develop a company without leeching on mainstream online market place/websites' popularity, a private label makes perfect sense. It will require a bit extra time to select a supplier since you must do the job yourself and guarantee that you work for the right supplier. Still, you will also gain a better profit when you take responsibility for the client support and are willing to negotiate the supplier's rates. A private label is where a person or corporation paying another business to make a commodity without its name, emblem, etc. The person or business then applies to the packaging their name and design. So, what sorts of items should be labeled privately? From skincare and dietary treatments and infant essentials, pet products, and kitchen utensils, pretty much all under the sun. The benefit of private labeling is that nothing innovative needs to be produced or developed by you. You can add your mark on it as long as it's not a proprietary commodity and label it yours.

3.1 How to Start Your Private Label Brand from Scratch?

Because of its profitability and consumer benefits, private labeling has boomed in prominence in recent years. To distinguish between larger vendors, more and more sellers create their products on and off e-commerce marketplaces. With 50 percent of one of the online markets, private labeling vendors, the rivalry is fierce. You need to realize what you're doing if you want to excel. To start a strong private label, you need the know-how, expertise, and money. When you place your logo and name on a standardized commodity, private labeling is. This separates the brand from related rivals and retailers. You have full power over your brand, with a private label. You establish a distinctive identity that is essential for successful promotion and the acquisition of consumers. Customers, not goods, are faithful to labels. Customer satisfaction and repeat business may be created through the private label. In the market, you still have the power of your price and place. A private label on the online marketplace enables you to build a different collection of items only for your product. This gives real estate devoted to your brand and assures that you are not vying against other retailers for the Buy Box. Since they get higher value, clients love private labels. Private-label goods are usually cheaper, but major stores' efficiency is the same, if not higher. In reality, at least one form of private label product is purchased by approximately 98 percent of customers.Depending on their lifestyle, customers may even buy goods. One study showed that clients prefer private labels for the price and choose them based on expertise. They buy from private labels that they most associate with. Ultimately, in a sea of rivals, a private label separates the name, allows you greater leverage over your revenues, and appeals to a niche client target. So, you have agreed to launch a private label of your own. The measures to take to help you start a profitable private label from design to launch are below.

3.2 Understand the costs of private labeling

Before digging deeper into a private label, it's important to consider the initial start-up costs. In comparison to reselling, private tagging is more costly. However, this capital input usually results in a better return on your expenditure in the long term.

Manufacturing

Typical development expenses, such as supplies, processing, manpower, and transportation, would have to be accounted for. You may need to consider the customization charge, too. For customizing a product with your mark, packaging, or specs, most manufacturers will charge a fee.

Brand

Even to design the brand itself, you would require money. To create the logo and package template, you'll definitely want to employ a graphic artist. To stress the voice of your company, you will also want to develop a content strategy.

Marketing

Marketing is a significant part of private labeling. Customers don't know about your company, so to become more noticeable, you need to spread knowledge. A large cost may be generated through ads such as promoted and boosted blogs. A website creator and domain name would presumably both need to be charged for. For any other unforeseen fees or modifications that pop about at the beginning of the start of a new company, you can also add a sizable buffer.

- **Choose the products you want to sell**

The majority of corporations and labels start with a commodity. The brand is how you create your cash and profits. The item is the guiding force of your business. Starting a commodity with your name helps determine your margins, demand, and availability. The brand is the consumer service, but you will need to offer your consumers a valuable product in the end. You would typically choose a branded commodity that you place your own logo on while you market a private label. This suggests that a single generic product begins with your "brand." How do you further build and broaden your branding using that product? You want high-rank and high-margin units when buying a commodity. To lower warehousing and shipping costs, you will want thin, lightweight goods. If the first product you offer doesn't work out or you choose to shift paths, you can still move goods. The aim is to stick less to one commodity than to use product testing as a prism in your overall business and niche instead. You should also accept complimentary commodities with this in mind. If you market key items, you want to think of a range of similar goods that would still blend with your brand when choosing key products. For starters, you can grow inside the travel domain or beverage industry if you sell travel mugs. You will market some eco-friendly home products as well if you sell environmentally efficient cleaning products.

- **Define your target market**

Who is the perfect consumer for you? Who would be more willing to buy your unique product? This can assist you in deciding the sorts of goods you are trying to produce and how you are going to promote such products. The consumer is your market and your brand's secret. Getting a well-defined target demographic is more relevant than ever, considering the current condition of the economy. No one is willing to afford to target everyone. By approaching a niche segment, small enterprises may successfully compete with big firms. Many firms say they are targeting "anyone interested in my services." Others say they are targeting buyers, renters, or stay-at-home moms in small businesses. These priorities are all too common. Targeting a certain market does not mean that you exclude entities that may not follow the standards. Instead, focus marketing helps you to concentrate your advertising money and brand message on a single demographic that is more inclined than other markets to purchase from you. This is a means of meeting prospective consumers and creating a business that is far more accessible, accessible, and effective. For instance, an interior design business might opt to sell to households between the ages of 34 and 63 with incomes of $160,000-plus. The business could opt to approach only those involved in kitchen design remodeling and conventional designs in order to define the segment any better. This business may be broken into two niche markets: parents on the move and baby boomers leaving. It is much simpler to decide where and how to advertise your brand with a well-specified target audience. To help you identify your target market, here are some ideas.

Look at your current customer base.

Who are your new clients, and why are they buying from you?
Look for features and desires that are popular. What ones do other
businesses carry in? It is also possible that your product/service
will also help other individuals like them.

Check out your competition.

What are your adversaries targeting? Who are the clients at
present? Don't try the same business. You might discover a niche
market they are missing.

Analyze your product/service

Write up a description of each of the product or service specifications. List the advantages it offers next to each function. A graphic artist, for instance, provides high-quality design services. The advantage is the picture of a professional organization. More clients would be drawn to a professional image when they perceive the business as professional and trustworthy. So, basically, attracting more clients and earning more profits is the advantage of high-quality design. When you have your advantages identified, make a list of persons that have a need that suits your benefit. A graphic designer may, for instance, opt to approach organizations involved in increasing their consumer base. Although this is already too common, you now have a foundation on which to proceed.

Choose specific demographics to target.

Find out not only who wants the products or service and also who is most willing to order it. Consider the reasons that follow:

- Location

- Education level

- Occupation

- Gender

- Ethnic background

- Marital or family status

- Age

- Income level

- Ethnic background

Consider the psychographics of your target.

Psychographics is a person's more intimate traits, including:

- Personality

- Values

- Interests/hobbies

- Attitudes

- Lifestyles

- Behavior

Assess how your service or product would blend with the lifestyle of your destination. How and where is the item going to be used by your goal? What characteristics are most enticing to your goal? What media for details does your goal switch to? Can the newspaper read the destination, check online, or attend unique events?

Evaluate your decision

Make sure to consider these issues after you have settled on a target market:

- Are there enough individuals that meet my criteria?

- Is my goal actually going to benefit from my product/service?

- Are they going to have the use for it?

- Do I know what guides my aim to make choices?

- Can they afford my service/product?

- With my post, may I meet them? Are they readily accessible?

Don't smash the goal so far down there. Know, there is more than one niche opportunity you may have. Consider how, for each niche, the marketing message can be different. If you can successfully hit all niches with the same post, then maybe you have broken down the market so much. Also, if you notice that there are only 50 individuals that match all of your requirements, you may need to reevaluate your objective. Finding the right combination is the trick. You might be wondering, "How do I gather all this data?" Attempt to look online for analysis that others have done on your aim. Look for posts and blogs in publications that speak to or around the target group. Check for blogs and sites where thoughts are shared by people in the target market. Check for sample findings, or try doing your own survey. Ask for input from the new clients. The hard part is identifying your target demographic. It is much simpler to find out which platforms you should use to attract them, and what advertisement campaigns can connect with them if you know who you are approaching. You should give it only to people that suit your requirements instead of delivering direct mail to anyone in your ZIP code. In identifying the target demographic, save money and have a greater return on investment.

• Consider your differentiating factor.

You've settled on demand and a commodity. Now, what is going to make you distinctive in your business from your competitors? Look at the rivalry. What is their emphasis? And where are they missing? A perfect spot for you to put the brand is the field that they struggle the most. You could find, for example, that all of your rivals have a formal language; with your brand, you might take a goofy and enjoyable tone. In order for it to become a good differentiator, it doesn't have to be a big improvement. The core of your identity becomes your differentiator. Keep in mind that price may also be a defining factor. You would get a different demographic and competition than a cheap or discounted commodity, whether you are quality or luxury product.

- **Create your brand look**

Your "brand" consists of the goods, the demand, and the distinguishers. Yet, it is your material and aesthetic as well. You need a clear emblem that represents the name while private labeling is used. How you are and where the stuff comes from, the logo tells. This emblem can be included in all communications, packaging, and marking. Be sure it's accessible as a corporation and website prior to picking the brand name. This would mean that you do not infringe on any patents or fight with companies with identical names. To build the logo and package template, you'll definitely want to employ a graphic artist. This is the perfect approach to make things look respectable and trustworthy to the private label.

- **Create an experience**

A brand is, ultimately, more than a slogan, though. Your "brand" is how your business is experienced by the client. It's a consistent way for your audience to communicate. You need to work out how consumers can uniquely perceive your brand based on brand differentiation. What is your content going to look like? What could you provide that is unique to the experience of your brand? You may produce visually enticing social media photographs, for instance, that contribute to the lifestyle around your dog collars. Or you should make sure that you react to and respond to any social network statement or post. To keep your label on the edge, you can use special and exclusive packaging. Build an atmosphere, and you can turn your one-time consumers into long-term customers.

- **Find a supplier**

Acting with a good provider is an important aspect of private marking. The manufacturer must have private labeling expertise so they can help you make a return from your products. For a variety of consumers, several overseas factories will produce a standardized commodity and modify such items with private packaging for marking. You collaborate with a retailer, for instance, that produces bottles of water and T-shirts. They have ten buyers, each with their own special emblem written on the bottles, that offer water bottles. A customization and packing fee will normally be paid by the factory.

- **Build the brand**

You have put yourself in a role, built a differentiator, and found a supplier. It's time to start developing your organization now. You have to:

- Name and image copyright.

- Website configuration

- Creating a voice on social media

- Shape an LLC

Just like you would like any other legal corporation, recognize your e-commerce firm. You need yourself, your goods, and your income to be covered. You would also like to start naming the lists with online items. A private label means you don't have to fight for a Buy Package. "With a different page for your branded goods, you hold your own "real estate." In line with the brand background, this is a good chance to customize the listing.

3.3 Choosing the Right Products

Choosing the best market and the right goods to spend your efforts on is the greatest challenge you would have to conquer. This decision is vital to the success or failure of your company. The only biggest mistake you're going to make is selecting a product based on your own interests or personal preferences, particularly if you want to create a genuinely profitable company. You have to provide what other customers want, not what you want. Especially if you are not the type of individual to embrace patterns or the type of individual that is always perceived to be "outside of the box." We can't tell you what products to offer, but we can definitely give you some ideas about how to pick the right ones.

How to choose the right product

Your organization would have an uphill struggle to become profitable without a strong product portfolio. It may seem impossible to try to find out what you are trying to market, with potentially millions of items out there. The item you chose will also pose other concerns that you may need to work on. For starters, shipping may become an issue if you are planning to sell freezers.

Depending on where the clients work, whether you are selling alcohol, there could be regulatory limits. Market analysis can sound daunting, but knowing the product can cater to the people you are going to attract through your site is important. You should monitor the industry dynamics if you already have an understanding of what you intend to do to see how the commodity is actually performing on the market. If you are really not sure what you'd like to offer, trends can still be helpful to you. Business dynamics will offer you an indication about what items consumers are purchasing or are interested in buying at the moment. Look for items that address a dilemma the target group is experiencing. If your consumer is fed up with the current product range, open a unique and better product to deliver them. Choosing a commodity that is not reasonably available nearby or a national brand that is coveted by a region outside of where it is actually accessible may also be a brilliant choice. Another recommendation is to find a service/ product based on your target audience's interests. This may be in the shape of a new TV show that is beginning or a fashion trend. It often applies to aiming for a difference in chances. If you choose a product that many different competitors are already selling, find something that you can do differently or better than everybody else. This can be an enhanced product characteristic, a market that your competitors totally miss, and maybe something in your marketing plan. If you are trying to market a commodity-based on something that is trending at the moment, ensure that you capitalize early on the pattern. There tend to be more individuals who buy the product at the beginning of a trend. Everybody else is now also moving along to the next thing if you get on the hype train at the end of the trend. Do not wait too long to profit on a trend in the market unless you think that you're going to revive a dead trend. When you make your choices, it is important to take into account product turnover. It would take a lot of time and resources on a product range that varies year after year to guarantee that the product selection is held up-to-date and does not include last year's choices, which could no longer be eligible. A reduced churn product would enable you to engage in a more informative website that will be applicable for a longer time span. Don't be frightened of looking at smaller segments and niches of products. Although there may be fewer prospective customers, there will also be less competition, making it easier to get it to the top of the search engines and much more cost-effective in terms of marketing. The right product is an essential part of your success. Take your time and also don't rush into the first good-looking product.

Looking for Product Ideas

There is no need to start a shop without a commodity to sell. Begin with something you already have, or how you can fix your own issues or the challenges of people you meet before you start looking for fresh ideas on what you can sell. There are some ways to consider:

- Which items or niches are you involved in?

- What items are your mates excited about?

- Which challenges do you have with your own life?

- Whose goods can address this?

- What kind of firms are based in your community?

- Can they be translated into a definition online?

- What will organizations in your culture cater to individuals outside of your community?

- In other areas of the planet, what items are trending?

- Is there a need inside your society for them?

- Will you build in your society a market for them?

- Is there a certain sector you like to be interested in if you are confused regarding products? In that industry, what products are popular?

- What items can you find useful from that industry?

- In other online retailers, what items are popular?

- Will this commodity have a niche that you should specialize in in sales?

- What's the social curation website trend?

- Is there an undiscovered thing out there that individuals would want to see open to them?

3.4 Building a Team and Starting your Personal Brand

Choosing the Right Supplier

It can be tricky to pick a supplier for your private label company, but it can help you to realize that there are a variety of suppliers who have been doing this for several years. Some lead the industry in broad industries, and this may be the perfect place to get started in your new company since the goods you offer are already established and have gained appreciation from the market. You can have to trade-off or work in restricted strategies with your profitability, and you need to be careful in reviewing the terms and conditions of each corporation, but each of these can create a backdoor into which you can start a profitable long-term business. Not all private labels are made equally, and to guarantee that your organization is effective, you want to make sure you chose the best provider. There are certain items that your provider wants to provide and some things that are less essential but can have greater convenience. Any of the items you'll be searching for in a provider include:

- Will the retailer have members who are knowledgeable?

- Will the supplier devote them to a particular entity committed to your account?

- Are they invested in being advanced technologically?

- How can you send orders?

- Where are they situated?

- Are they a coordinated business?

- How fast are their orders shipped?

- How are they keeping you throughout the loop on product returns and items out of stock?

- How fast can they send you the tracking details and purchase order?

- What payment types do they approve?

- What kind of fees are they charging?

It may seem impossible to locate the legal firms and distinguish them from the fraudulent as you are searching for a provider. There are some tricks to choosing a decent provider for private labels. One crucial point to bear in mind when you start approaching suppliers is that they could very well be the secret to selecting the best supplier, even though they are not the right match for you. Make sure you always ask every supplier you meet if they can guide you in the appropriate path to reach a supplier that suits your company. As they're in the business, they are sure to have connections that will help you and are typically prepared to share the details. Looking at social media is another way one can improve the chances of having a reliable supplier to deal with. Often, through a family member, neighbor, or acquaintance who might be in the industry or meet someone in the industry, you may find a lead. Any lead is a successful lead, even though it leads to a dead end. In order to strengthen the partnership, you have with your supplier, there are a few items you should do:

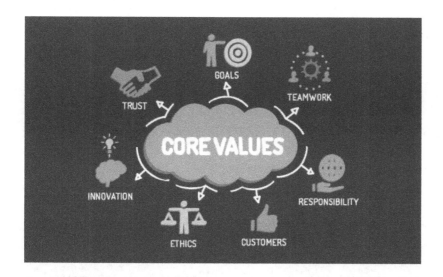

- Pay on time to develop trust and then become a reliable client.

- Set simple and realistic targets if an estimation of the goods you plan to sell in a specified period is requested

- Remember that they have other clients and do not belong to you alone.

- Learn what you need when you put orders to speed up the operation.

- If there is a malfunction, do not accuse the representative, but collaborate with them to find a remedy.

- Knowing somebody on a personal level seems to make them more likely to help you out. Build relationships with your delegate

- Train them to identify what you need, such as fresh product photos and product update updates, items out of stock, and products were withdrawn.

Finding the Right Suppliers and Working with Them

The one crucial part you have to do before you continue the quest for the right suppliers is learned how to say the difference between a true wholesale supplier and a department store that works like one. The manufacturer orders their stock from a genuine wholesaler and delivers far higher deals than a supermarket would. To create a good organization, you need to be able to do all of the following:

Have Access to Exclusive Distribution or Pricing

Being able to negotiate unique product agreements or exclusive prices would offer you the advantage without the need to import or produce your own product to sell online. These are not quick items to arrange, and you can notice that you are still out-priced, and at wholesale rates, some private label brands would still offer the same or equivalent. You need to find a way to persuade the buyers that the commodity you sell is of greater quality than the competitor, whether you can have exclusive distribution, particularly if the competition sells a knock-off product at a cheaper price. This is where the website's "about us" page becomes much more useful as it is a good way to share the fact that you are unique to the product.

Sell at the Lowest Possible Price

You will rob clients from such a chunk of your niche market if you are willing to sell your goods at the lowest costs. The main thing is that since you actually won't be able to appreciate the gain, you are destined to struggle. The low price is not often the primary motivating factor behind the choice of a consumer to shop. Customers seem to choose to invest their cash on the best benefit and lowest cost of a commodity. This suggests that you ought to persuade them that the best decision is to invest a little extra cash in your goods, so there is less downside and more appeal to them.

Add Your Value Outside of the Price

Think in terms of having data that complement the items selected. A real capitalist can fix challenges, and at the same time offering goods at high rates. In your unique niche, make sure you give suggestions and insightful recommendations. Your customer support is one extremely efficient way to bring value to the goods outside of the costs. If you are willing to address all the queries of your consumer without needing to call you and are willing to respond to any emails easily, your store website will stick out from the rest.

Conclusion

A private label is where a person or corporation paying another business to make a commodity without its name, emblem, etc. The person or business then applies to the packaging their name and design. So, what sorts of items should be labeled privately? From skincare and dietary treatments and infant essentials, pet products, and kitchen utensils, pretty much all under the sun. The benefit of private labeling is that nothing innovative needs to be produced or developed by you. You can add your mark on it as long as it's not a proprietary commodity and label it yours. Dropshipping is a convenient method for private-label goods to be distributed. You will find a dropshipping provider if you are an online shop owner who can offer items directly to you and incorporate your branding. Dropshipping is an e-commerce market concept in which no inventory is held by the manufacturer. The retailer, instead, manages the packaging, packing, and delivery of goods to the end customer. In other terms, for dropshipping, the goods are delivered directly to consumers, and they are never used by stores. There is a legitimate explanation for retailers that are involved in flooding their stores with items with their brand name. Third-party suppliers operate at the behest of the supplier, providing full influence over the ingredients and consistency of the goods. In reaction to growing consumer demand for a new feature, smaller stores have the opportunity to move rapidly to bring a private label product into development, whereas larger firms might not be involved in a product or niche category. You should concentrate on creating a reputation before you start your company, one that is recognizable and valued, and a private label benefits both you and the retailer or supplier you select. The first move with your organization is importing the goods you choose to market, products that do not crack easily, which have satisfaction for the customer. The second and most significant move is to make your brand known to current and future clients. The more customers remember your brand, the higher it is possible that your revenue rate will be. Through selecting producers or suppliers who will submit your goods via Private Label, you will help this along. This operates by encouraging the consumer to position their orders with you, then deliver them to the retailer and directly dispatching the product. To sum up, while you are looking to get your brand out and develop a company without leeching on mainstream online marketplace/websites' popularity, a private label makes perfect sense. It will require a bit extra time to select a supplier since you must do the job yourself and guarantee that you work for the right supplier. Still, you will also gain a better profit when you take responsibility for the customer support and are willing to negotiate.

Youtube, Tik-Tok and Instagram Made Easy

A Collection of Filters, Entertaining Topics and Viral Trends to Gain 10k Followers and Generate Passive Income

By

Marcus Wayne

Table of Contents

Introduction

Don't think you can compete against millions of creators and influencers? Well, let's set one thing straight, not only can you do it but also how you can do it. Working smarter, not necessarily harder, makes all the difference.

This book is for those who wish to make a name of themselves by leaving behind a reputation, legacy on social media platforms. Or maybe, all you want is to be able to do what you love for a living and offer that to the world. Either way, you're in the right place.

If you haven't been able to make much of a passive income from these social platforms for a while now, you should know it's probably not you; it's the platform. This book aims toprovide an insight into these social platforms by teaching you how to increase your audience by changing some basic habits and teach you a few new tips, tricks, and tactics you can use by first understanding their working. 10,000 is perhaps the right number of followers to be considered literally as an influencer/brand, get paying offers, and raise your account's value.

It may be sluggish as you try to win the starting few followers, but it does get a little easier after that. Understanding the algorithm plays a crucial role in enlarging your audience. YouTube, Tik Tok, and Instagram use algorithms to recommend various creators. Once you understand how their algorithms work, you can easily reach a larger variety of users. By gaining an active audience of about 10K, YouTube, Tik Tok, and Instagram may consider paying attention to your content, and you could even gain more than 10,000 depending on your consistency.

Now, you are probably thinking "easier said than done", right? Well, don't worry, this book is solely there to make these things easier. To provide a how-to gain 10K followers quickly, An easy-to-use reference to aid your growth on social media platforms (i.e., YouTube, Tik Tok, and Instagram.)

Try not to read this book as a novel; rather, truly study it and apply it in your daily practices to notice change and improvement in your channel/account/profile growth.

First, this book will teach you why earning a passive income through YouTube, Tik Tok, and Instagram is the way to go, especially in this day and age, next, how each platform has its own way of working and different method to win over the platform to your side. And then, if you're having a tough time generating content for these platforms, the last part will teach you how you can remove your creativity block and let yourmuse come to you.Last but not least, Afterthoughts will give you that push you need to get cracking, radiating motivation and energy to really get you started.

CHAPTER I: Why it's One of the Best Ways to Earn

In current times, the Internet is available in almost every part of the world. People interact, learn, and enjoy through platforms. More specifically, YouTube, Tik Tok, and Instagram. Since 2020, most people have spent their time at home, and so usage of these social media platforms has grown excessively. People discovered hidden talents, curiosity, and inspiration so much more than before.

Even if people hadn't spent half their time on their phones or other electronic devices, there are so many advantages of working on YouTube, Tik Tok, and Instagram for a passive income.

1.1: Freedom of Speech

YouTube, Tik Tok, and Instagram are the kind of social media platforms that allow an individual to really do anything and everything they want, needless to say, as long as they follow community guidelines.

"I do not agree with what you have to say, but I'll defend to the death your right to say it." ~ Voltaire

From a thriller,a short film to kids toy reviews, from gameplays to reactions, whatever.These are platforms where even the smallest of people have a voice, and they can make it known. Your creativity can literally pay the bills and put food on the table. And there can always be an endless supply of creativity, that is if you know where to look.

What could you possibly want more than being able to do what you love for a living? It's the ideal dream.And there are so many advantages of being able to do what you enjoy for a living.

High Efficiency

You become more useful and productive with your work as you can be excited for the next day. Your work won't even feel like a job,and so you would find yourself more relaxed as it wouldn't feel like a burden, finding other things to do in your spare time would be exciting too.

Inspiration

When you're having a tough time, doing what you love can spark inspiration and motivation in you. Once you feel inspired, your ideas run like a high-qualitycar engine, and it can sometimes even get difficult to do all these amazing things you have in mind.

New Perspectives

When you are following a boring schedule every single day and spend most of your time thinking about what you would do once the weekends here, you should realize you're doing it wrong. When working on a social media platform, you don't have a boss; in fact, you are your own boss, much like running a business. You set timings that are best suited for your work, and as being a public figure is constantly exciting, you won't find yourself in the same routine each day. Sure, you would probably have some ups and downs, but at the end of the day, you work for your own satisfaction and so view life from a different point of view than those who work solely because they feel they have no choice.

Better Wellbeing

Working on your chosen niche on these social platforms sounds fun and enjoyable, and it is. What you probably didn't know that being happy is great for your health. In fact, it's a lot cheaper than being miserable and stressed for everyday of your life. It even

relieves all that stress, mental and physical tension.

1.2: Fame

An Audience

Working on being a public figure or influencer gives you an audience that cares for you; they show an interest in your content. It could make you a role model for them, or they see your content to put a smile on their faces, it could help them in some basic struggles they didn't know they had until they saw your work.

Your followers/subscribers may value your opinions on certain topics and appreciates you and your content in the respective niche. And being validated for your effort would make anyone happy.

They even help you grow by giving honest feedback and so you can easily tell what it is they like about your content.

Opportunities

Fame grants you several chances to work with well-known brands or companies. Whether that be in sponsored advertisements or partnerships for products(i.e., perfume, apparel, electronic gadgets, games, etc.)

For example,maybe you're a sports-focused content creator, you could get offers from sportswear companies to model with their products!

Not only brands but also popular public figures would notice you, and you'd be given numerous opportunities to work with them, especially if you're in the same niche as them. When an already successful creator acknowledges and validates your content, they bring in their fans to your work, ultimately broadening your audience.

Forinstance, YouTuber Lilly Singh, also known as superwoman, grew so big on YouTube that she now hosts a late-night show called "A Little Late with Lilly Singh" on NBC. She not onlyreleased a film that entailed her world tour but also a book named "How to Be aBawse: A Guide to Conquering Life," which made it to New York Times best-seller list. She also won a substantial number of rewards on multiple award shows over the years and made her own music videos, and so much more.Her Niche? Entertainment.And it's an understatement to say she entertained.

@lilly with @malala Via Instagram

Of course, it didn't come easy to her, but with time, her channel grew and not only on YouTube but also across other platforms like Instagram.

Like her, once you obtain that loyal audience, you could try new things whenever you want, but not too much, or you may drive your audience away. You'd be able to work on creative projects. (i.e., Liza Koshy acted in a tv show and other showbiz related content, PewDiePe who made not one but two games with another company as well as a YouTube original show called "Scare PewDiePie", Joey Graceffa who made his own YouTube original show called "Escape the Night".)

1.3: Money

The obvious reason for earning through YouTube, Tik Tok, and Instagram? The Money.Succeeding on any social platform often promises good fortune. Influencers often buy new cars, houses, editors to help them with their work, maybe even a new oven!

You'd finally be able to finish that bucket list. Get something for the people you care about! And most importantly, once you get that money you've been waiting for, be grateful and don't take it for granted.

YouTubers like Lilly Singh made use of their money by making her profile a little more professional by hiring a team and basically becoming a CEO of her team. A lot of influencers do live charity streams, raise money, or donate for the poor and needy in several ways as well.Well, that's not all she did with her money she spent it for fun too as I'm sure you can as well do whatever you want with it.

Merchandising

You would be able to sell your own products, which would be your signature merch (people would recognize it as yours). Often influencers get sweatshirts, T-shirts, caps, posters, phone covers, etc. This increases your profits as well as advertising yourself. You get something to represent yourself with and receive more recognition.

CHAPTER II: YouTube

2.1: How it Works

To know how to easily get 10,000 subscribers on YouTube, you first need to be able to understand the YouTube software's working and how you can use it to your advantage.

Video

YouTube is a free space where creators can store videos, pictures, and posts. But their main focus is the videos that various people of all types upload. Google owns it, and its search engine is the second largest around the globe. YouTube videos can be embedded into other websites as well.

Moreover, YouTube recommends videos that are viewed by a similar audience to the one a user is currently watching.

Being successful through YouTube won't happen in a week. You have to be prepared to go through the rough patches as well as the smooth ones.

Analytics

There is a reporting, and self-service analytics tool on YouTube which provides intel regarding every video you upload so YouTube can help you easily keep track of how many views each video receives, what type of people are watching your content (age group, where they are from, and such).

It can provide data about:

1. The age groups and genders it is commonly seen by.

2. The statistics: comments, ratings, and views.

3. The countries your content is mostly seen in.

4. The first time your video was recommended to a user, either when they are watching something similar or when your video was recommended when they search a keyword.

5. In the first instance, your video was embedded in a website by a third party.

Advertising

YouTube embeds features that allow various businesses to promote their content to users who may have an interest in it, aiming at clients by subject and demographics.

The advertisers pay you each time someone in your audience views their Ad. They can decide the areas in which the Ad will show, the amount of payment, and the format.

Channels

Create your own niche, don't constantly jump from one genre to another, or your audience will never remain consistent.

2.2: The Content

Watch Time

Videos that consist of a higher watch time get recommended frequently on the main YouTube homepage. So how do you increase it? Pattern Interrupts.

These result in making your videos more vibrant, which prolongs the viewers' attention span.

A pattern interrupt can be jump cuts, graphics, different camera angles, and cheesy humor. It can put a smile on the watcher's face or catch them off guard, which keeps them watching.

Trends

Keeping up with the current times is vital for small channels to grow. Trends are one of the catalysts of increasing your audience.

PewDiePie Via YouTube

As of February 2021,most YouTubers stream live, do how-to tutorials, DIY's, etc.

Things like the chubby bunny challenge, Reddit reactions (cross-platform), spicy foods challenge, etc., gives more room for the creator and audience to get to know one another. The goal is to make them feel like your friend, so they feel comfortable enough to come back.

Create longer videos.

Making long videos (10+ minutes) actually gives your video a higher rank in YouTube's search results in most cases. Of course, if you make the video longer with not much to add, then it will still be lowly ranked as users will prefer not to waste their time.

And definitely avoid making videos longer than an hour because it's likely the viewers' attention gets diverted.

Like, Share, and Subscribe

At any point of the video, remind your viewers to subscribe, but make sure you don't keep mentioning that along with 'Like, Share, and hit the notification bell' as this tends to irritate the viewers due to the fact that they just want to watch the video. Keep the message short and maybe even humorous to attract the viewers.

Link more videos at the end.

If the users watch more of *your* content, they will probably subscribe. So, promoting your videos will definitely increase the chances of them watching it as it would be convenient for them to just click on that instead of going to your channel and surfing through there.

Quality over Quantity

Viewers can never be fooled by the number of videos you upload every week, they value the effort and time put into each piece of content, and they are well aware that you are as human as they are.

Do try maintaining a schedule just to let your viewers know when they can expect a video, but don't force it, or it will not be valued.

Thumbnail and Video Title

Your thumbnails should be eye-catching and interesting, as it is the first thing they see when they are introduced to your channel. It's your first impression. Make sure it's a high-quality image.

If it's a professional website, a simple and sleek thumbnail will do. If it's a vlog or an entertainment purpose video, an exciting title with an image of the most important part of the video in place of the thumbnail would fit nicely.

For example, if you want to give your review on a certain product, give a strong statement as a title that would be intriguing for people to watch (i.e., 'Why I think the new Tesla cars are amazing', 'Why Harry Potter actually makes no sense', 'Public Speaker Reacts to PewDiePie')

More Content

At the end of your videos, hint at what you'll be doing next so your viewers can come back for more.

Keep track of your subscriber magnet. In analytics, creators can see what type of videos made by you have the most views. So, start by focusing on those. Obviously, don't make a hundred parts on the same topic, but keeping track of your subscriber magnet can help a lot.

2.3: Channel Profile

Keep an attractive and creative Channel with intriguing art styles, so it shows the work put in your banner. It welcomes the viewers. Here are some examples:

Jaclyn Lovey Via YouTube: here,Jaclyn made a minimalistic banner with her video update schedule and her genre of videos mentioned, so newcomers do not have to search for it; convenience.

jacksepticeye Via YouTube: Jack, a successful YouTuber with over 20 Million views, categorized all his videos in playlists so users can access any genre of his videos anytime. Also, notice a signature logo, and he mentioned all his handles, brand links too.

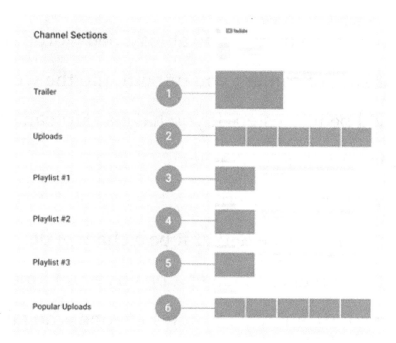

Make an exciting and persuading channel trailer. Preferably short and catchy, show the best you can here because these viewers came specifically to your channel, and you want to keep them there.

Organize the Channel page in a way that's convenient to the viewers.

Check out this basic layout:

Mention other platforms you use so they keep up with you if they don't rely on YouTube.

In 'About', make sure you provide at least 300 words about yourself, what kind of content you put out into the world, and why you think they'd be interested. If you have an upload schedule (please do), then mention that as well.

Persuade the viewers to subscribe by the end of it. Keeping a polite tone in your descriptions, whether it be a channel description or video description, gives the viewer a positive and kind tone. They wouldn't particularly enjoy watching someone who talks in a manner of giving orders rather than guiding or entertaining (depending on your content subject).

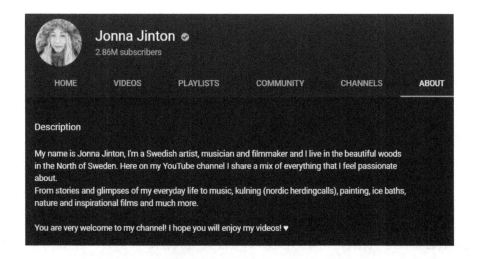

Make sure you use well-known keywords that describe your content. (i.e., Crash courses, funny, motivational, etc.) so the YouTube algorithm can detect these things.

Here's an easy comparison:

A:

Via YouTube

B: Via YouTube

Which is a better Description of the YouTuber? I hope you say B, because it is, in fact, B.

Categorize your videos into playlists. For example, if you are running a gaming channel, make sure long gameplays are divided into separate videos but put together in one playlist after you upload them. Not many people watch 4-hour gameplays all at once, especially when you are starting as a small channel. But suppose you divide your gameplays into videos and edit them to cut out the boring bits. In that case, they may enjoy watching multiple short videos, which would be around 15-20 minutes each-depending on your preferences.

2.4: Interactivity

Replying to comments is the best and simplest way to gain more subscribers. The more you interact with your viewers and give importance to their feedback, the longer they stay.

"When creators take the time to interact with their local community, it can encourage audience participation and ultimately result in a larger fanbase." ~ YouTube.

Creator Hearts- you can heart your favorite comments to recognize comments from your public. By doing this, the viewer gets a notification, and this keeps interactivity high by leading them back to your channel. These notifications receive 300% additional clicks than normal.

Once you get a handful of people that are consistent in watching your content, you can even ask for their opinion on anything related to the video or even an idea for the next video. To engage yourcommunity is perhaps the most important thing, especially when you are a growing channel. Doing Q&A videos every once in a while acknowledges the audience and engages them more.

Recently, YouTube updated, and now Creators can interact with their audience with polls and posts as well as comments. Using these frequently to keep your audience there is vital.

Shine Theory

Needless to say, they'd be more excited by a famous YouTuber replying to their comments, but you could be famous soon enough too! So, building a community that promotes each other does help. This concept comes from the Shine Theory.

Shine Theory is a long-term investment, where two individuals, creators, or consumers, help each other by means of advertising or engagement depending on the platform it is being used.

CHAPTERIII:Tik Tok

3.1: Down the Rabbit Hole

Over 2 billion people have downloaded Tik Tok all around the globe. Especially during the global pandemic, literally, everyone seems to have this app on their phone- and even if they don't have the app, it is taking over the apps they *do* have.

Tik Tok is super addicting, and the main reason for this is that each video is no longer than one minute, which gives viewers quick entertainment /tips /motivation.

Tik Tok famous is a word the vast majority seems to be throwing around as if it is a solid career, but the problem is, they all act as though it's a comfortable ride without even putting their back into it! Though it's a little more complicated than that, and you'd know that. But don't worry, here's a step-by-step guide to how you can be Tik Tok famous in no time.

This is the kind of platform that anyone can get into, from a 7-year-old to a 70-year-old *anyone.* Most people follow overnight after one of your Tik Tok's go mega-viral. Without further ado, let's start with all the things you need to remember to get 10 000 followers on Tik Tok.

3.2: The Algorithm

The Tik Tok algorithm was updated recently at the start of 2021, due to which a number of views on Tik Toks have started to go down. They did this because Tik Tok realized Tik Toks could go viral for almost anyone and a lot of creators' content was against community guidelines, so the early adopter advantage is lost. A way to tackle this is- keep pumping out more content. These algorithms will keep updating throughout the years, but the best you can do is give the viewers a reason to watch.

3.3: Your Profile

Username

Choose a simple yet unique username. One that is familiar to your niche would be most preferred as it would make users find you conveniently. (i.e., if your Tik Toks are travel-focused, you can call yourself JourneysInLife)

Bio

Think of an intriguing Profile Bio. Something welcoming, relatable, original, fun, and interesting your followers would enjoy. And definitely mention your niche to clarify your target audience. Often really good bios consist of a call to action (i.e., follow for a cookie).

Upload a Photo (high-quality image not to look cheap). Link your other social media handles like Instagram, YouTube, etc.

3.4: The Content

Target Audience

Before blindly making videos, you need to consider what kind of audience you're aiming for. Firstly, they use Tik Tok. If you think editing videos the same way you'd edit a YouTube or IGTV video will work, you're wrong. Every platform is unique in its own significant way,so you need to pay attention to how Tik Tok is entertaining and focuses on that.

Is it family-friendly content for youngsters? Short tutorials for artists? Perhaps it's professional cooking for beginners. You need to think about your audience's geolocation, age group, gender, so on and so forth.

This is an approximate age breakdown:

- Age 55+: 5%

- Age 44-53: 2%

- Age 34-43: 7%

- Age 24-33: 15%

- Age 17-23: 41%

- Age 13-16: 26%

What's your Niche?

Delivering high-quality videos (in both quality of the video and content) is the most basic important thing. Don't steal content from other underrated creators, or it will have dire consequences like getting banned.

Make it unique, edit your videos with your ability if you can because people get tired of seeing the same editing design used by the Tik Tok app. There are various editing apps like ViaMaker, Zoomerang, Quik, InShot, Funimate, etc.

Quality

You need a really powerful hook in the first 3 seconds the keep the viewers wanting to watch more. Your job is to do everything and anything to keep the viewers from clicking away then make them interested enough to follow!

To do this, you need a significant number of pattern interrupts-graphics, different camera angles, etc. It could be as easy as starting with a greeting or as concrete as taking the time to explore or finishing your wish list. A trend disrupts you to exciting new locations, both visually and psychologically. It jolts you away from your comfortable perceptions and rituals and then into broad freedom of possibilities.

Better quality videos are pleasing to the eye, and they will likely continue watching until it ends. Sometimes Tik Tok degrades your videos' quality, and the reason this happens is thatthe data saved on your app has been turned on often than naught. This feature is on means the Tik Tok application downloads your mobile data while you watch videos. This decreases the resolution of your clips too. So, to tackle this, you can turn off the data saver feature.

Collabs

Collaborating with some people you have good chemistry with really improves shares as it would be increasing both your and the other Tik Tokers views/follows another branch of Shine Theory.

Not just that, but Tik Tok allows you to reply to other influencers Tik Tok with your own, right? Use that! Make your reply unique and interesting to get them and other viewers to notice.

When it comes to collaborations with companies, sponsorships sound nice but try not to overdo it. While looking for new celebrities to partner with, be sure to review how many supported videos are posted. When a majority of their latest material is paying for updates, their commitment rate will not last. Alternatively, search for influencers with a decent amount of organic, non-sponsored material. As they probably have fans interested and involved.

Going Viral

When you post a video on Tik Tok, your creativity has the potential to ignite a chain reaction.

To get a decent amount of exposure, engage in trends, challenges, and duets. Put your own twists on patterns that captivate individuals. Paying attention to and bookmarking popular clips can prove useful to use it for inspiration. In Tik Tok, there are so many viral challenges. Engaging in various challenges will increase your visibility to the network and encourage you to get far more follows.

On the majority of your Tik Toks, for now, at least, use recommended and trending songs. Positive content almost always has more views, something quirky and enjoyable with a warm tone. Using a trending song is the next move (except when your music is original or a video idea in particular to a kind of sound.)

This is the reason why using trending songs is clever: basically, Tik Tok is a little wired in regard to trending songs to promote videos. It wasn't a random occurrence that Tik Tok also works with record companies; they work together to promote the artist's music in the app to improve the sales of the album and raise the likelihood that the song can hit the top rankings. Tik Tok practically dominates the music world. A mere peek at the week's Top 100 tunes. Most of those best hits on Tik Tok are those that are mega-famous. How do you know what tunes everyone's listening to? Simply choose one of the suggested tracks the platform recommends when you make your film.

Get on top of all those trends, except with a surprise. Do the idea of popular dances or rising clips, but add a twist on it and make it something of your own. You need to balance trending videos with fresh material when you're a small producer. A Tik Tok clip received millions of views, and that account got about 10,000 Tik Tok followers; it just happened overnight.

However, once you receive those views, you shouldn't anticipate the next day to be filled with that much fame, because you will probably be disappointed. Once you get over a million views, then you need to keep up the work or probably work even harder than before to keep everyone there.

Make sure you don't take part in really cringe trends, though!

Using Hashtags

Utilize hashtags as much as you can, especially hashtags that are trending. This actually matters because the Tik Tok algorithm detects these hashtags and recommends your content accordingly.

The cleverer and simpler your hashtags are, the higher your videos get ranked on Tik Tok, which in result increases your views and likes. Along with being in contact with record labels, Tik Tok often works with companies/brands, and their drives are almost always attached with a hashtag. This encourages your videos on people's For You Page during the duration of the campaigns.

1-2 hashtags are preferred. Go to the Discover tab and take 1-2 trending and 1-2 broad hashtags or tags related to your related to you exclusively and trendy.

Most Popular: #tiktokers #lfl #bhfyp #follow #explorepage #followforfollowback #explore #meme #tiktokdance #viral #memes #tiktokindia #photography #tiktokindonesia #k #cute #art #youtube #instagood #fashion #likes #bhfyp #likeforlikes #trending #music #funny#tiktok #instagram #love #like

Timing Matters!

What time you decide to post your content actually matters. When most people are online is when you'd want to put out videos and this depends on your geolocation heavily. If you're careful, you can get twice the followers you'd normally get.

Posting late at night (not too late), afternoon, and early morning tend to be the best times as most people would be looking through their phones then.

But that's just an average. To be more specific, go into your account analytics and content section, look at the past 7 days and what times your content was viewed most often, then make your posting times according to when your most interactive followers were active to make it as convenient for them as possible. Also, take into consideration the timings more well-known Tik Tokers in your niche are posting.

Repost and Share.

Sometimes, your video doesn't do as well the first time but reposting it several times a day and week can drastically change that because sometimes your followers just miss it. Saying things like 'Posting again till it goes viral' or 'Reposting since it didn't do too well last time' can really make a difference.

Sharing your videos on every other social media platform (i.e., Instagram, Twitter, Facebook, etc.)

Engagement

You need to turn your viewers, commenters, and likers into followers, especially at such an early stage. Basically, your early squad needs the spa treatment. To do this, perhaps the most important thing is engaging with your community. Interacting with them as much and as often as you can is vital to Tik Tok's growth.

Credits: wired

Reply to each and every comment.People love viewing comments seeing their opinion was acknowledged would be a satisfying feeling foreveryone. Follow everyone, and I mean everyone that has interacted with your account in anyway.

Go Live every single day, and it really boosts your page. Even if you're super busy, go live and work!

If you receive hate comments, reply back with a bit of humor! However, if it's constructive criticism, show interest, and try actually considering their opinion, this can really help your account develop.

Ask questions in your videos, so they feel the need to reply in the comments. This is a little trick most creators use.

Staying Consistent

Posting regularly is important. Post multiple times a day (considering the timings) and try avoiding uploading content right after each other, or it will not be pushed to the For You page.

Stockpile videos: If you have a day off, film as much content as you can so you can still upload videos if you're too busy another day. Posting 3-6 times a day is an ideal amount.

Duration

The duration of each video is preferred to be 11-17 sec long. The ideal time for something to be pushed out into the algorithm. And you'd get a good amount of watch time. Keep it shorter than you think it needs to be.

Tik Tok revolves around fun and concise videos, so if yours is too long than they would like, Tik Tok may decrease your rank on the For You page.

Ask them to follow, like, and comment.

The easiest method to improve the number of followers you have is by asking the viewers to 'double tap!' or 'let me know what you think in the comment section'; these things remind viewers to give you some sort of feedback on the content you create.

Asking for engagement in every video for a *very* brief period of time in the video and saying it in the description is important. Make sure it isn't mentioned for longer than 2-3 seconds, or the viewer will get bored and click away.

Keep all your content accessible.

Never delete any of your Tik Tok videos because it's likely your posts won't do well right away; you need to give it time. Your previous posts can go viral any time, so never keep them private or delete them.

There have been many times a Tik Toker posts a video, and it gets hardly 500 views in the first night, but about a few weeks later, it starts to become trending again, and you get a thousand more views.

Judge Yourself

Not to the point, you put yourself down, of course, but realistically judging yourself to keep track of your work is important.

How will this video contribute to your growth?

Is it interesting for people in my own niche?

Why would it be interesting?

What themes can I use to make this better?

If the most popular Tik Toker in my niche saw this, would they be impressed?

Take these things into consideration when you're done with certain Tik Toks.

Follow Guidelines

Especially with the recent 2021 update, you don't want to get on Tik Tok's bad side. Make sure you aren't copying someone else's work on your own profile, as that would really degrade your account.

Funded partnerships may not be as clear to Tik Tok as they are to other social networking sites, but that wouldn't imply that the very same FTC laws do not apply. Tik Tok celebrities are expected to report advertising with a transparent and obvious message that the material is funded or promoted.

Do not, under any circumstance, attempt to get free followers. This will never help you really grow. And it can have really adverse consequences later on if you are serious about Tik Tok as this is seen as a way to steal from Tik Tok. Trying to buy free followers will never get you the triumph you thrive for.

Stitch- The Tik Tok Feature

This adds yet another way for the user to interact with material that is created and posted every day by the creative Tik Tok users. Stitch is a feature the company called which enables a user to put in snippets of another Tik Tok video in yours.

How can you use it?

1. Search for the video you want to stitch and then click on 'Send to'.

2. Click on 'Stitch'

3. You can pull only 5 seconds out of the video, so choose wisely.

4. Make the rest of the video you want to put in with the stitched snippet.

5. Stitch them all together!

In the settings menu, you may select if you want to allow others to stitch your material. This is accessible on the Security and Confidentiality tab underneath "Settings and Privacy." You could allow or remove Stitch for any of your clips. Conversely, this feature can be customized for every clip you post.

Stay Stress-free

Don't try to push out more content forcefully, if your audience sees that you are, they would easily be able to get that your content came from a negative mindset. Keep it fun, enjoy making the clips, actually show your positivity.

Having a healthy mindset further nurtures your creativity and gets your ideas flowing, and you need as much of that as possible. Being authentic with your followers is key.

A few different tactics that have proved effective, such as constructive self-discuss and positive envisioning, can achieve encouraging thought.

Here are a few tactics that would prove beneficial for you to prepare your brain in thinking positively to get you started with generating content.

Concentrate on the good stuff. A part of our life is inconvenient situations and obstacles. Look at the constructive stuff once you're faced with one, regardless of how minor or relatively meaningless they are. You may still discover the ultimate positive aspect of any inconvenience if you search for it, even if it's not readily apparent.

Train with appreciation. Studying kindness has been shown to alleviate depression, boost self-esteem and promote endurance in some very trying situations. Image friends, experiences, or stuff that give you any type of warmth or delight, and struggle to convey your thanks at least once every day. This could be a thank you to a co-worker for assisting with a job, to a significant one for cleaning dishes, or to your cat for the affection they have provided.

Keep a diary of thanks. Research studies have reported that putting down stuff you're thankful for will boost your motivation and your state of wellness. You could do that by writing in a thankful diary daily or by setting down a range of items that you're happy for the days when you're going through a rough time. Using this to generate ideas even if it's really far-fetched should prove useful.

Find your motivation, whether that be intrinsic or extrinsic. You get to create the kind of content you like on Tik Tok, any kind! Use that as your passion and drive to work harder and do better.

Let's take a look at a few Tik Tokers

Daniel here has already made 10 parts of the same category and he still has millions of views. Why? Because he doesn't do the *same thing each* time of course, he changes it up, builds better for the next parts. His idea is original, unique, and entertaining!

But be careful not to overdo it, you can't go making 50 parts of the same theme as that would really just stretch it out too much and no one enjoys a guest who overstays their welcome.

daniel.labelle ✔ Daniel LaBelle

If people lagged. Part 10

♫ original sound - Daniel LaBelle

daniel.labelle Via TikTok

Zach shows a clip of the most absurd idea there is: fishing in your house, using these surprises and then a pattern interrupt which involves him falling into the water really is an odd sight to see though very entertaining and unique.

Because of this, a large number of people shared his video and commented in it to share their thoughts.

zachking Via TikTok

CHAPTER IV: Instagram

4.1: About You

Instagram is used by everyone in almost every part of the world. It's so popular because Instagram uses imagery rather than text, and people are extra quick to respond to that. It's easier to understand and process visual data rather than heaps of words. And so, visual marketing is blowing up.

The main focus on Instagram is are images. Captions are put out of the way and under the image for that exact reason.

Portrait photography is perhaps the most popular amongst the flock of imageries on Instagram. And most of these images are almost always edited by third-party applications (i.e., Snapseed, VSCO, Adobe Photoshop Express, Polarr).

Not just images, but also Boomerangs, IGTV videos, filters (of which most are created by users), stories, etc. These things push engagement to the front lines.

Naturally, every time Instagram's algorithm changes, it impacts every person who accesses it. You need to make sure youaren't going against the current of those waves. Becausethe fact is that their algorithm is constantly judging posts all over the globe and deciding which users can see each moment they open the app.

Instagram's algorithm works on machine learning, which makes the way your posts are ranked constantly changing. This book has the most recent details about how to deal with the algorithm to push you further in the marketing campaign and to keep developing engagement with your followers.

Ever since Instagram halted the inverted response in 2016, each specific feed on the site has been arranged as per the algorithm's guidelines.

As per the official @creators handle of Instagram, this concluded in a pleasant result for everybody. Basically, saying they won't be changing it back.

4.2: Ranking Factors

Genre/Niche

Design your account, configure it in a way people can know precisely what they can expect from you. After which, you post intriguing content that your audience will enjoy instantly. If people have liked those kinds of posts before, the system is much more likely to display them.

For example, Let's say Steven came in contact with a verified account. He will probably see more posts from that account, especially if he saw more content from there.

Simply put, users who communicatewith content similar to yours are probably going to come across your account as well.

Timing

Recent posts are always going to be recommended more than others. So,just like Tik Tok, posting in timing when your followers are normally active is vital.

People who spend over an hour scrolling on Instagram are obviously going to see numerous kinds of posts from top to bottom compared to someone who spends hardly a few minutes will only see only the top-ranked ones.

Instagram portrays the best at the top of users' feed every time the user activates the application. So, someone who follows hundreds of thousands of accounts will most likely miss a fair number of posts from people they are even really close to.

Engaging Your Audience

Just like every other social media platform, Instagram wishes for users to stay on the app as much and as long as possible as long as they are interested. As anend result, the software cranks up profiles in which the followersare already conversing. This guarantees that the stress on community participation is essential for advertisers and developers.

Credits: mavsocial.com

Sliding in DMs, tagging one

another in blogs, and consistently posting comments all are acts thatimply a strong bond among users as well as likes, shares, and views.

4.3: What You Need toDo

Pay Attention.

Seeing your Instagram stats is, perhaps shockingly, a few of the easiest ways to get insight into not only how your viewers think but also how the application looks at you.

Could you send everyone much of the same, or twists on the subject? Will they want better photos or videos? Just how many views come from hashtags? What kind of content is going to wow the audience?

Insights tell you did well, so it's up to you to work out where to run from that performance.

Keep It Coming

Some type of involvement, and figuring out where the intended crowd is. To have a grip on the Instagram algorithm, you have to create bonds with your followers first. And because the volume is simple to compute and accomplish than performance, the first item on the agenda is to create a social media posting schedule to stay on track.

What is consistency? Mean for Instagram? This is exclusive to your niche. As you just started, start with the way you want to progress. Think about what's affordable for the team to create.

If you draw viewers with a spark, three stories, two posts, and one IGTV video per day produced a certain amount of perception. Volume and layout selections would depend on the resources you currently have. And what's most critical, however, is to concentrate on publishing posts that you feel proud of regularly.

Reposting is Key.

Even after you have a nice schedule, you're following and knowing what your followers expect, pushing content out into the world isn't simple like butter on jam.Recycle, change-up your best work. Now, not only do you know Instagram wants it, but it also saves a lot of time.

You could transform the videos to gifs, similar pictures to a slideshow,and use pictures used in another photo shoot for multiple reasons, throwbacks, and repost on stories.

Just use the same thing but be extra creative with it.

Collaborating withOther Influencers& Brands

Keep an eye on what other public figures in your niche are up to, and if possible, try to do a collab with them.

Perhaps the easiest way to naturally broaden your scope to fresh eyes is to seek a suitable friend with a complimentary following while still attracting the viewers' interest with appropriate different perspectives.The outcome may very well provide an added strength from Instagram if the partnership is as enjoyable for your community as it would be for you.

Though you need to make surethat the person you choose to partner with is suitable and legitimate, as other influencers will judge you based on who you collab with, it is probably best if you do a detailed background check before setting a collab date with them.

As that influencer will be bringing in their audience, you need to see what kind of followers they have and their analytics. Making sure you don't bring in the wrong crowd who would go away as soon as they came. You could check this by looking at their engagement on posts. If the person you are intending to collab with is genuine and interactive with his/her audience, you should probably go for it.

As searching through every single person, you could collab with would take a significant amount of time, you could use means likeNinjaoutreach, Meltwater, GroupHigh, Newswire, Cision Communications Cloud, etc.This software allows you to make your listing in its database, making things a lot more convenient for you as time is, in fact, of the essence.

The kinds of sponsorships you could get fall into three basic categories: large accounts (120K followers) get at least $400 per sponsored post, middle-class (3K-100K followers) get at least $150, and small accounts (less than 3K)get around $100 or less.

After making a list of the sponsorships you'd like to go for, you need to send each one your pitch. But not in the first text, of course, that would be not polite. Tell them why you're interested in the subject they put out and communicate with them. Once you know what they want exactly, you could develop an amazing pitch.

Next, you need to plan your influencer publicizing campaign. Makesure you keep interacting with the influencers so you can get an insight into what they think. Consider other people's opinions to make a master plan using the influencers and your creativity.

As soon as you have initiated your campaign, please keep track of how it's doing and keep adjusting it accordingly.

An example:

@omayazein partnered up with a brand calledModanisa and gave her audience a discount code, which in turn gets a lot of shares, and she has about 1 Million followers!

@omayazein Via Instagram

Reward Them

As discussed before, Instagram values engagement A LOT, so give your audience what they want! When your audience shares your posts on story or DM, comments and likes push your posts to the top instantly.

The goal should be to create a kind of commitment and passion that motivates individuals to advocate and empower themselves. The service could do the job for you if you already have an outstanding Business-to-consumer service. Anything other than that, you would need to find means of subtly encouraging individuals.

Please stop posting everything sent to you from your community. Compile the latest and integrate material into the digital plan of your content whenever appropriate. And bear in mind that merely reposting the stories of other users has also been specifically noted as something that would not include your stories on the Explore List, so make sure you remain imaginative and on topic.

Like your followers' and viewers' comments, reply to each one, even the haters. Try getting into a conversation with them. Interact with them through stories, polls, use trending filters.

Ask questions on your stories and share them, be humorous, genuine, everything and anything interesting. It could be 'what's your opinion on....' Or 'what's your most embarrassing story!', etc.

If they reply to your stories, make sure you reply!! And not after days at a time, but as soon as you can. Enjoy your time with them. Really try and understand what they wish to see from you. Unless they're just there to hate on you, then you should probably ignore it or if you could do something creative with it (while following community guidelines), go for it.

Follow influencers that are familiar with your niche. This can link other people that are interested in your type of content to you. Not just follow, but also like and comment on their posts, share it! (Another way of utilizing the Shine theory). Showing interest in other people's content can help you too.

Use the Hashtag System

Just like Tik Tok, hashtags are an important part of Instagram. It is the middleman between you and the right audience. It's the lowest building block, especially when you're just starting out.

If you think using heaps of hashtags, including ones that do not correlate with your niche, will help, you might be wrong. It would be misusing the hashtag system, and that leads you to a direct road to the bad side of Instagram because they do, in fact, notice those who try abusing the algorithm. And not to mention, you are not gaining anything by trying to show it to people who have no interest in your niche.

The maximum quantity of hashtags you are allowed to use is 30 per post, and yes, use all those 30. Try writing those hashtags in the first comment rather than in the caption, so it looks a bit more well put together.

Perhaps not all hashtags that you assume are nice would be suitable for your own use. It is why every last one of you would want to verify to see whether the material is important to your subject.

When deciding whether a hashtag is right for your post, there are two key considerations to have a look at Niche and Dimension.

Never use only the most famous and vague hashtags, thinking you would be able to reach a larger crowd because you won't. You'll just be a hidden needle in a haystack. An invisible need at that. Why? Because they aren't specific enough, and a lot of popular influencers already use those so you wouldn't be too noticed yet.

Please make sure you have certain hashtags that you use in every post (with fewer follows) so that you can be noticed by at least one familiar audience (needless to say, they need to be your target audience too).

It would be best if you would be able to find a middle ground between hashtags that not one soul has ever heard of before and hashtags that everyone knows about. Both would reward you little. Try hashtags that have about 90,000-900,000 post range.

Sorry, But Buying Is NOT the Way to Go

You can purchase double-taps or follows in due to despair just to see whether a lift is what they needed to get moving all along. But while this may make you appear popular to random people; it couldn't be farther from the facts.

Finally, they consider giving up both as a waste of time on Instagram and stop bringing in any considerable effort to expand, since they just do not see what else there is to do. Don't purchase likes, fans, and also, don't try the old trick of interaction pods.

Yes, even Instagram notices it if you buy followers/likes/views. Not only Instagram but also your followers. Which makes things a lot worse. And so, you won't gain any kind of income from that.

Using Highlights

Utilize the highlights feature and make/or find suitable cover photos for each to maintain consistency.It is making a profile that's pleasing to the eye and fitting for your niche and target audience.

4.4: Seeing is Believing

You may think this is all talk and no action, so let's drive that notion away by looking at a few of the many influencers on Instagram.

Notice the overall layout of this account. The username and profile instantly tell the users what the account is about.

Just the username would do this for us too but @wedarkacademia further described what it was about as well as threw in a bit of personality to the description as well as handles for other social platforms.

Their posts are consistent and related to one another. See the Highlights categorized neatly too.

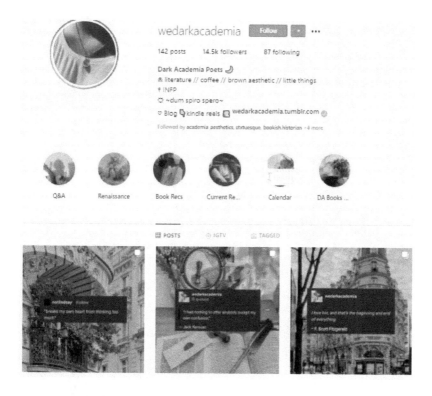

@wedarkacademia Via Instagram

Responses like these encourage so much growth and engagement amongst the target audience.

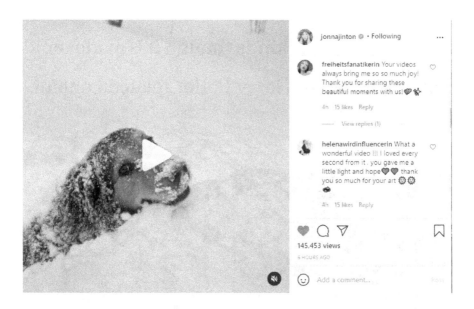

@jonnajinton Via Instagram

@madeyemoodswing interacting with their audience. Their username being humorous and instantly getting the attention of Harry Potter fans who understand the reference.

Drawing in users of various kinds though if @madeyemoodswing doesn't involve any kind of Harry Potter related content, those fans may lose interest.

@madeyemoodswing Via Instagram

Jonna Jinton, blogging her art, photography and life on Instagram whilst also mentioning that she works on another platform (YouTube). Her posts are coherent and in sync with nature and mostly winter in her home country.

Her description and highlights are simple and straight to the point which a lot of users would find convenient and contemporary.

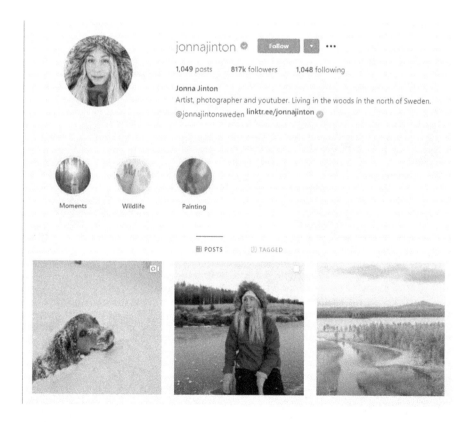

@jonnajinton Via Instagram

CHAPTER V: Ideas for Newbies

5.1: Idea Generation

There is not much to implement without ideas, and since the implementation is the secret to progress, creative ideas are required to enable some sort of change. It is clear that thoughts alone are not going to make creativity possible, since you need to be able to construct a structured mechanism to handle such innovations. The concept is not only about producing lots of it but also about bringing care to the nature of it.

It's not easy to create grade A content 24/7. Often people find it difficult to break out of their usual routine and habits when thinking about working on something new. In order to get out of the negative spiral, you need to glance at the development of creativity altogether and incorporate a few of the most key factors, strategies, and procedures that could be used more routinely to produce fresh concepts.

Perhaps you need original thoughts so a new possibility can be thoroughly explored?

Maybe you are trying to find a new way of solving a creativity barrier, or are you hoping for a decent answer to the dilemma?

Why does it matter?

Generating ideas is the outcome ofcreating complex, tangible, or conceptual theories. It's at the top of the funnelfor concept organization, which works on seeking potential alternatives to true or suspected challenges and possibilities.

Ideas are, as stated, the very first move into change. Fresh theories rely on you progressing as independent individuals. From the point of view of a person, whether you feel stuck with a job or otherwise unable to resolve that one dilemma, fresh solutions will motivate you to push ahead.

The aim of fresh concepts is to reinforce the manner in which you work, irrespective of your priorities or the kinds of things you're searching for.

To fuel productivity and improve nature on a broader scale, societies rely on creativity. Creativity improves emerging innovations and enterprises. They are providing creators with more opportunities.

How do you do it?

Chances are, you brainstorm. However, it's been found that brainstorming requires more time and tends to fewer ideas as ofplanning, logging, and managing the meeting would take a lot more time than it should. While there are certain approaches to boost the quality of brainstorming, it's preferred if brainstorming isn't your first thought.

Nevertheless, certain methods are worth taking a look at. As you're searching for various kinds of ideas, it is beneficial to have methods in mind that help in developing them. Several of these concept development approaches may be used for further productive brainstorming and another creativity type.

5.2: The Techniques

Challenging proposals

This concept is when you bring an issue or opportunity into view due to the possibility of innovatively solving it. It can let you make a certain doubt about your content and aim it at your audience to get more ideas and useful opinions after you have identified what you intend to gain from it.

These idea challenges come in handy, especially when you're looking to engage a large audience of up to 10000. When you plan an idea challenge, pre-define the outcomes you'd like, the niche, followers, subscribers, etc. Make sure you keep track of the time with this technique to make sure it's working.

Similarities

You can use data and statistics from previous posts or videos on social media platforms to improve on ideas for another piece of content; this is thinking simultaneously.It is the simplest way of generating fresh content as it's often experimented with and succeeded.

In Example, YouTuber's making reaction videos continually but of various kinds of content.

SCAMPER

This method applies critical thinking to alter creativity, which is already present — adjusting open-sourceideas to improve and agree on the best answer.

1. Substitution – Your old content being substituted with others to gain improvement.

2. Combining- Merging two or more ideas into one master idea for your content.

3. Adapting- Evaluates the options to make a method more versatile and works on the design, system, or principle alongside other related gradual changes.

4. Modification- From a broader context, changing not only the concept but also changing the concept looks at the challenge or potential and tries to change the outcomes.

5. Improvising by putting to another use- Searching for opportunities to use the concept or current content for some other reason and, if applicable to other areas of your profile or channel, analyzes the potential advantages.

6. Elimination- This technique studies all the possibilities, and if you find more than one fragment was removed.

7. Reversal- The emphasis of this procedure is to reverse the order of factors that can be swapped of your idea.

This technique was originatedfrom the idea of brainstorming, but it applies to your thinking technique too. If you make generating ideas a daily activity by a series of trivial things, you could have a decent chance of winning the main breakthrough. Occasionally all it takes is really to reflect on what you already have. Sometimes, creators want to worry about the next remarkable thing being discovered. It is easy to overlook that the endless gradual changes are the aspects that can have a difference in the medium haul while creating fresh concepts. As a baseline, utilizing your existing theories or methods will explain a lot in relation to your present content, and that is what the SCAMPER strategy is really about.

Reverse Psychology

This method will make you challenge your content-related perceptions. Reverse thinking comes in handy when you feel you are trapped in the traditional mentality, and it appears to be impossible to come up with such unique ideas. It helps in checking our routinely-habits as the answer to finding more content isn't always a straight-to-the-point road. You consider the possibilities of what the opposite would do for your profile or channel, even if you end up thinking of the most peculiar of solutions.

5.3: Once You've Got It

Organizing Ideas

Once you've got all those ideas down, planning and organizing them can be difficult if you don't know where to start. Creators need to collect this creativity as soon as it comes to them instead of using it as soon as it comes up.

Jotting down all your ideas in a notebook or on your phone can be helpful, and most people do this as it's only for personal use. But if you wish for other people's opinions on the matter to know their judgment, this could be a hassle. Not to worry though, there are things like idea management tools to aid you with that.

Management

A concept tool for effective functions as the foundation of the method of idea planning. This is how you can assemble the ideas, analyze them, debate, prioritize them, take account of their success, and the overall course of the operations of your idea generation.

Since concept planning is such a huge subject and famous influencers or public figures are likely to have loads of suggestions, it often makes perfect sense for most influencers or creators to use a designated idea management system.

It is just as productive to handle ideas with a designated method as the underlying mechanism at the back end. You could create a mechanism that makes it a lot easier to produce and refine fresh concepts and create ideas a persistent practice. The methods that are too confusing can infuriate people, so try not to make things too difficult.

5.4: Winning at Creativity

The Appropriate Crowd

It is necessary to include the right individuals in the equation for the content to be as efficient as possible. Start engaging all influencers who know about the content creation and are sincerely involved in you making a difference.

Ensure your community is the target audience and well educated on the topic if the aim is to involve a wider community of users to produce ideas.

Determine Your Objective

Aim to collect as much relevant data as possible about the content you wish to make before you begin to understand the source. Define what you understand about it by now and what data is still required.

Though it sounds simple, the further you can clearly explain your actual idea, the greater the odds of producing practical ideas are.

Limits to Keep an Eye Out For.

It can impede imagination to convey that every idea is a valid idea, so ensure the aims are ambitious and precise enough. One approach to get some of the viewers' genuinely innovative thoughts is to set limits.

If the ultimate aim is to cut prices, suggestions such as investing truly little on content would certainly come to mind when you want to save up. The thoughts you get, though, would vary greatly if you ask yourself: "How could I save 50% on expenses and create unique and engaging content?".

Deduction

The goal of creating original approaches is to improve what is already present as well as to produce something new.

From a different angle, coming up with entirely novel solutions will help you tackle your creativity block. It helps you to widen the spectrum of thoughts beyond the present style of learning, which inevitably leads to much more ideas.

Sometimes, creators, influencers, and public figures use current ideas or behavioral templates while attempting to get started on a social media platform instead of attempting to think of the latest ideas. The concern with this technique is that it does not encourage you to pursue multiple options and limits the number of possibilities.

5.5: About Yourself

Who are you?

Create a clip of yourself being introduced. Who are you, what are you doing? On your YouTube channel, Tik Tok, or Instagram profile, what should viewers hope to see? How frequently do you upload photos or videos? Create videos to let them know exactly what they should expect, inviting viewers to your channel or page. Aim to give a convincing argument for audiences to click on the subscribe button on YouTube and follow on Instagram or Tik Tok.

Vlogging

Making Vlogs can be informative, fun, intimate, anything you would like to create of it, much like traditional writing. Almost all influencers and public figures may use material from vlogs to involve fans and expand their communities.

A Day in Your Life

YouTubers love to walk through The Day in your Life videos from another's perspective. Once you wake up the next morning and lead audiences to a normal day in your schedule, start filming.

Matt D'Avella Via YouTube

Behind-the-curtainContent

Showcase to the viewers what's going on at the back end of your Instagram account, YouTube channel, or Tik Tok account. With this famous video style, let your audience see behind the curtains. You can display your room, your house, your workplace, your city, anywhere else you enjoy.

20 Questions

You could make short clips or long clips (depending on your preference or niche) playing a game of 20 questions. These questions can be personal or silly, and the best have a little bit of both. Letting your audience be closer to you is what this accomplishes.

'Draw My Life.'

These kinds of videos are often found on YouTube, where the creator essentially draws their life often on a whiteboard with stick figures and narrating their life so far. Of course, you decide how much or how little you wish to say about yourself. Majority 'Draw my life' videos include key events or milestones in their lives.

You can even introduce your family, background, and friends in these.

5.6: Trending Content Ideas

Teach them How to Cook (or how not to)

This kind of content is often made by entertainment-focused or cooking influencers. You can make it an A grade cooking tutorial, or you could completely twist it depending on your creativity and teach people how not to cook but let them have an enjoyable time watching creators do it wrong.

For example, YouTuber 'Simply Nailogical' made a video called 'Baking a cake with Nail Polish' on 18th September 2016, which got over 5 Million views. The cake was quite inedible but still entertaining to watch to over 5 Million people.

You can make this an Instagram post, a Tik-Tok video, or a YouTube video.

Workout Routine

As it's time to start working out, lots of folks look towards YouTube videos, quick Tik Tok hacks, or Instagram posts/IGTV videos for specific fitness routines, as well as how to do those workouts. Both common subjects are exercise, stretching, or shape footage.

Understanding the Complicated Mess

Informative and aurally captivating means of presenting data and figures that could otherwise be dull or difficult to grasp is infographics related content. Content that helps your audience's day a little easier. Every genre of content has specific things that not everyone understands, so try finding the most commonly found problem in yours and present content on that!

Reviewing other People's Products

One of the most common kinds of information on these social media platforms is product reviews. Before deciding to buy, thousands of viewers check out this insightful content. Tech gadgets and make-up items are common themes, but reviews can be sought for all types of goods.

For example, YouTuber Marques Brownlee's Niche is tech gadgets, and a majority, maybe even all, of his video's reviews on really expensive gadgets so often people who think about buying a new phone or the PS5 watch his videos to see his opinion on it. His video called 'PlayStation 5 Review: NextGen Gaming!' received almost 6 Million views!

You can make review videos on any and every genre of content! Games, movies, books, food, universities, perfumes, songs, shows, even countries! So, search for things you can review in your niche.

Comedy Videos

In the event that you need to turn into a web sensation, an entertaining video may very well assist you with getting there. A sizable number of the most mainstream recordings on YouTube, Instagram, and Tik Tok ended up in such a state since this sort of content made watchers chuckle or laugh.

Pranks

Viewers love watching tricks. Pull a trick on somebody (innocuous tricks, please) and share the outcomes on your social media platforms.

Tricks have not been altogether contemplated; however, scientists have discovered that individuals find being deceived an extremely aversive encounter. Trick based humor can be coldblooded or kind, cherished or detested; however, it's not straightforward.

Furry Creatures Content

Dogs, little cats, child elephants, the Internet loves charming/interesting creature recordings are considerably more popular than recordings of human children. So, if you have a pet, share it with the world! Everyone loves animals.

Music Videos

Singing a song cover, and original, or even lip-syncing is always a fun sight to see. Indeed, even late-night TV gets in on the good times. Pick a mainstream tune and give it a shot!

If you have a bad voice, don't worry; try making it hilarious by a funny parody where you impress the audience with clever and witty lyrics rather than your vocals.

Fact Check

What are some myths that are commonly believed by the vast majority regarding your niche? Compile all the misconceptions and make a post or video on the matter. Show emotion and teach your audience the stereotypes believed about your niche by the public.

As the internet is filled with so much information, a fair share of it is fake news, so spreading awareness about it would be intriguing for your audience (as long as you stay on topic).

Often people are found spreading rumors without even knowing they are rumors and not facts, so content that addresses the rumors is an interesting concept for anyone.

Needless to say, double-check whether the information you are giving your audience is proven with evidence to be right. Or else those mistakes can decrease your followers/subscribers quick.

Write a catchy caption or thumbnail with a question that quickly catches their interest. For example, '10 Myths you probably believed about professional cooks' or '6 reasons why you should not believe every thing you're told'.

Speed-run

Can you play games as fast as humanely possible?Finish your make-up in under 2 minutes? Or maybe you can make a 3-course meal in under an hour? Show off those skills on social media!

Speed-runs are commonly found on gaming channels so viewers can quickly experience a gameplay without having to play it themselves due to the cost of the game or less time of time.

Time-slip

@jonnajinton Via Instagram on April 17th , 2020

Time-lapse is a method where the casings of the video are caught at a far slower speed than expected. Traffic, mists, and the sunrise all will, in general, be well-known time-slip by subjects. The outcome is frequently hypnotizing.

Some creators make time-lapses of their artwork to show progress quickly as an art piece can take at least a few hours.

Shopping/Mail Hauls

This type of video is particularly well known with style vloggers and beauty. After an outing to the shopping center, flaunt your take piece by piece. From the freshest iPhone to an in-vogue membership box or the most trending toy, individuals love to watch others open boxes. So next time you do another package, don't simply tear into it; make sure you are recording first!

You could even give out your address and your audience would send you mail. Often YouTubers make mail opening videos reviewing all the heartfelt gifts their watchers send them.

Go Live

Why trust that the recap will show individuals what's happened? Take your watchers to the occasion with you by live-streaming to your Instagram Live, Tik Tok Live, or YouTube Live. Even after the session is over, the stream would still be accessible online.

You can schedule a certain day for every week in which you go live and make sure you let everyone know through all your social media platforms, so they are aware and wait for you to go live.

What Most Do

A substantial number of the top Instagrammersare singers, sports brands, actors, footballers, models, and ofcourse, Instagram themselves.The most famous YouTuber channels are often among the genre oftrailer channels, singers, gamers, kids show, hack tutorial channels, and so on.Tik Tokers are often found to be comedians, musicians, artists,etc.

The best content? Ones that are so good that people feel the need to see it on other platforms too, Tik Tok video compilations on YouTube, and Tik Tok videos on Instagram, Live videos on Instagram recorded and put-onYouTube. The type of content that is put across various platforms are the ones that have gone viral or loved enough that users wish to see it almost everywhere.

Conclusion

First things first, it would be beneficial if you ask yourself, what do you have to offer? Why would people want to watch your videos? What are they getting out of the time they spent on your video?

Is it educational? Hilarious? Scary? Relaxing? Silly?Helpful? Inspiring or motivational? Perhaps very random, either way, would your target audience enjoy or show any interest in it?

Maintain originality- the charm of social media is that you can express your thoughts and add a little more to *you*, so to speak. You can grow on YouTube, Tik Tok, and Instagram, only if you have something no one else has to give out. The basic rule to starting a business, 'what's so special about you?' or 'what do you have that no one else does?'. Write down all that comes to mind when answering these questions.

You can not copy peoples' ideas, only your own significant expression of those ideas into your videos, posts, stories, etc.However, if your content seems to be matching someone else's a little too much, change it up, brainstorm a little about what you could do to make it unique, and choose the best one. And be certain you aren't tuning out any other possibilities due to your fears.

Honesty- be honest about your opinions and where you stand. This can be a random video about car reviews or your opinion on white supremacy; it need not matter. Maybe you feel like changing your genre after a long time, but you're afraid of losing the number of followers/subscribers you've gotten so far. Your fear is valid, but you can't force yourself to put out content on something you have no more interest in anymore because you followers/subscriber will notice eventually, and they'll just fade out on their own. So, try being honest, raw, and authentic from the start.

However, being honest does not amount to being insensitive. You're trying to be the person people look up to or look forward to viewing when they're having a difficult day, so try to fill those expectations without disregarding your bad days, of course. Ending things on a positive note and be accepting of the honest truth your followers/subscribers/viewers offer in return.

Humility- Try not to overthink each comment they make because what seems like an hour of thought to you was probably not more than five minutes to them. When you start noticing your growth, don't become egotistic about it, or the people that put you where you are today will leave as fast as they came. Nobody likes a showoff.

Setting boundaries- deciding where you draw the line between your public and personal life is vital. You don't need to broadcast every minute detail about your personal life to the entire world, and you need to value the privacy of the people close to you if you wish for the same.

Motivation- find that mechanism that triggers, leads, and retains your aiming habits. Whether it be intrinsic or extrinsic motivation, keep a daily reminder for it, so you keep that drive and motivation to continue working hard. Grabbing a coffee, chocolate bar, reading, or some inspirational quote is what puts you in a nice mood and sparks wisdom, do it every day.

The physical, internal, cultural, and mental factors which trigger action are involved in motivation. Introjected motivation is when you are driven to work out of the guilt of procrastination or laziness. Identified motivation is when you know you have got work to do, yet you haven't determined anything in regard to it. Try to avoid introjected and identified motivation as it originates from a negative space.

Don't give up if you feel like you are not getting enough growth, stay consistent and keep at it no matter what. If you still feel like there has been no effect, try going over the points again and make sure you keep track of how you have been doing by statistically analyzing yourself.

Soon enough, you will catch yourself with 10,000 followers/subscribers on YouTube, Instagram, and Tik Tok. It is more or less a smooth ride from there. Good Luck!

Short Stays Real Estate with No (or Low) Money Down

The 7+1 Creative Strategies to Create Passive Income from Home Using the AirBnb Business Model in 2021

By

Marcus Wayne

Table of Contents

Introduction

If you are a forward-focused person, you can dream of leaving the profession to enjoy a retirement life that is simpler, or you might even consider early retirement. But a dream is only a wish without a plan. You need to contemplate passive income to put a few wheels on the dream. There are also plenty of different options for passive income and rationales of how to build it. Passive income is the money you collect that doesn't cause you to do a lot of "active" work in order to continue to earn it. In essence, you may do much of the work in advance and do some extra effort to earn an income. For instance, to keep the money flowing, if you develop an online course, you only need to update the content. Likewise, passive income strategies like renting out property and/or building a blog can take some effort to get up and running, but while you sleep, they would eventually earn you cash. You've already heard the word, "make money when you're sleeping." This is the main attraction that allows individuals to generate passive income. Even when you're not working, you can develop something (a course, a blog, e-book, videos, and/or an online store) which generates income. Or you can own something that helps you to earn passive income (property or stocks).

So why do you need to build passive income?

In the presence of a full-time job, your salary is your biggest income tool, a tool that usually requires your active involvement. Even if you enjoy your career, you wouldn't mind making some additional money without the tears, blood, sweat, and time commitment of another job. If you lose your job or want to generate an extra source of income when you are no longer productive or if you outlive your retirement fund, developing a passive income will improve your wealth-building strategy, create the opportunity to retire early, and save you from a total loss of income.

And how much money can passive income generate?

Generally, passive income won't make you wealthy overnight, so ignore those get-rich-quick schemes you've read about. But, over the long term, consistent, profitable passive income strategies will produce some serious money. Depending on the income stream, we're talking about anything from two to three thousand dollars to thousands of dollars.

Some people like to think of investing when we mention "passive income" because, with the least amount of effort, it can yield the greatest returns. But you should think about your retirement plan & passive income as two distinct subjects. The entire premise behind the long-term investment is to produce retirement income. If your fund options are good and they offer a match, you want to make sure you invest in your company retirement plan, like that of a 401(k). These are great choices for establishing a powerful pension plan, but before a certain age, you will face taxes as well as penalties for every withdrawal. You need to let your money grow only for the long term with retirement planning and not touch it. However, a form of low-effort income which can be accessed at any time should be passive income. After you are debt-free and have some cash left, one way to build passive income is by buying real estate and leasing it out to tenants. Rental property may be a fantastic source of additional income, but it is not the most passive option because, unless you employ a property management company, you will have to put a lot of effort and time into maintaining the property. You need to be incharge of your property if you go on the rental property route. Pay off your own home first before you buy a rental property, and buy your investment property with cash. You must not go into debt in order to purchase property for rent. You could develop something like an informative blog and/or a YouTube tutorial series to be able to generate online traffic if you have a bright idea that appeals to a particular audience.You might sell commercial space on your blog or ad spots on your channel if your content is engaging and it sees ample regular traffic. You can sit back, relax, and reap sources of passive income after you put in the heavy lifting. The list of ideas for passive income could go on indefinitely. Never go for any passive income strategies that promise a fast return or require large sums of money upfront. Your other financial targets would be sabotaged by them. In this book, we will present ideas that are steady, profitable, and trustworthy.

CHAPTER 1: Understand Income and Importance of Passive Income

There are three main categories of income:

Active income

Portfolio income

Passive income

1.1 Active Income

Active income alludes to money made as a result of the provision of service. Examples of active income are wages, tips, salaries, fees, and income from companies in which there is material involvement. The owner must meet the criteria for "material participation," which is based on hours worked or other factors, in order for income from a company to be considered active rather than passive. The most popular example of active income is income earned in the form of a paycheck from an employer. "Money from business activities is deemed "active" for the self-employed or someone else with an ownership interest in a corporation if it meets the criteria of material participation by the Internal Revenue Service (IRS). That implies one of the following is valid, at least:

- The taxpayer works during the year in the corporation for 500 or more hours.
- The taxpayer performs the majority of the company's work.
- Over the year, the taxpayer works for more than 100 hours in the company and no other employee works more hours than the taxpayer.

However, income earned is treated as passive income if someone earns income from a company in which they do not actively participate. Meanwhile, portfolio income is income from investments, like dividends and capital gains. Depending on the legislation at the time, these various forms of income can be taxed differently. At present, for instance, portfolio income is taxed at lower rates than active income.

Example of active income from a business

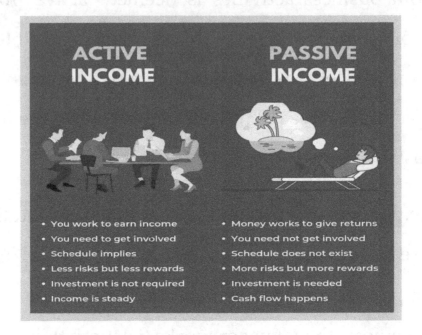

John and Laura are not married to each other. They have a 50% interest in an online business. John performs the majority of the day-to-day work in the business. Therefore, his income is considered active by the IRS.On the other, Laura helps with the marketing activities. She, however, works less than 100 hours a year in the business. It is for this very reason that her income from the business is considered passive income by the IRS. The material participation rule was established to prevent individuals that do not actively participate in a business from using it to generate tax losses which they, otherwise, could have written off against their active income.

1.2 Portfolio Income

Income from the portfolio is money received from investments, interest, dividends, and capital gains. Portfolio income streams are often known to be dividends received from investment properties. It is one of three main income groups. Active income and passive income are the others. Most income from the portfolio enjoys favorable tax treatment. Dividends and capital gains are charged at a much lower rate as compared to active income. Furthermore, portfolio income is not subject to Medicare or Social Security taxes. Income from the portfolio contains dividends, interest, and capital gains. Compared to active or passive income, portfolio income typically enjoys favorable tax treatment. Money from the portfolio is not subject to withholding from Social Security or Medicaid. One way to maximize portfolio income is to invest in an ETF that purchases dividend-paying stocks. Income from the portfolio does not come from passive investments. Moreover, portfolio income is not received from daily business activity. It is earned because of dividends, taxes, and capital gains or interest paid on loans. For tax purposes, the categories of income are important. Passive income losses can not necessarily be offset against portfolio or active income.

Ways to Increase Portfolio Income

Following ways can be employed for increasing portfolio income:

Purchase High-Paying Dividend Stocks

Investors can enhance their portfolio income by purchasing stocks that pay above-average dividends. Dividends can be paid directly to the shareholder. Moreover, dividends can also be used to buy additional shares in the company.

Purchase Dividend Exchange-Traded Funds

A cost-effective way to maximize portfolio income is to buy ETFs that explicitly track high-paying dividend stocks. For example, the FTSE High Dividend Yield Index is tracked by the Vanguard High Dividend Yield ETF. There are 396 stocks that have high dividend yields and are included in the index. For other dividend ETF options, the selection criteria concentrate on how many consecutive years the company has paid a dividend and/or on companies that have a history of raising their annual dividend payments.

Write Options

An investor can write call options against their stock holdings to enhance his portfolio income.

1.3 Passive Income

Passive income are earnings that come from a limited partnership, rental property, or another enterprise in which an entity is not actively engaged, such as a silent investor. Proponents of passive income tend to be boosters of the working lifestyle of a work-from-home and/or be-your-own-boss. Colloquially, it has been used on the part of the person receiving it to describe money being earned periodically with little or no effort. When used as a technical term, passive income is defined by the IRS as either "net rental income" or "income from an enterprise in which the taxpayer does not participate materially" and may include self-charged interest in some cases. Passive income is a source of income that may require some initial effort or investment but continues to generate payments in the future. Examples are music and book royalties and house rent payments. Passive income is the return on savings accounts. Passive income is created by a limited partnership in which a person owns a share of a company but does not engage in its functioning. Passive income consists of earnings generated from rental property, a limited partnership, or some other enterprise in which a person does not engage actively. Usually, taxes are charged on passive income. Portfolio income is perceived by a few analysts as passive income, and interest and dividends will also be considered as passive income. In order to earn and maintain, passive income needs little to no effort. When an earner puts in one of those little efforts to produce income, it is called progressive passive income. In many ways, a passive income investment can make an investor's life easier. This is true when a hands-off strategy is followed. Examples of passive income investment strategies include - Peer-to-Peer Lending, Real Estate, Dividend Stocks, and Index Funds. These four choices suggest different risk and diversification levels. As with any kind of financial investment, calculating the anticipated returns in relation to a passive income opportunity versus the loss potential is important. The main types of passive activities are explained below:

Cash flows from property income, including cash flows from a property or from any piece of real estate, capital gains, rent through resource ownership such as rental income, and in the form of interest from financial asset ownership.

Trade or business-related activities in which an individual does not engage in a company's operations other than investing during the year.

Royalties, that is, payments initiated by one corporation (the licensee) to another firm/person (the licensor) for the right to use the intellectual property of the latter (music, video, book).

Standards for Material Participation

The standards for material participation include:

- Five hundred plus more hours toward an activity or a business from which you are earning

- If the participation for that tax year has been "substantially all."

- Up to 100 hours of commitment and at least as much as every other person involved in the operation

- Material involvement in at least five of the past 10 tax years

- For personal services initiatives, material engagement at any point in three previous tax years

According to the IRS, there are two passive activity categories. Rentals, including equipment and real estate, are the first type; and businesses are the second type, where the individual does not engage materially on a daily, continuous and significant basis.

Examples of passive activities

The following are considered passive activities:

- Equipment leasing
- Limited partnerships

- Partnerships, S-Corporations, and LLCs where the individuals do not materially participate
- Rental real estate (some exceptions apply)
- Sole proprietorship or farm where the individual does not materially participate

1.4 Taxing of passive income

There are various forms of passive income, ranging from capital gains and dividends. Then the question arises whether the passive income is taxable or not. The brief response is, yes. Tax rates can differ depending on how long the assets are kept, the amount of benefit gained, and/or net income on each form of passive income.

Short-Term Passive Income Tax Rates

For assets retained for a year or less, short-term gains apply and are taxed as ordinary income. In other words, at the same rate as your income tax, short-term capital gains are taxed. The prevailing tax rates for short-term gains are as follows: 10 percent, 12 percent, 22 percent, 24 percent, 32 percent, 35, and 37 percent.

Long-Term Passive Income Tax Rates

Long-term capital gains (assets that are held for more than one year) are taxed at three rates: zero percent, fifteen percent, and twenty percent, based on your income bracket.

Taxing of real estate income

With lower tax rates, investing in real estate and high yield rental assets is now even more advantageous for individuals. The authorized business income deduction is now a twenty percent deduction on the taxable income while buying and holding real estate. This deduction of 20 percent now requires investors to subtract a portion of the real estate investment holdings, which may lead to a higher ROI.

1.5 Why Passive Income Beats Earned Income

income Earned is the income that you earn when you work the job full-time or run a business. Notice that, in most instances, "running business" doesn't require rent real estate corporate. Money gained from royalties,rents, & stakes in the limited partnerships is passive income. Income from the portfolio is the income from interest, dividends, and stock sales capital gains. Earned income would be subject to heavy taxation at all levels. Earned money should be utilized to rapidly create wealth, but your wealth must be transferred into the portfolio and passive income pools in order to reduce your tax position. Earned incomes are subject to FICA taxation and the full marginal income tax rate. There are undoubtedly ways of minimizing tax liability, such as operating an S-earned Corporation's revenue, investing in the firm and currently earning deductible expenditures, etc., but high marginal tax rates would also be subject to net income. The issue with earned money is that you still have to spend more cash in order to minimize tax liability. Passive incomes from the rental property aren't subject to the high operational tax rates. Rental property income is privileged by amortization and depreciation and contributes toa much lesser effective rate of tax.

Let's assume, for instance, you now own a rental property,which nets 10,000 dollars before the depreciation & amortization. Let's just say that $8,000 is the total amount of depreciation and amortization. It leaves with a taxable revenue of $2,000. You can paya tax equivalent to 740 dollars if you fall in the 37 percent tax bracket. Yet you see an effective rate tax of just 7.4 percent as we equate the $740 with the amount raised ($10,000). If you made the same 10,000 dollars in the earned income, inorder to minimize the amount available to tax, you would need to expend more. Otherwise, with $10,000 into taxable income, you'd pay $3,700, meaning you're in 37 percent tax brackets. With the rental real-estate, every year, you don't have to be paying for depreciation. It's a ghostly cost which you have to claim. That's why, from a tax standpoint, passive income knocksout earned income.

1.6 Reasons Why Passive Income Is So Important

It's no wonder passive income's, and for a good cause, one of the most thought about, sought after aspects of personal finance. Passive income will have an incredibly positive effect on only about any financial situation, from creating vast wealth to avoiding a paycheck-to-paycheck lifestyle. But that posesthe question: why does passive income matter so much? In short, passive income's essential because in financial life, it provides flexibility, prosperity, and independence. In addition, because your time & resources do not limit passive income, it may havea beneficial and important impact on the ability to build wealth. Passive income, in different words, is 1 ofthe easiest ways to upgrade the financial condition. But if that's not compelling enough, we've listed the top reasons whypassive income's important.

Improved financial stability

One ofthe most significant milestones you will hit on the road to prosperity is monitory stability. In different words, even if you really can see your financial position and realize, with certainty, that you're capable of coping with a powerful financial storm, so then you're on a very stable path. If you may count on the money rolling inside without having to fight for every cent of it, even more than that, so financial security is just a nearby corner. More money which comes in more you can be secure and comfortable in the finances. It helps you in relaxing, look atthe bigger picture, & make smarter financial decisions because you don't have to grind for every dollar you earn, which, in turn, increases your financial health. This is a magnificent little cycle & one of key reasons whypassive income is playing such a major role inpersonal finance.

Less reliance on a paycheck

The discomfort that comes with living paycheck to paycheck is not comparable by any means. And if it is your case, then one of the best moves you can take is to adda bit of the passive income in your life. There is no secret in that sometimes it may get a bit stressful as you trade time for dollars. And the more you will distance yourself froma focus on the next paycheck, the lighter it can be in your life. One ofthe greatest advantages of passive income is avoiding the paycheck-to-paycheck lifestyle.

It's easier to achieve your goals

Did you ever say to yourself, " only If I made extra money, then I could accomplish my monetary goals much more quickly..."? Well, that's just another explanation why the passive income's so awesome. It doesn't what financial targets you're trying to attain; you can accomplish your goals much quicker if you build certain passive income sources that enable you to make money allthe time of day.

More freedom to pursue your passions

You will unexpectedly find yourself with the opportunity to pursue your passions or, for that matter, your ideal job, along the same line as avoiding the paycheck to the paycheck lifestyle, while you get some ofthe passive income flowing through the bank account. Remember that it's easy to end up trapped in a position you can't bear when you focus on the active income to make ends meet. It is tough enough to leave a career. But it is particularly tough to leave a job if you don't have sufficient money to pay the rent that is due in two weeks. On theother hand, you have the opportunity to do the things you really want to do when you have a stable stream of passive income running into the finances of yours. Passive income, to put plainly, offers you choices. & with those choices, independence comes.

Location independence

Likewise, in many ways, passive income encourages you to live and working from anywhere you like. Since you don't have to work constantly to earn a passive income, so you don't have to be working from a particular position either. You could tour the world if you like, as far as you earn passive income sufficient to support your lifestyle. And plenty of people do.

Early retirement

Retirement is,to some degree, for many people, that may only be done later inlife. Although, if you're building any passive income sources, retirement may not be far away as you thought. Really, if you love the thought of retirement at a young age, so then your primary financial priority should be passive income. If it means creating a company that operates even without you needing to be present there, participatingin real estate, or a mix of few different sources of income, if you desire to stop working at a young age, passive income is necessary.

More financial margin

 more financial margins you will build in life, better off you will be in personal finance. In different words, the more distance you've between the expenditures & your income, the better it will get for financial life. And when you produce a constant stream of the passive income per month, it becomes much simpler to build the financial margin. Let's say, for instance, that your monthly gross expenditures increase upto 3,000 dollars. Now, if you're earning $4,000 inactive household revenue, then the monthly margin is $1,000. Yeah, that's not bad. However, if you add an additional $2,000 in passive monthly income in to the mix, life just got a lot better.

Reduced stress

There's one unity between all, after everything we've spoken about so far. It's plain; passive revenue has a distinctive way to reduce the financial burden. A passive income life is considerably less difficult than a life deprived of it. Because your financial security, margin, independence, and too much more are improved by passive income, it's only logical that it will help alleviate your financial burden. So, if financial condition makes you feela little tightened around the collar, you may just want to give passive incomea little more priority.

It's exciting

Passive income is not constrained by the effort and time that you can put into it. In different words, at all the hours of night and day, passive income can be earned, including while you are sleeping. Yet, at the same time, making money is incredibly thrilling. There's nothing like waking up inthe morning thinking that you've won a few hundred bucks while you're sleeping. And the more you are enthusiastic about the financial condition, the more probable you are to continue to improve it.

CHAPTER 2: Passive income ideas to help you make money in 2021

Passive income may be a wonderful way of helping you produce more cash flow, & global upheaval created primarily by the pandemic isevidenceof the importance of having many income sources. Passive income lets you cross the gap whether you unexpectedly become jobless or even whether you willingly take the time from work away with the pandemic tossing the working condition of most people into disarray. You might get the cash rolling in from passive income even while you follow your primary career, or if maybe you can build up a good passive income pool, you may needa little to kickback. Anyway, you are granted additional protection from passive income. And if you are concerned about being capable of saving enough money to reach your retirement objectives, accumulating capital throughpassive income also is a tactic that could be appealing to you. Regular earnings from a party other thanthe employer or the contractor are counted as passive income.IRS (Internal Revenues Service) notes that passive revenue will come from 2 sources: a company or a rental property in whichone is not directly participating, such as paying book royalty or dividends on securities. Most individuals agree that passive income's about getting more for nothing. It's got get-wealthy-quick charm, but it also includes work inthe end. What you offer is work upfront. You may do any or all the job upfront in practice, but the passive income also requires some extra labor alongthe way too. To keep the passive dollars flowing, you might have to saveyour merchandise updated orwell-maintained rental property. But if you're dedicated to the approach, it could be a perfect way to make income, and by the way, you'll build some more financial stability for yourself.

2.1 How many streams of income should you have?

"When it comes to generating revenue sources, there is no "one size fits all" advice. How many revenue streams you have can depend on where you are financially and what your potential financial targets are? But it is a decent beginning to get at least a handful. "With multiple lines in the sea, you'll attract more fish. Rental assets, revenue-producing shares, and company ventures are a perfect way to diversify your income stream, in addition to the earned income produced by your human capital. You'll want to make sure, of course, that bringing work into a new passive income stream would not cause you to lose sight of the other sources. So, you want your efforts to be aligned and make sure you pick the right options for your time.

2.2 Passive income ideas for building wealth

So,if you're considering building a passive income source, look at these techniques and absorb what this takes to succeed with them, whereas still recognizing the dangers involved with each strategy.

2.3 Selling information products

One common passive income approach is to produce information products, such as e-books, orvideo or audio lessons, and then kick back while cash rolls inside from product sale. Via platforms such as Skillshare,Udemy, and Coursera, courses could be distributed & sold. Otherwise, you may think of a "freemium model"-making a free content follow-up and only charging for the more comprehensive details or for the ones who wish to learn more. Language teachers or / &stock-picking guidance, for instance, can use the model. Free material serves asa demonstration of talents and can draw those who want to be going tothe next stage. You may use advertising (or sponsor) to make your revenue as the third alternative for this concept while offering information or material ona free forum like YouTube to a growing audience. Take the love of music or video games, for instance, and transform it into the content.

Opportunity

The Information products will have an outstanding revenue stream, so after the initial time outlay, you quickly make money.

Risk

development of this product typically requires a huge amount of effort. And it needs to be good in order to make great money off it. There isn't space out there for trash. If you wish to be competitive, you must create a strong base, advertise your products & prepare for other products. Unless you get very lucky, one product isn't business. Generating more outstanding products is the easiest way to market an established good. You could create a strong income stream once you understand the business model.

2.4 Rental income

A successful way of earning passive income is to invest in rental properties. But more work is always needed than people expect. You could risk your money if you do not take the time to know how to create a profitable venture.

Opportunity

If you want to earn the passive incomes from the rental properties,then you must determine three things:

- Financial risk of owning property.

- Property's total expenses and costs.

- How much profit you need on investment.

For example, suppose your objective is to make $10,000 ina year in the rental income. At the same time, your property has monthly mortgages of 2,000 dollars and charges another 300 dollars in one month for the taxes & other expenses. In this scenario, you will have to cost 3,133 dollars in the monthly rent foraccomplishing your objective.

Risk

few questions should be considered: Is there a marketplace for a property? How if you have a homeowner who pays off the property late or harms it? Suppose you cannot rent the property out? The passive income could be significantly impacted by any of the variables. And pandemic also has raised new threats. You could suddenly have occupants who could no longer afford their rent because of the economic crisis, although you may already have a mortgage of your own to be paying. Or, if earnings fall, you couldn't be capableof rentingout homes for as far as you did before. So, to secure yourself, you'll want to consider these threats and have a contingency plan in place.

2.5 Affiliate marketing

However,with affiliate advertising, website owners, "influencers" on social media or blogs support the goods of third parties by including a link to the product on the forum or the social media network. The best-known associate partner maybe Amazon, but Awin,ShareASale and eBay, are all among the bigger brands. And for those watching to developa following and sell goods, TikTok and Instagram have become major websites. To attract attention to the blog or else steer people to goods and services which they may like, you might also start growing an email list.

Opportunity

The site owner receives a fee if visitors click on the link and make a transaction froma third-party associate. The commission may vary from 3-7 %, so it would obviously need substantial traffic to the site to produce serious revenue. But you could be able to make some serious coin if you may expand the following or even have a more profitable niche (like tech, fitness, or financial services). Affiliate advertising is deemed passive, and, in principle, only by addinga link to your social media platform or website, you will gain money. In fact, if you cannot draw readers to the site to tap onthe link and purchase anything, you won't earn anything.

Risk

You'll have to be taking time to develop content and generate traffic if you're just starting out. Building a following will take important time, and you'll need to discoverthe best formula to reach the crowd, a task that could take a while on its own. Worse, the audience might be likely to fly to the next famous influencer, topic, orsocial media site after you've expended all that energy.

2.6 Flip retail products

Make use of online sales sites like Amazon or eBay, and offer goods you find nowhere at prices of cut-rate. You will arbitragethe difference between the prices between your purchase & selling, and you will be able to create a following of the people who monitor your transactions.

Opportunity

The price disparities between what you'll find & what average customer will be capable of finding would encourage you to take advantage of them. If you've contact that may help you obtain affordable goods that some other individuals can locate, this might work extremely well. Or you might be capableof uncovering useful products which others have completely missed.

Risk

Although deals can happen online at any moment, you'll probably have to rush to find a reputable source of goods to help keep this strategy passive. And you're just going to have to knowthe competition so that you don't buy ata price that's too much. Otherwise, in order to market, you can finish up with goods that nobody needs. Moreover, you may be forced to slash the price drastically inorder to make the product worthwhile for the buyers.

2.7 Peer-to-peer lending

Peer-to-peer (or P2P) loan's personal loan supports bythe intermediary of third-party like LendingClub or Prosper between you &borrower. Funding Circle that targets firms & has greater borrowing caps, and Payout, which targets better collateral losses, are other players.

Opportunity

You generate income as a lender from interest payments made on loans. Yet, you face the possibility of default because the loan is insecure, implying you might end up with nothing. You must do two things to cut the risk:

By paying smaller sums on different loans, diversify the lending portfolio. Minimum investment for each credit is $25 at Prosper.com and LendingClub.

To make educated choices, evaluate old data on the prospective borrowers.

Risk

It takes time to learnthe lending metrics of P2P because it's not completely passive, and you'll want to vet your prospective borrowers closely because you ought to pay particular attention to payments earned when you're engaging in several loans. If you intend to create profits, whatever you make for interest can be reinvested. Economic recessions may also make the high-yielding personal loans more likely to default candidates because if the COVID-19 manages to harm the economy at higher than historical rates, these loans will go bad.

2.8 Dividend stocks

The Shareholders in companies with dividend-yielding securities receive a payout fromthe company atregular intervals. The Companies pay the cash dividend out of the earnings on a quarterly basis, and what you need to be doing is to own stock. Per-share of stock, dividends are funded, meaning the more shares that you hold, the larger your compensation.

Opportunity

Since stock income is not linked to any operation other than the actual financial investment, it may be one ofthe most passive ways of money-making to own dividend-yielding securities. In your bank account, the money will simply be deposited.

Risk

Choosing the correct stocks is a tricky aspect. Without carefully researching company issuing stock, too many novices leap into the market. You have to study the website of each organization and be acquainted with their financial statements. 2 to 3 weeks you can spend researching each venture. That said, without wasting a massive amount of time analyzing firms, there are some ways to participate in the stocks dividend-yielding. ETFs, or Exchange-traded fund, are strongly recommended for income generation. ETFs are hedge vehicles containing collateral such as equity, commodities & bonds but trading like stocks. The ETFs arean excellent alternative for novices because, due to much lower prices than mutual funds, they are easier to understand, affordable,highly liquid, and offer much higher potential returns. Another key risk's that the stocks or the ETFs will decrease dramatically over short periods of time, particularly in times of volatility, such as when the financial markets were shocked by the Coronavirus crisis in 2020. Economic uncertainty may also cause certain firms to fully cut the dividends, while the diversified funds can experience less of a pinch.

2.9 Create an app

Creating an app may be a method to invest time in advance and then enjoy rewards over time. Your software may bea game or one that allows smartphone users to execute any feature that is difficult to do. Users download it once the application is public, &you can generate revenue.

Opportunity

There's a big upside to an app if you can create something that captures your audience's fancy. You'll think about how it's best to generate revenue. You could run in-application advertisements, for example, or else make users paya small fee to use the app. You'll definitely add incremental improvements to keepthe product current and popular as the app gains attention or you get feedback.

Risk

Perhaps the greatest risk here's that you spend your time unprofitably. You have no financial drawback here if you contribute little to no money to the project (and/or money which you'd have spent otherwise, for instance, on hardware). It's a competitive market, though, and genuinely popular applications must give consumers a persuasive benefit of experience. If your app gathers some data, you would also want to ensure that it is in accordance with privacy rules, which vary across the globe.

2.10 REITs

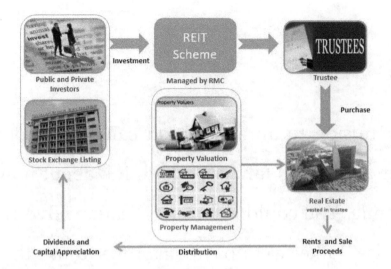

For a corporation that owns and manages real assets, REIT is a real estate investment trust, which is a fancy word. REITs have a special legal arrangement such that although they pass over any of their income to owners, they pay no or little corporate income tax.

Opportunity

In the stock exchange, you can purchase REITs much as every other business or dividend stock. You're going to earn whatever the REITs payout as a payout, and the strongest REITs have an annual record of growing their dividend, meaning over time, you might have an increasing supply of dividends. Specific REITs could be more expensive, like dividend stocks, than buying an ETF composed of hundreds of REIT stocks.Fund offers instant diversification, which is inherently much better than owning specific stocks & you can always earn a good return.

Risk

You'll have to be capable of selecting good REITs, much like dividend stocks, that means you'll have to evaluate any of the firms you might purchase, which indeed isa time-taking process. Also, while it isa passive activity, if you do not know what you're doing, you might lose a lotof money. And neither are REIT dividends safe from difficult economic times. If REIT does not produce enough income, this would possibly have to slash or totally remove its dividend. So just when you want it, most of the passive income could get hit.

2.11 A bond ladder

 bond ladder's sequence of bonds maturing over a number of years at various periods. The phased maturities help you to reduce the risk of reinvestment, which isa risk of locking up your cash as bonds offer interest rates that are too low.

Opportunity

bond ladder's a traditional passive investmentthat for decades has attractednear-retirees and retirees. You will sit back to collect the interest payments, and you "extendthe ladder," transferring the principle into different package of bonds as the bond matures. For starters, you could start off with one year, three years, five years, and seven years of bonds. In the year that 1st bond matures, you have two years, four years, and six years of bonds left. You may use proceeds from the newly aged bond to purchase another one year or roll out an eight-year bond with a longer-term, for example.

Risk

Bond ladder reduces one ofthe big dangers of purchasing bonds, the possibility that you may have to purchasea new bond as the bond develops when the interest rates will not be attractive. Bonds, too, come with the other risks. Althoughthe federal government backs Treasury bonds, corporate bonds aren't, meaning you could risk your principal. And to diversify the exposure& eliminatethe risk of someone bond harming your total portfolio, you'll want to buy multiple bonds. Many investors move to bond the ETFs because of these issues, which include a diversified fund of bonds that you may put up on a ladder, removing the possibility that a single bond will harm your returns.

2.12 Invest in a high-yield CD or savings account

Investing in an online bank's high-yield deposit certificate (CD) or savings account will help you to produce passive income and get one ofthe country best interest rates as well. In order to make money, you won't even have to leave home.

Opportunity

You'll want to do a fast check of the nation's great CD rates or the top savings accounts to make the most of your CD. Going to the online bank instead ofthe local bank is typically far more advantageous since you will be able to pick the highest rate available inthe region. And if the financial firm is backed by the FDIC, you will also receive a fixed return of principal of up to 250,000 dollars.

Risk

Your principal is secure as far as the bank is backed by FDIC and under limits. So, it is just as secure a return as you'll find to invest in a CD or savings account. Nevertheless, though the accounts are secure, these days, they return even less than before. And with Federal Reserve aiming at 2% inflation, the least in the short run, you're going to miss out on inflation. A savings account or CD can, though, yield less than keeping your cash in cash or in a non-interest paying checking account where you will earn about zero.

2.13 Buy Property

Real estate can be a decent way to make a passive income, depending on where you invest and when. There has been a rapid growth in the value of property in common cities such as Toronto-44 percent in Canada alone in the last five years. You will find some lower-cost properties by purchasing pre-construction condos, which will rise in value by the time it is eventually completed, enabling you to sell the property once it is complete for a profit. Like for all investments, it can be dangerous, so if you're new to the market, it's better to talk to a real estate agent to help you purchase the correct investment property.

2.14 Rent out your home short-term through Airbnb

This simple approach takes advantage of space that you don't need anyway, and converts it into an opportunity to make some money. Whether you're leaving for summer and/or have to be outside of the town for sometime, or maybe even you want to fly, try renting your present space out while you're gone.

Opportunity

On a variety of websites, including Airbnb, you may list space and set rental conditions yourself. With limited additional work, you'll receive a check for efforts, particularly if you rent to a tenant who might be in place for a couple of months.

Risk

You do not have a lot of financial downsides here, but it's a gamble that's atypical of the most passive investors to let strangers stay in your house. Tenants can, for instance, even deface or ruin your property or steal valuables even.

2.15 Air BnB Business as a Passive income Strategy

Airbnb is an online website for selling and renting urban homes. It ties hosts and travellers and promotes the rental process without owning any rooms on its own. Moreover, it cultivates a cooperative economy by allowing private flats to be leased by property owners. Airbnb is an internet platform which links individuals that wish to rent the homes to an individual in that area who are searching for a room. It currently surrounds more than 100 thousand cities in the world and 220 countries. The name of the business derives from the "air mattress B and B." Engaging in Airbnb is a way for hosts to gain some money from their home, but with the possibility that it may be damaged by the visitor. The benefit could be comparatively cheap lodging for visitors, but with the possibility that property wouldn't be as advisable as the listing has made itlook. For less than the cost of a hotel bed, travellers may also book an Airbnb. The traveler's biggest concern is that the property could not live up to its listing. The primary concern for hosts is that their property may be badly damaged by guests.

Airbnb

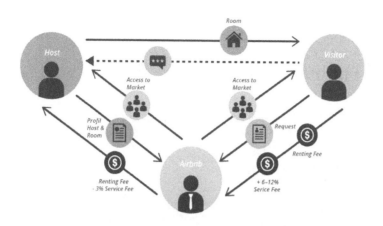

Business Model **Toolbox**

The Advantages of Airbnb

It offers the following advantages:

Wide Selection

Airbnb hosts list several different categories of properties on theAirbnb website, like single rooms,a suite ofrooms, moored yachts, , whole homes, studios, houseboats, even castles.

Free Listings

In order to list the assets, hosts don't have to be paying. Listings may contain written descriptions, captioned photographs, and user profiles so prospective visitors canhave the knowledge about hostsa little better.

Hosts Can Set Their Own Price

It is the host's prerogative to decide how much to charge per night, per week, or /and per month.

Customizable Searches

The Guests can filterthe Airbnb database and not only through date & location, however also by price, property type, amenities, and the host's language. To further limit their search, they may also add keywords (such asclose to the Louvre').

Additional Services

Airbnb has increased its services to include events and restaurants in recent years. In addition to a list of available hotels for the dates they expect to visit, individuals searching by the venue can see a list of opportunities provided by nearby Airbnb hosts, like classes and sightseeing. Restaurant listings also contain Airbnb hosts' reviews.

Protections for Guests and Hosts

As a protection for customers, before transferring the funds to the host, Airbnb keeps the guest's payment for 24 hours following check-in. For guests, Airbnb's Host Guarantee program "provides security for up to $1,000,000 in damage to covered property in eligible countries in the rare incident of guest damage."

The disadvantages of Airbnb

It has the following demerits:

What You See May Not Be What You Get

Booking Airbnb accommodation is not like booking a space with a big hotel chain, where you have a fair promise that the property will be as described. Individual hosts, though some may be more truthful than others, create their own listings. Previous visitors, however, often post updates about their experiences, which may offer a more critical perspective. To make sure the listing is correct, review the reports of other guests who have stayed at the Airbnb house.

Potential Damage

The greater concern for hosts is potential that their property will be damaged. Although most stays go without incident, when the Airbnb hosts assumed they were renting to a peaceful household, there are reports of entire houses being trashed by thousands of partygoers. Some insurance is offered by Airbnb's Host Guarantee program, mentioned above, but it does not cover anything, like cash, rare artwork, jewellery, and pets. Also, hosts whose homes are destroyed can experience significant inconvenience.

Added Fees

A number of extra charges are imposed by Airbnb (just like, of course, hotels and other lodging providers). To cover Airbnb's customer care and other programs, travelers pay a guest management fee of 0 percent to 20 percent on top of the reservation fee. Prices are shown in the currency that the customer chooses, provided it is sponsored by Airbnb. Banks or issuers of credit cards can, where applicable, add fees. And though listings are free, to cover the cost of handling the transaction, Airbnb charges a service fee of at least 3 percent for each reservation.

It Isn't Legal Everywhere

Would-be hosts need to review their municipal zoning codes before listing their properties on Airbnb to make sure it is legal to rent their properties. To receive special permits or licenses, hosts may also be required.

2.16 Advertise on your car

By merely driving your car across town, you can be able to raise some additional income. Contact a specialized advertisement firm to determine your commuting patterns, like when and how many miles you drive. The firm will "wrap" your car with the ads at no cost to you if you're a match with one of their advertisers. Newer vehicles are being searched by agencies, and drivers should have a clear driving record.

Opportunity

If you're still putting in the miles anyway, though you may have to get out and drive, then this is a perfect way to earn hundreds every month at little to no added expense. It is reasonable to pay drivers by the mile.

Risk

Be extra cautious about locating a reputable operation to work with if this idea seems good. In this space, many fraudsters set up schemes to try to bilk you out of thousands.

2.17 Invest in Stocks

When you look at the wealthiest people in the world, it's pretty fair to conclude that their deep, endless savings accounts are a result of their major investment in stocks. Warren Buffett reads 500 pages a day, but he doesn't read your usual mystery novel. He reviews the annual corporate reports. He better knows whether or not a company is doing well by reviewing annual reports each day, which helps him improve his decision to invest in stocks. While the act of investing in stocks is very passive, the analysis that goes into it is active. Nevertheless, investing in shares will help you gain passive income that goes well beyond what your value is worth at your 9 to 5 work. So, if you enjoy reading about the success of different firms, consider this passive income approach.

2.18 Make Your Car Work for You

Driving is another everyday practice that you can translate into passive income. When you're just walking around, why not pick up a commuter or two to run errands? Uber can help you make money by taking people to their designated destination by driving your vehicle. You may also put ads on your vehicle to collect cash as you drive around. When your car is not used while you're on holiday, driving, or just during a normal workday, it will still make money. You will make thousands of dollars with an app like Getaround by renting out your car if you're not using it. Plus, drivers of Getaround vehicles get the best parking spaces in town, a $50 monthly rental credit on any vehicle they want, and one million U.S. dollars in primary insurance coverage.

2.19 Sell your Videos

We live in a day and age where video content fascinates hundreds and thousands of humans. You would want to take out your phone and hit the record if you still find yourself in the middle of drama and excitement. To allow you to make some passive income, you can sell stored content. Why? It is because the video can be sold to a news site. And you can make some recurring income for weeks, months, and maybe even years if the video takes off. Of course, being at cultural gatherings such as marches, rallies, and festivals is the best way to get in on the action. You'll find ways for your material to be sold anywhere there's controversy. And corporations will pay you to make viral videos along with providing a share of total earnings if you are successful at creating engaging content.

2.20 Create YouTube Videos

The passive income source that just keeps on giving is YouTube. You'll find that you can make a regular income from your YouTube channel, from funded videos to ad sales. Creating videos on a regular basis for a long time is the key to creating a profitable YouTube channel. If you stick with it in the long run, you will finally start reaping the benefits of passive income.

2.21 Write an eBook

In 2009 and 2010, e-books came onto the scene and are now a hugely successful content medium. While they first became popular a few years ago, to this day, there is still a very decent chunk of individuals who make passive income from writing e-books. It's an insanely dynamic business, of course. Yet, you might find yourself with a nice slice of the profits if your writing chops are stellar. You could build a fanbase of loyal readers by designing how-to e-books on famous niches and marketing them.

2.22 Sell Digital Products

You can make digital goods if you're trying to create your own products rather than selling someone else's. You can sell your digital goods online using Shopify. From e-books, educational classes, PDFs, custom graphic templates, stock images, or some other digital goods, digital products will contain anything. Selling these items is the epitome of passive income, and with immediate updates, the whole operation can be streamlined on Shopify.

Car Wash

Car wash is a perfect way to earn a semi-passive income. Although a car wash will need daily cleaning, it is something you can either contract out or do once a week. We are talking about the very simple car wash that is cinderblocks, a pressure washer, and the powered coin, as a side note. It's certainly a corporation vs. a passive income stream if you're trying to run a drive-through car wash.

2.23 CPC Ads (Cost Per Click)

You get really paid whenever anyone clicks on your link and signs up for something or orders something through affiliate ads. On the other hand, show advertisements charges depend on the volume of traffic and eyeballs that you receive on their ads. On the other hand, for CPC advertisements, also known as "cost per click" ads, anytime someone clicks on an ad, you get paid no matter what they do after that. You don't have to hope or pray that they're buying anything or signed up for something. Any single click takes money into your account with the bank. Does that mean that all day long you can go to your own website and click on ads? It is not realistic since the corporation will inevitably find out what you are doing and cut you off. With all that in mind, it should not be a part of your plan here to click on your own ads. Instead, aim to build up traffic so that more and more viewers every day see the ads.

2.24 Minimize your taxes on passive income

A passive income may be a wonderful side-income generation strategy, but you can still create a tax burden for your effort. But by setting yourself up as a business and building a savings portfolio, you can reduce the tax bite and plan for your future, too. However, this solution will not work with all these passive strategies because to qualify. You will have to be a legal organization.

Register with the IRS to make your company receive a tax identification number.

Then call a broker, such as Charles Schwab or Fidelity, who will open a self-employed retirement account.

Determine the type of savings account that will fit well for your needs.

CHAPTER 3: Airbnb Offers The Best Passive Income Generation Strategy

rental vacation industry is rising quickly. It is real quick indeed asa matter of fact. The sector is currently generating 57,669 million dollarsin sales, according to recent analysis reports from Statista.com. The revenue is awaited to grow to a market value of 74,005 million dollars by 2023 and is projected to see an average growth rate of 6.4 percent. This data illustrates just how broad & robust the holiday rental management industry is. And you should expect demand for Airbnb property management to pursue to grow overthe coming years with the growth of Airbnb rental properties in recent years. Therefore, if one day you are aiming to become amanager of Airbnb property, now is a great time to be entering the business. But how are you able to get started? We will supply you with what you have to know regarding how to be an Airbnb vacation rental property manager. We're going to teach you what this takes to handle rental Airbnb properties, particular instruments you're going to be needing before you start, andstop points for the beginners for achieving successful property management. So, without further ado, over here are all six steps to beginning an Airbnb property management career inreal estate.

3.1 Understand the Vacation Rental Industry

Just like some other business, without learning at leastthe fundamentals of this area, you can't succeed. However, no formal qualification is necessary to become an Airbnb property manager,and many find success with the onlydiploma of high school in this profession.Thorough knowledge of howthe holiday rental industry & Airbnb run is what you need to have.So, if you don't already have it, having this information now is the 1st step to being the manager of the Airbnb properties. Ideally, as Airbnb hosts yourself, you should have some experience. If you've already hosted your rental property on Airbnb, run it yourself, you can show to potential buyers which you know exactly what you are doing. Furthermore, this will allow you to be prepared better to predict challenges, recognize potentially troublesome travelers, and cope with common issues. But if you don't have the experience, through online guides and classes, you can empower yourself about the rental vacation industry &how Airbnb works. There are plenty of those out there that can help you create a good base on which you have to learn. For instance, you may take marketing coursework to know how to extend your scope and get bookings more and business courses to know how to manage a company, keep records, &file tax. As an Airbnb property manager, it'll help you improve your creditability. Before you start, another significant point to learn is where the Airbnb hosts invest in rentals for the short-term. You'll know the place to find customers looking for management support with this detail.

3.2 Create a Maintenance Management System

Managing rental of short-term rentals ensures that you'll get visitors checking in & out repeatedly. One of many duties of the property managers, of course, is to review property before visitors visit &after they depart. Every now & then, operators of holiday rentals must also conduct repairs to ensure that the properties are in perfect shape. This is vital to ensure the happiness of both your customer and guests. For instance, imagine having visitors who had parties and had rental property trashed before leaving. Nobody with such a situation is going to be happy to step intoa rental. As a consequence, before addressing the issue, themanager of Airbnb property can never leave the maintenance as an afterthought or even wait forthe property owner to receive several inquiries. In addition, to offer high-quality care on their behalf, great short-term property rental operators often work alongside a dependable maintenance team. Your staff should include, among others, plumbers, house cleaners, and electricians. For any check-in, these entities will ensure that Airbnb assets you handle are tip to top.

3.3 Put Together a Vacation Rental Marketing Strategy

The most significant tasks of property managers are promoting and selling holiday rentals to attract prospective visitors. Today, there are millions of listings on Airbnb & morerental sites for the short-term, which is creating rivalry among the Airbnb hosts. It is why one of the first things potential users would like to know is how you're going to get reservations and increase their occupancy rates for Airbnb. As a consequence, you must havea basic comprehension of tactics and methods for property marketing. Therefore, having a marketing campaign that will draw Airbnb visitors to the holiday rentals you run isthe next step towardsbeing Airbnb properties manager. Start by writing an enticing listing that will maximize the probability of retaining a high rate of occupancy

&a positive flow of cash. To make rental properties under your management stand out, think about investing in advanced photography & videography facilities, also branding services. Moreover, selling holiday rentals suggests that you have to go outside the listing platform. It is why active rental managers of Airbnb use social media and also SEO to meet the target tenant audience. If you don't know how it works, before you begin handling rentals inthe short term, we strongly suggest that you begin to read about real estate marketing.

3.4 Invest in Property Management Tools

You can handle them with hard work and a few spreadsheets as you becomemanager of Airbnb property for the first time when you have only some rental properties underneath your belt. This becomes difficult, though, as you continue to add more assets to manage. How are thirty check-ins & cleanings going to be done in 1 day? At an early point, it is best to begin thinking about it so thatyou're planning yourself & your company for success and expansion. Using real estate management ofproperty software that allows to automate & remain structured is the best approach for this.

In order to operate their businesses more effectively, modern holiday rental property supervisors rely a lot on technology. There are several high-tech solutions that make it easy to handle Airbnb rental, from the smart lock to invoicing, pricing, and the guest screening software systems. You will even find holiday rental apps which will synchronize schedules and handle multiple Airbnb profiles for free from different platforms. Not only does the use of such instruments make your life more effective asa manager of real estate properties, but they can also give youthe strategic edge to keep rising. Mashboard, for instance, is a software that lets managers of Airbnb property connect with their customers and findthe right properties for those to expand their business.

3.5 Outline Your Guest Management Strategy

Amazing client care is one of the abilities that any manager of real estate property wants to provide when handling both conventional and holiday rentals. It is how effective operators of Airbnb assets set themselves away from the audience. A good selling point, particularly for Airbnb travelers, is customer service that goes beyond and beyond. Getting a guest engagement plan ensures that during their visit, the services can be open to visitors and their demands at whatever time. Expect the short-term visitors to have to inquire or inquire over something. You must be capable of responding in a timely way to such unannounced requests. How can you treat a case, for instance, where the visitor has misplaced keys toa holiday rental and can't get in? There will be a contingency in it and other cases for a successful Airbnb property manager. In addition, to manage communication with visitors, managers of top-performing properties also have automation tech systems in place. Airbnb guests really enjoy great customer service & show this by posting favorable feedback. This, in essence, helps to get more bookings & boost cash flow, that will surely make the customers happier. As you could see, oneof the most critical skills for good management of Airbnb property is definitely customer service, so don't consider it asan afterthought.

3.6 Set a Reasonable (But Competitive) Price

To becomea manager of Airbnb property, the only thing you need is a pricing plan. Usually, the holiday rental manager takesa percentage cut from the real host's secured rental fee. A selection of online outlets recommends anywhere from ten to twenty-five percent. At the same time, others believe that more consumers would be drawn by charging the lowest price; that isn't the case. Customers base their options on the quality o facilities rendered by property managers-not dependent on costs. Thus, providingthe lowest price means that you don't have top-tier facilities for owners of Airbnb property. You need to take several factors into account in order to fix the correct price. First of all, as stated, is what kind of services you are providing. Naturally, for something that you don't sell, you do not charge. Look at experience instead, what distinctive points of selling you may give, and set rate accordingly. The local economy and what the other rental property (short-term)managers in the area charge, the seasonal demands, also current events, you will need to remember. Ultimately, you need to seta fair price which you are sure will be getting you back that your serviceis worth.

3.7 How an Airbnb Business Works

Nearly everyone has listenedto Airbnb or has used it. It is the platform for online home rentals that helps hostsrenting vacant private short-term accommodation from asingle room to whole homes. Airbnb launched in 2007 &has expanded exponentially to have listings in further than 65 thousand cities in the world with more than three million available properties. Here is how tostart a sustainable Airbnb company if you have sufficient rental space and are searching for additional revenue. Through uploading photographs and details of the room for rent, the first move is to bea host on Airbnb and register the home. When an Airbnb property's listed, travelers searching for a room inthe host area will access it. Guests may use a number of requirements to check for Airbnb listings, like:

- Availability dates
- Destination

- No. Of rooms, such as bedrooms and washrooms

- Price

- Host language

- Amenities such as hot tub, breakfast, pets allowed, and etc.

- Facilities like air conditioning, parking,etc.

Prior to booking the chosen space through the Airbnb guest may establish a contact withhosts directly for gathering additional information through the Airbnb service of messaging.

Access

Along with browser access, Airbnb offers mobile applications for Android and Apple IOS devices.

Security

For security purposes, the hosts are expected to provide Airbnb with appropriate identification. Travelers should post the reviews of hotels to create a trustworthy group (and the hosts may review the guests). The Reviews aren't anonymous.

Guest Services

Airbnb offers a stable payment platform for the guest's calmness of mind, and fees to the hosts are deferred until 24 hr after the arrival of the guest. In the event that any difficulties are faced during the renting time, Airbnb hasa 24-hour hotline forthe guest.

Fees

Host sets the price for lodging. Moreover, Airbnb chargesunder-mentioned fees:

Host: Three% transaction payment fee

Guest: six to twelve% booking fee

The Hosts can also ask fora security deposit&couldwell charge a cleaning fee.

Taxes

Airbnb could apply provincial, state, or city taxes for guest bookings depending on the jurisdiction.

Travelers Prefer Airbnb Rentals

One ofthe best things about operating an Airbnb company is that, for several reasons, travelers choose Airbnb over motels, hotels, or hostels:

Cost: Usually, Airbnb rent is much inexpensive thana similar hotel room. In certain instances, an entire house may be rented through Airbnb forthe cost of a single suite of the hotel, depending on the location.

Living locally: Living the life of a local person is the key advantage ofthe Airbnb service. Most guests of Airbnb choose to stay inside the community and explore the destination way the locals do, instead of renting a generic hotel room.

Privacy: customers of Airbnb are not continuously surrounded by visitors and workers at the hotel.

Peace & quiet: the Airbnb rents are usually more secure and do not suffer from loud hotel events, such as guest exits early in the morning, young children, maid service, and traffic.

Witness what you get already: Unlikea hotel where you can see a snapshot of similar rooms on their Airbnb page at best, you get full images and explanations of the real premises.

Diversity: From yachts and boathouses to castles and lighthouses, Airbnb has an immense variety of available accommodations.

Home comforts: Airbnb hasa homey atmosphere of a real living space instead of generic hotel spaces (few haveresident pets even). Kitchens allow the guests to cook their own food if they desire to save money on outside dining or have dietary issues.

Friends or Family: Through Airbnb, you may savea lot of money by renting a whole apartment/ house/condo rather than the multiple rooms of a hotel for family and friends.

Is Renting Your Space Permissible or Advisable?

Ensure you're legally permitted to bean Airbnb host into jurisdiction before you plan to start an Airbnb business, & you're prepared to respect local laws &regulations. Depending on the state/ cityor regional rules, municipal laws governing the hosting of paid visitors will vary greatly; they are absolutely banned in some areas whilst they're subject to occupancy tax in others if space is condominium or apartment,check to view if it is allowed to sub-let the premises. There are also regulations in place for apartment landlords & condominium societies to prohibit an owner from renting the units out as Airbnb rooms. Renting your apartment out without the knowledge of your landlord will have you evicted. Neighborhood ties are also a significant concern. In the area, a few inconsiderate or loud Airbnb guests will easily turn you in a pariah. If none of the challenges are insurmountable, it could be an outstanding opportunity of home-foundbusiness to become an Airbnb host.

Are You Committed to Becoming a Host

There are a variety of additional concerns to remember prior to making a definitive decision to host Airbnb:

Would you like to starta business? Then Startingan Airbnb company is like establishing any business- that you need enthusiasm, entrepreneurial spirit, &the ability to make the required effort, starting off with doing relevant background analysis and developing business plans.

Do you've energy? It could takea great amount of time to be a landlord, particularly for the short-term rents. You'll have to:

- Manage reservations and reply to interactions with prospective tenants.

- Plan to meet the guests to give out or receive keys

- ensure the property, including fresh linen, breakfast supplies, is cleaned properly and ready for the arrival of the guest (if applicable)

- Fix some property maintenance problems such as plumbing and pest control, electrical & appliance repair

- Be accessible to the visitors on a 24 into 7 basis if the property has any problems.

Demand: The deciding factor inthe popularity & price of rented accommodation is visitor demand. The highest places for rental returns are:

sought-after tourist destinations with high hotel rates (famous neighborhood ranks higher on the Airbnb searches)

situated Centrally, close to visitor attractions, shops & public transport,

Featuring panoramic views and facilities like parking, balconies, etc.

Seasonality: Demand for the property in the northern hemisphere will definitely drop drastically in winters (unless you're renting a ski chalet). In comparison, rental accommodation demand in colder southern locations (like Arizona) decreases dramatically in summers.

What are the marketing aims? Are you trying to earn a little cash or create a stable income onthe side? The financial portion ofthe business plan must show target market analysis and reasonable forecasts of your property's future rental income. The income from the Airbnb contract depends upon:

Before you start thinking about leaving your job& making a living through runningan Airbnb company, make sure that by seeingrental prices & booking regularity for comparing Airbnb listings of your area, you carefully examine the revenue potential of your property.

Extra costs: In addition to booking fees paid by Airbnb, there are extra costs involved with Airbnb hosting, including:

Insurance: Standard insurance plans for homeowners do not includethe use of the property for commercial uses, including renting on Airbnb. Airbnb has a free host compensation insurance policy in Canada, U.K., U.S., and many other nations, offering up to 1 million dollars in guarantees against personal harm or property loss. If your place is not protected by Airbnb policies, please contact your insurance provider to see if there is sufficient coverage.

Business Licenses: Airbnb hosts are being required by more & more cities to holda business license.

Repair and Cleaning: You want to keep rental properties in top condition all the time in order to keep your Airbnb host ranking at a high standard, which includes extensive cleaning during guest stays and daily repairs. The charges will contribute to your expenses if you have to sub-contract cleaning and repair duties.

Listing and Pricing Your Property on Airbnb

Accurately describe the place and make this stand out. Note that Airbnb is an online marketplace & you have to be thinking likea realtor to make listing stick out fromthe competition in order to optimize guest interest in your house. Start by looking at the same Airbnb listings insidethe region and consider the amenities/features and prices listed. If this works, makea spreadsheet. The definition of your listing must be precise, comprehensive, complete, and highlight, which makes it special. Comprehensively define the facilities and functionality of your room also as any regulations or preferences of visitors. Providing high-quality photographs of the room is incredibly necessary. Airbnb has specialist availability of photography service in certain places if you are unable to do this yourself.. You don't want visitors to be upset because the room isn't as advertised or you've exaggerated amenities. Note that the guest rankings would be partially dependent on the accuracy of your listing description.

Price Your Listing Competitively

You should also get an ideaof how to market your listing from your analysis of similar listings. It needs to be competitively priced to keep the property consistently booked (and increase profits).

Improving Your Host Ranking

Higher the property pops up in rankings, the more probable it's to be chosen by visitors, so having good rankings of Airbnb is crucial to the success of Airbnb business. Airbnb rankings are like internet search rankings.Andby building confidence and offering a fantastic experience to your visitors, you will boost your rankings.

Build Trust

Airbnb community's based on trust and guests would be searching for hosts with contact information, credentials, and favorable feedback.

Verification

For the new hosts, verification is highly essential: change your profile and include other details like the email address, phone number, Facebook profile, and etc. For giving prospective visitors some confidence that you're a reliable host.

References

You should post the references from colleagues, co-workers, relatives, business partners, etc., to build more trust. For the other Airbnb users, you may even write references.

Provide Great Customer Service

Like any entrepreneur would tell you, the cornerstone of any successful business is customer care, and becoming an Airbnb host has no difference. Positive ratings, better search scores, and more bookings reward hosts of Airbnb who havethe best experience of the guest. The hosts with the most popular are:

Responsive

The Hosts that can not be bothered for responding in a timely manner (or at some) to inquiries are a big turnoff for visitors. In reality, Airbnb keepstrack and rates your replies to guests accordingly. With higher search rankings and improved bookings, the host who hasthe highest ratings of response is awarded. At all times, Airbnb mobile application will help you to keep connected. All the time when visitors are present, be available through phone and check up with them on extended trips and see if there's something more you may do to maximize the services.

Update Their Calendars Regularly

Keeping your calendar current, also enhancing the guest experience, boosts the Airbnb rankings of search.

Fix All Problems quickly

When a guest mentions problemslike leaky taps or a burned-out lightbulb, it should be repaired promptly and render an apology to the guest. Sure ways to boost the guest rankings is to provide five-star service.

Act on Their Reviews

Fix the issue and benefit from the failures if a visitor writes a critical review. React to complaints all the time in a respectful way.

3.8 The Bottom Line

In real estate, there are many ways of earning profits. The growing success in the U.S. housing sector of Airbnb and other short-term rentals has created opportunities not just for real estate developers but also for property managers. Today, there is a great demand for vacation rental managers, and industry analysts expect that over the coming years, there will be national growth. Therefore, imagine being an Airbnb property manager if you're looking for a profitable means of generating passive income.

Conclusion

In a nutshell, passive income is money that comes at regular intervals without having to invest a large amount of work into generating it. By blogging, one method of producing passive income may be achieved. If you've figured out how to produce content that attracts sufficient traffic to the host advertising, you can makea product that your customers would want to purchase. From a basic e-book toa sophisticated app that produces sales for several years after it is released, passive income could be anything. Similarly, people have a lot of things, and they still look for cheap places to store this. What might be simpler than asking people to pay you for storing their things? An investment ona large-scale in purchasing storage facilities (with the cash) or anything simple like offering the basement or the shed might entail creating passive income by offering storage. All you'll need is to make sure their goods are clean and stable. You will make money by selling them to others against such charges if you've any things that you don't use at all times, which others will love to borrow. As rental items, useful items such as a tractor, trailer, kayak,trampoline, or your own lawneven may give youpassive income. With the support of platforms like Airbnb, this also involves renting spare rooms out in your home. Upload the pictures of items, fix a date, and tellthe world they're ready for the rent on your favorite social networking site. The reason why it is necessary to have passive income is that it will help increase your financial consistency. The more passive income you make, the easier it becomes to be consistent with your financial life, from consistently saving to consistently spending to consistently donating. One of the strongest and most relevant aspects of a sound financial condition is passive income. It is beneficial for you in several ways, from enhancing your financial health to reducing your financial burden.

The Cryptocurrency Investing | Advanced Guide

Study, Anticipate the Crypto Market and Raise the first Million Dollar from Bitcoin, Ethereum, Cardano and other unknown Altcoins that costs less than 1$

By

Marcus Wayne

Table of Contents

Chapter1. Understanding cryptocurrency

A cryptocurrency ("crypto") is a digital currency that may be used to shop for items and offerings but makes use of an online ledger with robust cryptography to relaxed online transactions. Much of the hobby in these unregulated currencies is to trade for profit, ith speculators at times driving prices skyward. A cryptocurrency is a form of payment that can be exchanged online for goods and offerings. Many organizations have issued their own currencies, often called tokens, and those can be traded especially for the best or provider that the employer gives. Think of them as you will arcade tokens or casino chips. You'll want to alternate real forex for the cryptocurrency to get entry to the best or carrier.

Why Cryptocurrency Is So Popular

Cryptocurrencies have gone from a difficult to understand part of finance to centre-level over the past 12 months. In the space of twelve months, bitcoin has exploded from buying and selling at $8,166 on 8 March 2020 to hit all-time highs of over $58,000 in February 2021 and now trading at $54,011 as of 9:31 am GMT on 9th March.

Their meteoric upward push has been observed by means of elevated institutional interest, consisting of big names like HSBC, Goldman Sachs, BNY Mellon and JPMorgan.

There are hundreds of cryptocurrencies around the sector but the core group of 20 coins constitutes around 99% of the marketplace through quantity, according to crypto internet site CoinDesk.

In the primary week of March — the quietest week for the reason that early January — inflows into digital asset investment products had been $108m, in step with James Butterfill, an investment strategist at CoinShares. Of these inflows, 90% had been bitcoin, with $4m invested in ethereum. Trading volumes for bitcoin, but, remained high, with each day average of $11.8bn for 2021 in comparison to $2.2bn in 2020.

As cryptocurrencies hold their rollercoaster rally into 2021 and hitting record highs in February and March, Financial News has compiled a list of the ten largest cryptocurrencies by using market capitalization.

Following are some reasons why cryptocurrency is popular for:

Low Fees

One of the reasons why cryptocurrency is famous around the world is that there are very few fees associated with using it. When you're using alternative options of online payment options, you're often going to incur massive costs. The very low charges that you have to deal with while the use of numerous cryptocurrencies will be a far higher deal for you. It makes the experience for many people to use cryptocurrencies to pay for items online and people also find it to be safe.

No Associatation of Cryptocurrencies with World Governments

Another reason why people have placed faith in cryptocurrencies is that those currencies aren't associated with world governments. This means that cryptocurrencies have the capacity to remain strong even if there is turmoil in a particular country. Some investors see cryptocurrencies as a terrific way to guard their wealth and that is one motive why cryptocurrency has persevered to upward push over time. The capacity that cryptocurrencies will be safer than some government currencies makes them extra appealing.

It's Getting Easier to Use Cryptocurrency

Using cryptocurrency is getting less complicated all of the time, thanks to greater online companies adopting it. You'll find that more web sites are beginning to accept cryptocurrencies as a fee and this could simplest emerge as more widely widespread in the future. It's also thrilling to notice that there are now things that include cryptocurrency debit cards popping up in certain locations.

This won't be widespread right now however it's far something that is very much occurring.

As cryptocurrency keeps turning out to be greater, not unusual, it's going to reach increasingly more people. This leads to a growth in consciousness and a common surge in popularity. More people remember the fact that that is an alternative now and some of the questions about what cryptocurrency is are being answered. Lots of people have at least a bit of understanding approximately what things such as Bitcoin are and this makes it extra ideal.

There Is Potential for Profit

Of course, the potential for profit is another huge reason why people get involved with cryptocurrencies. If you <u>buy Bitcoin</u> while it's at a low price, then you can potentially profit when that price rises. Lots of people who invested in cryptocurrencies before they got super hot wound up making huge profits. Investors are still making money from cryptocurrencies because the market has not cooled in recent years.

Overall Security Is Important

Protecting your identity and your money is important, and you know how hard cybersecurity has become in modern times. Using cryptocurrency to pay for things online is actually a lot safer than many other traditional payment options. If you're at all worried about cybersecurity issues, then deciding to use cryptocurrency might be a good idea. The security of cryptocurrency is one of the things that has helped it to become so popular over time.

It's Easy to Get

Getting cryptocurrency isn't some difficult thing that you're going to have to jump through a lot of hoops to do. It's actually possible to get the cryptocurrency that you want from reputable sources and the ease of getting cryptocurrency has helped it to grow in popularity. In the past, people might have thought of cryptocurrency as some type of shady and unknown entity but it's become a common thing in many circles now. If you have yet to purchase cryptocurrency, then you'll find that the process is decidedly simple and customer-friendly.

It's Seen as the Future

Finally, you could say that cryptocurrencies are seen as the future of money by many individuals. People who adopt cryptocurrency now are also adopting major technological innovations such as blockchain. This allows you to be on the cutting edge and it makes sense for many to get ahead of the curve. Blockchain technology is supposed to change the world in many ways and it's going to make trading a much more transparent process.

Types of Cryptocurrency

The first blockchain-based totally cryptocurrency became Bitcoin, which still remains the most popular and most valuable. Today, there are lots of alternate cryptocurrencies with diverse features and specs. Some of those are clones or forks of Bitcoin, while others are new currencies that were built from scratch.

Bitcoin was released in 2009 by an individual or group known by the pseudonym "Satoshi Nakamoto.1 As of March 2021, there had been over 18.6 million bitcoins in flow with a complete marketplace cap of around $927 billion.

Some of the competing cryptocurrencies spawned by means of Bitcoin's fulfilment, known as "altcoins," encompass Litecoin, Peercoin, and Namecoin, in addition to Ethereum, Cardano, and EOS. Today, the mixture price of all of the cryptocurrencies in life is round $1.5 trillion — Bitcoin currently represents more than 60% of the total value.

Advantages and Disadvantages of Cryptocurrency

Advantages

Cryptocurrencies preserve the promise of creating it less difficult to switch funds immediately among two parties, without the need for reliance on a third party like a financial institution or credit card enterprise. These transfers are alternatively secured through using public keys and private keys and distinctive kinds of incentive structures, like Proof of Work or Proof of Stake.

In modern cryptocurrency systems, a consumer's "wallet," or account address, has a public key, at the same time as the private key known only to the owner and is used to sign transactions. Fund transfers are finished with minimal processing expenses, allowing customers to keep away from the steep costs charged via banks and financial establishments for wire transfers.

Disadvantages

The semi-anonymous nature of cryptocurrency transactions makes them well-suited for a host of illegal activities, such as <u>money laundering</u> and <u>tax evasion</u>. However, cryptocurrency advocates often highly value their anonymity, citing benefits of privacy like protection for whistleblowers or activists living under repressive governments. Some cryptocurrencies are more private than others.

Bitcoin, for instance, is a relatively poor choice for conducting illegal business online, since the forensic analysis of the Bitcoin blockchain has helped authorities arrest and prosecute criminals. More privacy-oriented coins do exist, however, such as <u>Dash</u>, Monero, or <u>ZCash</u>, which are far more difficult to trace.

Special Considerations

Central to the appeal and functionality of Bitcoin and other cryptocurrencies is <u>blockchain</u> technology, which is used to keep an online ledger of all the transactions that have ever been conducted, thus providing a data structure for this ledger that is quite secure and is shared and agreed upon by the entire network of an individual node, or computer maintaining a copy of the ledger. Every new block generated must be verified by each node before being confirmed, making it almost impossible to forge transaction histories.

Many experts see blockchain technology as having serious potential for uses like online voting and crowdfunding, and major financial institutions such as JPMorgan Chase (JPM) see the potential to lower transaction costs by streamlining payment processing.4 However, because cryptocurrencies are virtual and are not stored on a central database, a digital cryptocurrency balance can be wiped out by the loss or destruction of a hard drive if a backup copy of the private key does not exist. At the same time, there is no central authority, government, or corporation that has access to your funds or your personal information.

Criticism of Cryptocurrency

Since market prices for cryptocurrencies are based on supply and demand, the rate at which a cryptocurrency can be exchanged for another currency can fluctuate widely, since the design of many cryptocurrencies ensures a high degree of scarcity.

Bitcoin has experienced some rapid surges and collapses in value, climbing as high as $19,000 per Bitcoin in Dec. of 2017 before dropping to around $7,000 in the following months.2 Cryptocurrencies are thus considered by some economists to be a short-lived fad or speculative bubble.

There is concern that cryptocurrencies like Bitcoin are not rooted in any material goods. Some research, however, has identified that the cost of producing a Bitcoin, which requires an increasingly large amount of energy, is directly related to its market price.

Cryptocurrency blockchains are highly secure, but other aspects of a cryptocurrency ecosystem, including exchanges and wallets, are not immune to the threat of hacking. In Bitcoin's 10-year history, <u>several online exchanges</u> have been the subject of hacking and theft, sometimes with millions of dollars' worth of "coins" stolen.

Nonetheless, many observers see potential advantages in cryptocurrencies, like the possibility of preserving value against inflation and facilitating exchange while being easier to transport and divide than precious metals and existing outside the influence of central banks and governments.

What Is Bitcoin?

Bitcoin is a digital currency that was created in January 2009. It follows the ideas set out in a white paper by the mysterious and pseudonymous Satoshi Nakamoto. The identity of the person or persons who created the technology is still a mystery. Bitcoin offers the promise of lower transaction fees than traditional online payment mechanisms and, unlike government-issued currencies, it is operated by a decentralized authority.

Bitcoin is a type of cryptocurrency. There are no physical bitcoins, only balances kept on a public ledger that everyone has transparent access to.

All bitcoin transactions are verified by a massive amount of computing power. Bitcoins are not issued or backed by any banks or governments, nor are individual bitcoins valuable as a commodity. Despite it not being legal tender Bitcoin is very popular and has triggered the launch of hundreds of other cryptocurrencies, collectively referred to as alcoin. Bitcoin is commonly abbreviated as "BTC."

Peer-to-Peer Technology

Bitcoin is one of the first digital currencies to use peer-to-peer technology to facilitate instant payments. The independent individuals and companies who own the governing computing power and participate in the bitcoin network — bitcoin "miners" — are in charge of processing the transactions on the blockchain and are motivated by rewards (the release of new bitcoin) and transaction fees paid in bitcoin.

These miners can be thought of as the decentralized authority enforcing the credibility of the bitcoin network. New bitcoin is released to the miners at a fixed, but periodically declining rate. There are only 21 million bitcoin that can be mined in total. As of January 30, 2021, there are approximately 18,614,806 bitcoin in existence and 2,385,193 bitcoin left to be mined.3

In this way, bitcoin other cryptocurrencies operate differently from fiat currency; in centralized banking systems, currency is released at a rate matching the growth in goods; this system is intended to maintain price stability. A decentralized system, like bitcoin, sets the release rate ahead of time and according to an algorithm.

What is Blockchain?

Blockchain seems complicated, and it definitely can be, but its core concept is really quite simple. A blockchain is a type of database. To be able to understand blockchain, it helps to first understand what a database actually is.

A database is a collection of information that is stored electronically on a computer system. Information, or data, in databases is typically structured in table format to allow for easier searching and filtering for specific information. What is the difference between someone using a spreadsheet to store information rather than a database?

Spreadsheets are designed for one person, or a small group of people, to store and access limited amounts of information. In contrast, a database is designed to house significantly larger amounts of information that can be accessed, filtered, and manipulated quickly and easily by any number of users at once.

Large databases achieve this by housing data on servers that are made of powerful computers. These servers can sometimes be built using hundreds or thousands of computers in order to have the computational power and storage capacity necessary for many users to access the database simultaneously. While a spreadsheet or database may be accessible to any number of people, it is often owned by a business and managed by an appointed individual that has complete control over how it works and the data within it.

So how does a blockchain differ from a database?

Storage Structure

One key difference between a typical database and a blockchain is the way the data is structured. A blockchain collects information together in groups, also known as blocks that hold sets of information. Blocks have certain storage capacities and, when filled, are chained onto the previously filled block, forming a chain of data known as the "blockchain." All new information that follows that freshly added block is compiled into a newly formed block that will then also be added to the chain once filled.

A database structures its data into tables whereas a blockchain, like its name implies, structures its data into chunks (blocks) that are chained together. This makes it so that all blockchains are databases but not all databases are blockchains. This system also inherently makes an irreversible timeline of data when implemented in a decentralized nature. When a block is filled it is set in stone and becomes a part of this timeline. Each block in the chain is given an exact timestamp when it is added to the chain.

Decentralization

For the purpose of understanding blockchain, it is instructive to view it in the context of how it has been implemented by Bitcoin. Like a database, Bitcoin needs a collection of computers to store its blockchain. For Bitcoin, this blockchain is just a specific type of database that stores every Bitcoin transaction ever made. In Bitcoin's case, and unlike most databases, these computers are not all under one roof, and each computer or group of computers is operated by a unique individual or group of individuals.

Imagine that a company owns a server comprised of 10,000 computers with a database holding all of its client's account information. This company has a warehouse containing all of these computers under one roof and has full control of each of these computers and all the information contained within them. Similarly, Bitcoin consists of thousands of computers, but each computer or group of computers that hold its blockchain is in a different geographic location and they are all operated by separate individuals or groups of people. These computers that makeup Bitcoin's network are called nodes.

In this model, Bitcoin's blockchain is used in a decentralized way. However, private, centralized blockchains, where the computers that make up its network are owned and operated by a single entity, do exist.

In a blockchain, each node has a full record of the data that has been stored on the blockchain since its inception. For Bitcoin, the data is the entire history of all Bitcoin transactions. If one node has an error in its data it can use the thousands of other nodes as a reference point to correct itself. This way, no one node within the network can alter information held within it. Because of this, the history of transactions in each block that make up Bitcoin's blockchain is irreversible.

If one user tampers with Bitcoin's record of transactions, all other nodes would cross-reference each other and easily pinpoint the node with the incorrect information. This system helps to establish an exact and transparent order of events. For Bitcoin, this information is a list of transactions, but it also is possible for a blockchain to hold a variety of information like legal contracts, state identifications, or a company's product inventory.

In order to change how that system works, or the information stored within it, a majority of the decentralized network's computing power would need to agree on said changes. This ensures that whatever changes do occur are in the best interests of the majority.

Transparency

Because of the decentralized nature of Bitcoin's blockchain, all transactions can be transparently viewed by either having a personal node or by using blockchain explorer that allow anyone to see transactions occurring live. Each node has its own copy of the chain that gets updated as fresh blocks are confirmed and added. This means that if you wanted to, you could track Bitcoin wherever it goes.

For example, exchanges have been hacked in the past where those who held Bitcoin on the exchange lost everything. While the hacker may be entirely anonymous, the Bitcoins that they extracted are easily traceable. If the Bitcoins that were stolen in some of these hacks were to be moved or spent somewhere, it would be known.

Is Blockchain Secure?

Blockchain technology accounts for the issues of security and trust in several ways. First, new blocks are always stored linearly and chronologically. That is, they are always added to the "end" of the blockchain. If you take a look at Bitcoin's blockchain, you'll see that each block has a position on the chain, called a "height." As of November 2020, the block's height had reached 656,197 blocks so far.

After a block has been added to the end of the blockchain, it is very difficult to go back and alter the contents of the block unless the majority reached a consensus to do so. That's because each block contains its own hash, along with the hash of the block before it, as well as the previously mentioned time stamp. Hash codes are created by a math function that turns digital information into a string of numbers and letters. If that information is edited in any way, the hash code changes as well.

Here's why that's important to security. Let's say a hacker wants to alter the blockchain and steal Bitcoin from everyone else. If they were to alter their own single copy, it would no longer align with everyone else's copy. When everyone else cross-references their copies against each other, they would see this one copy stand out and that hacker's version of the chain would be cast away as illegitimate.

Succeeding with such a hack would require that the hacker simultaneously control and alter 51% of the copies of the blockchain so that their new copy becomes the majority copy and thus, the agreed-upon chain. Such an attack would also require an immense amount of money and resources as they would need to redo all of the blocks because they would now have different timestamps and hash codes.

Due to the size of Bitcoin's network and how fast it is growing, the cost to pull off such a feat would probably be insurmountable. Not only would this be extremely expensive, but it would also likely be fruitless. Doing such a thing would not go unnoticed, as network members would see such drastic alterations to the blockchain. The network members would then fork off to a new version of the chain that has not been affected.

This would cause the attacked version of Bitcoin to plummet in value, making the attack ultimately pointless as the bad actor has control of a worthless asset. The same would occur if the bad actor were to attack the new fork of Bitcoin. It is built this way so that taking part in the network is far more economically incentivized than attacking it.

How is Blockchain Used?

As we now know, blocks on Bitcoin's blockchain store data about monetary transactions. But it turns out that blockchain is actually a reliable way of storing data about other types of transactions, as well.

Some companies that have already incorporated blockchain include Walmart, Pfizer, AIG, Siemens, Unilever, and a host of others. For example, IBM has created its Food Trust blockchain1 to trace the journey that food products take to get to its locations.

Why do this? The food industry has seen countless outbreaks of e Coli, salmonella, listeria, as well as hazardous materials being accidentally introduced to foods. In the past, it has taken weeks to find the source of these outbreaks or the cause of sickness from what people are eating.

Using blockchain gives brands the ability to track a food product's route from its origin, through each stop it makes, and finally its delivery. If a food is found to be contaminated then it can be traced all the way back through each stop to its origin. Not only that, but these companies can also now see everything else it may have come in contact with, allowing the identification of the problem to occur far sooner, potentially saving lives. This is one example of blockchains in practice, but there are many other forms of blockchain implementation.

Banking and Finance

Perhaps no industry stands to benefit from integrating blockchain into its business operations more than banking. Financial institutions only operate during business hours, five days a week. That means if you try to deposit a check on Friday at 6 p.m., you will likely have to wait until Monday morning to see that money hit your account. Even if you do make your deposit during business hours, the transaction can still take one to three days to verify due to the sheer volume of transactions that banks need to settle. Blockchain, on the other hand, never sleeps.

By integrating blockchain into banks, consumers can see their transactions processed in as little as 10 minutes,2 basically the time it takes to add a block to the blockchain, regardless of holidays or the time of day or week. With blockchain, banks also have the opportunity to exchange funds between institutions more quickly and securely. In the stock trading business, for example, the settlement and clearing process can take up to three days (or longer, if trading internationally), meaning that the money and shares are frozen for that period of time.

Given the size of the sums involved, even the few days that the money is in transit can carry significant costs and risks for banks. European bank Santander and its research partners put the potential savings at $15 billion to $20 billion a year.3 Capgemini, a French consultancy, estimates that consumers could save up to $16 billion in banking and insurance fees each year4 through blockchain-based applications.

Currency

Blockchain forms the bedrock for cryptocurrencies like Bitcoin. The U.S. dollar is controlled by the Federal Reserve. Under this central authority system, a user's data and currency are technically at the whim of their bank or government. If a user's bank is hacked, the client's private information is at risk. If the client's bank collapses or they live in a country with an unstable government, the value of their currency may be at risk. In 2008, some of the banks that ran out of money were bailed out partially using taxpayer money. These are the worries out of which Bitcoin was first conceived and developed.

By spreading its operations across a network of computers, blockchain allows Bitcoin and other cryptocurrencies to operate without the need for a central authority. This not only reduces risk but also eliminates many of the processing and transaction fees. It can also give those in countries with unstable currencies or financial infrastructures a more stable currency with more applications and a wider network of individuals and institutions they can do business with, both domestically and internationally.

Using cryptocurrency wallets for savings accounts or as a means of payment is especially profound for those who have no state identification. Some countries may be war-torn or have governments that lack any real infrastructure to provide identification. Citizens of such countries may not have access to savings or brokerage accounts and therefore, no way to safely store wealth.

Healthcare

Health care providers can leverage blockchain to securely store their patients' medical records. When a medical record is generated and signed, it can be written into the blockchain, which provides patients with the proof and confidence that the record cannot be changed. These personal health records could be encoded and stored on the blockchain with a private key, so that they are only accessible by certain individuals, thereby ensuring privacy.

Records of Property

If you have ever spent time in your local Recorder's Office, you will know that the process of recording property rights is both burdensome and inefficient. Today, a physical deed must be delivered to a government employee at the local recording office, where it is manually entered into the county's central database and public index. In the case of a property dispute, claims to the property must be reconciled with the public index.

This process is not just costly and time-consuming it is also riddled with human error, where each inaccuracy makes tracking property ownership less efficient. Blockchain has the potential to eliminate the need for scanning documents and tracking down physical files in a local recording office. If property ownership is stored and verified on the blockchain, owners can trust that their deed is accurate and permanently recorded.

In war-torn countries or areas that have little to no government or financial infrastructure, and certainly no "Recorder's Office," it can be nearly impossible to prove ownership of a property. If a group of people living in such an area is able to leverage blockchain, transparent and clear timelines of property ownership could be established.

Smart Contracts

A <u>smart</u> contract is a computer code that can be built into the blockchain to facilitate, verify, or negotiate a contract agreement. Smart contracts operate under a set of conditions that users agree to. When those conditions are met, the terms of the agreement are automatically carried out.

Say, for example, a potential tenant would like to lease an apartment using a smart contract. The landlord agrees to give the tenant the door code to the apartment as soon as the tenant pays the security deposit. Both the tenant and the landlord would send their respective portions of the deal to the smart contract, which would hold onto and automatically exchange the door code for the security deposit on the date the lease begins. If the landlord doesn't supply the door code by the lease date, the smart contract refunds the security deposit. This would eliminate the fees and processes typically associated with the use of a notary, third-party mediator, or attornies.

Supply Chains

As in the IBM Food Trust example, suppliers can use blockchain to record the origins of materials that they have purchased. This would allow companies to verify the authenticity of their products, along with such common labels as "Organic," "Local," and "Fair Trade."

As reported by Forbes, the food industry is increasingly adopting the use of blockchain to track the path and safety of food throughout the farm-to-user journey.

Voting

As mentioned, blockchain could be used to facilitate a modern voting system. Voting with blockchain carries the potential to eliminate election fraud and boost voter turnout, as was tested in the November 2018 midterm elections in West Virginia. Using blockchain in this way would make votes nearly impossible to tamper with. The blockchain protocol would also maintain transparency in the electoral process, reducing the personnel needed to conduct an election and providing officials with nearly instant results. This would eliminate the need for recounts or any real concern that fraud might threaten the election.

Advantages and Disadvantages of Blockchain

For all of its complexity, blockchain's potential as a decentralized form of record-keeping is almost without limit. From greater user privacy and heightened security to lower processing fees and fewer errors, blockchain technology may very well see applications beyond those outlined above. But there are also some disadvantages.

Pros

· Improved accuracy by removing human involvement in verification

· Cost reductions by eliminating third-party verification

· Decentralization makes it harder to tamper with

· Transactions are secure, private, and efficient

· Transparent technology

· Provides a banking alternative and way to secure personal information for citizens of countries with unstable or underdeveloped governments

Cons

· Significant technology cost associated with mining bitcoin

· Low transactions per second

· History of use in illicit activities

· Regulation

Here are the selling points of blockchain for businesses on the market today in more detail.

Chapter2. Mining of Cryptocurrency

Mining is how new units of cryptocurrency are released into the world, generally in exchange for validating transactions. While it's theoretically possible for the average person to mine cryptocurrency, it's increasingly difficult in proof of work systems, like Bitcoin.

"As the Bitcoin network grows, it gets more complicated, and more processing power is required," says Spencer Montgomery, founder of Uinta Crypto Consulting. "The average consumer used to be able to do this, but now it's just too expensive. There are too many people who have optimized their equipment and technology to outcompete."

And remember: Proof of work cryptocurrencies require huge amounts of energy to mine. It's estimated that 0.21% of all of the world's electricity goes to powering Bitcoin farms. That's roughly the same amount of power Switzerland uses in a year. It's estimated most Bitcoin miners end up using 60% to 80% of what they earn from mining to cover electricity costs.

While it's impractical for the average person to earn crypto by mining in a proof of work system, the proof of stake model requires less in the way of high-powered computing as validators are chosen at random based on the amount they stake. It does, however, require that you already own a cryptocurrency to participate. (If you have no crypto, you have nothing to stake.)

History of Cryptocurrency

In 1983, the American developed a cryptographic system referred to as eCash. Twelve years later, they developed every system DigiCash, that used cryptography to make economic transactions personal.

However, the first time the concept or time period "cryptocurrency" turned into coined changed into in 1998. That year, Wei Dai began to consider developing a brand new payment method that used a cryptographic system and whose important feature was decentralization. In 2008, a funding crisis affecting everybody, together with America's superpower, changed into booming. The effects of such a large economic disaster were dormant and the coins were losing value faster and faster.

In 2009, the so-called Satoshi Nakamoto someone whose identity still remains secret, no person knows who invented bitcoin, or at the least no longer conclusively. Satoshi Nakamoto is the call associated with the person or organization of people who released the authentic bitcoin white paper in 2008 and worked at the authentic bitcoin software program that was launched in 2009. As you have already read, he was not the first person who came up with the idea to create it. In the years since that time, many individuals have either claimed to be or have been suggested as the real-life people behind the pseudonym, but as of January 2021, the authentic identity (or identities) in the back of Satoshi remains obscured. Although it's far tempting to agree with the media's spin that Satoshi Nakamoto is a solitary, quixotic genius who created

Bitcoin out of thin air, such improvements do now not normally appear in a vacuum. All foremost medical discoveries, no matter how original-seeming, have been constructed on previously present research.

There are precursors to bitcoin: Adam Back's Hashcash, invented in 1997, and finally Wei Dai's b-money, Nick Szabo's bit gold, and Hal Finney's Reusable Proof of Work. The bitcoin whitepaper itself cites Hashcash and b-cash, as well as diverse different works spanning numerous studies fields. Perhaps unsurprisingly, most of the individuals behind the other initiatives named above had been imagined to have additionally had a component in creating bitcoin.

There are a few feasible motivations for bitcoin's inventor deciding to preserve their identity mystery. One is privacy: As bitcoin has gained in recognition—becoming some thing of a worldwide phenomenon—Satoshi Nakamoto would likely garner a number of attention from the media and from governments.

Another motive will be the ability for bitcoin to purpose a major disruption inside the contemporary banking and financial systems. If bitcoin have been to advantage mass adoption, the device should surpass nations' sovereign fiat currencies. This chance to existing forex should inspire governments to need to take legal movement in opposition to bitcoin's creator.

The different motive is safety. Looking at 2009 by myself, 32,489 blocks were mined; at the praise fee of 50 bitcoin according to block, the total payout in 2009 become 1,624,500 bitcoin. One may additionally finish that best Satoshi and perhaps a few different human beings had been mining via 2009 and that they possess a majority of that stash of bitcoin.

Someone in ownership of that lots bitcoin should turn out to be a target of criminals, especially since bitcoins are much less like shares and more like coins, in which the personal keys needed to authorize spending may be published out and actually kept underneath a mattress. While it is likely the inventor of bitcoin could take precautions to make any extortion-brought on transfers traceable, closing anonymous is a superb way for Satoshi to restrict publicity.

Why you should consider investing in Cryptocurrency?

Investing in currencies such as Bitcoin and Ethereum is considered a "high-risk" investment. The price of cryptocurrencies is generally volatile; some can go wrong, others could turn out to be scams, while others may increase in value and produce a great return for the investors. If you are considering investing in Cryptocurrency, you need to find a trusted and reliable trading platform such as Bitfinex. You can read about the <u>trusted Bitfinex review</u>.

To some people, Cryptocurrency could remain niche or vanish just like that. But Cryptocurrency should be considered a high-risk investment just like any other investment. With more and more businesses accepting crypto, it is now evident that Cryptocurrency is here to stay and it will not disappear any time soon.

Some of the big brands that have accepted crypto include Starbucks, Tesla, and other top casinos. This proves that crypto will soon find its way into so many big brands, making it a worthy investment. But just like any other investment, before you invest in crypto, you need to do extensive diligence and don't pin your hopes on one Cryptocurrency or one company. The best decision is to spread your money across so that you can spread the risk. Again, remember to invest only what you can afford to lose.

Types of Risks Associated with Cryptocurrency Investing

Although Bitcoin was not designed as a normal equity investment (no shares have been issued), some speculative investors were drawn to the digital currency after it appreciated rapidly in May 2011 and again in November 2013. Thus, many people purchase bitcoin for its investment value rather than its ability to act as a medium of exchange.

However, the lack of guaranteed value and its digital nature means the purchase and use of bitcoins carries several inherent risks. Many investor alerts have been issued by the Securities and Exchange Commission (SEC), the Financia Industry Regulatory Authority (FINRA), the Consumer Financial Protection Bureau (CFPB), and other agencies.

The concept of a virtual currency is still novel and, compared to traditional investments; bitcoin doesn't have much of a long-term track record or history of credibility to back it. With their increasing popularity, bitcoins are becoming less experimental every day; still, after only a decade, all digital currencies still remain in a development phase. "It is pretty much the highest-risk, highest-return investment that you can possibly make," says Barry Silbert, CEO of Digital Currency Group, which builds and invests in Bitcoin and blockchain companies.10

Regulatory Risk

Investing money into bitcoin in any of its many guises is not for the risk-averse. Bitcoins are a rival to government currency and may be used for black market transactions, money laundering, illegal activities, or tax evasion. As a result, governments may seek to regulate, restrict, or ban the use and sale of bitcoins (and some already have). Others are coming up with various rules.

For example, in 2015, the New York State Department of Financial Services finalized regulations that would require companies dealing with the buy, sell, transfer, or storage of bitcoins to record the identity of customers, have a compliance officer, and maintain capital reserves. The transactions worth $10,000 or more will have to be recorded and reported.

The lack of uniform regulations about bitcoins (and other virtual currency) raises questions over their longevity, liquidity, and universality.

Security Risk

Most individuals who own and use bitcoin have not acquired their tokens through mining operations. Rather, they buy and sell bitcoin and other digital currencies on any of a number of popular online markets, known as bitcoin exchanges.

Bitcoin exchanges are entirely digital and, as with any virtual system, are at risk from hackers, malware, and operational glitches. If a thief gains access to a bitcoin owner's computer hard drive and steals their private encryption key, they could transfer the stolen bitcoin to another account. (Users can prevent this only if bitcoins are stored on a computer that is not connected to the internet, or else by choosing to use a paper wallet printing out the bitcoin private keys and addresses, and not keeping them on a computer at all.)

Hackers can also target bitcoin exchanges, gaining access to thousands of accounts and digital wallets where bitcoins are stored. One especially notorious hacking incident took place in 2014, when Mt. Gox, a bitcoin exchange in Japan, was forced to close down after millions of dollars' worth of bitcoins were stolen.

This is particularly problematic given that all Bitcoin transactions are permanent and irreversible. It's like dealing with cash: Any transaction carried out with bitcoins can only be reversed if the person who has received them refunds them. There is no third party or a payment processor, as in the case of a debit or credit card—hence, no source of protection or appeal if there is a problem.

Insurance Risk

Some investments are insured through the Securities Investor Protection Corporation. Normal bank accounts are insured through the Federal Deposit Insurance Corporation (FDIC) up to a certain amount depending on the jurisdiction.

Generally speaking, bitcoin exchanges and bitcoin accounts are not insured by any type of federal or government program. In 2019, prime dealer and trading platform SFOX announced it would be able to provide bitcoin investors with FDIC insurance, but only for the portion of transactions involving cash.13

Fraud Risk

While bitcoin uses private key encryption to verify owners and register transactions, fraudsters and scammers may attempt to sell false bitcoins. For instance, in July 2013, the SEC brought legal action against an operator of a bitcoin-related Ponzi scheme. There have also been documented cases of bitcoin price manipulation, another common form of fraud.

Market Risk

Like with any investment, bitcoin values can fluctuate. Indeed, the value of the currency has seen wild swings in price over its short existence. Subject to high volume buying and selling on exchanges, it has a high sensitivity to any newsworthy events. According to the CFPB, the price of bitcoins fell by 61% in a single day in 2013, while the one-day price drop record in 2014 was as big as 80%.

If fewer people begin to accept bitcoin as a currency, these digital units may lose value and could become worthless. Indeed, there was speculation that the "bitcoin bubble" had burst when the price declined from its all-time high during the cryptocurrency rush in late 2017 and early 2018.

There is already plenty of competition, and although bitcoin has a huge lead over the hundreds of other digital currencies that have sprung up because of its brand recognition and venture capital money, a technological break-through in the form of a better virtual coin is always a threat.

Imposter Websites

You may be following a solid tip from someone with a lot of expertise but still become a victim by accidently visiting a fake website. There's a surprising number of websites that have been set up to resemble original, valid startup companies. If there isn't a small lock icon indicating security near the URL bar and no "https" in the site address think twice.

Even if the site looks identical to the one you think you're visiting, you may find yourself directed to another platform for payment. For example, you click on a link that looks like a legitimate site, but attackers have created a fake URL with a zero in it instead of a letter 'o'. That platform, of course, isn't taking you to the cryptocurrency investment that you've already researched. To avoid this, carefully type the exact URL into your browser. Double check it, too.

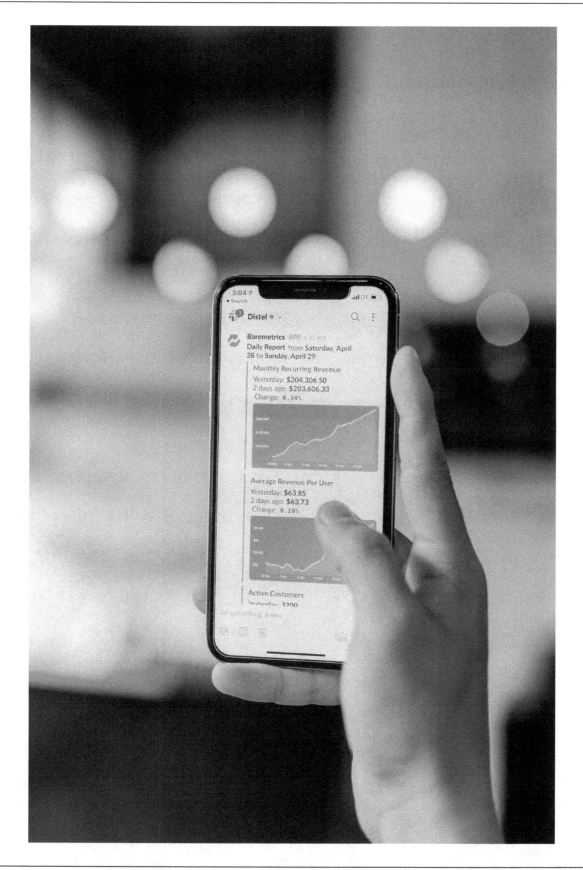

Fake Mobile Apps

Another common way scammers trick cryptocurrency investors is through fake apps available for download through Google Play and the Apple App Store. Although stakeholders can often quickly find these fake apps and get them removed, that doesn't mean the apps aren't impacting many bottom lines. Thousands of people have already downloaded fake cryptocurrency apps, reports Bitcoin News.

While this is a greater risk for Android users, every investor should be aware of the possibility. Are there obvious misspellings in the copy or even the name of the app? Does the branding look inauthentic with strange coloring or an incorrect logo? Take note and reconsider downloading.

Bad Tweets and Other Social Media Updates

If you're following celebrities and executives on social media, you can't be sure that you're not following impostor accounts. The same applies to cryptocurrencies, where malicious, impersonating bots are rampant. Don't trust offers that come from Twitter or Facebook, especially if there seems to be an impossible result. Fake accounts are everywhere.

If someone on these platforms asks for even a small amount of your cryptocurrency, it's likely you can never get it back. Just because others are replying to the offer, don't assume they aren't bots, either. You have to be extra careful.

Scamming Emails

Even if it looks exactly like an email you received from a legitimate cryptocurrency company, take care before investing your digital currency. Is the email the exact same, and are the logo and branding identical? Can you verify that the email address is legitimately connected to the company? The ability to check on this is one reason why it's important to choose a company that has real people working for it. If you have doubts about an email, ask someone who works there. And never click on a link in a message to get to a site.

Scammers often announce fake ICOs, or initial coin offerings, as a way to steal substantial funds. Don't fall for these fake email and website offers. Take your time to look over all the details.

Unfortunately, there are many ways that some Internet users exploit unsecure computing systems to mine or steal cryptocurrency.

How to Buy Bitcoin using PayPal

It is likewise feasible to shop for Bitcoin through charge processor PayPal. There are two ways to buy Bitcoin the usage of PayPal. The first, and maximum handy technique, is to purchase cryptocurrencies through the use of your PayPal account. The second choice is to apply the stability of your PayPal account to buy cryptocurrencies from a third-celebration issuer. This choice isn't always as handy as the first one due to the fact very few third party sites allow users to purchase Bitcoin with the use of the PayPal button.

Four cryptocurrencies – Bitcoin, Ethereum, Litecoin, and Bitcoin Cash – can be purchased without delay thru PayPal. With the exception of Hawaii, citizens of all states can both use their existing PayPal accounts or set up new ones.

To set up a crypto account with PayPal, the subsequent pieces of information are required: Name, Physical cope with, Date of Birth, and Tax Identification Number. There are some of the methods by which you may purchase Bitcoin via PayPal.

Some of them are:

- Existing balance in PayPal account.

-
- Debit card linked to PayPal account
-
- Bank account linked to PayPal account
-

It is not feasible to apply for a credit card to buy Bitcoin using PayPal. During the purchase system, PayPal will show a price. However, the inherent volatility of cryptocurrency charges method that those prices can exchange fast. You have to make sure which you have enough finances in your account to make the purchase.

When you buy Bitcoin without delay from PayPal, it makes cash off the crypto spread or the distinction between Bitcoin's marketplace charge and change fee among USD and the cryptocurrency. The enterprise additionally expenses a transaction fee for each purchase. These charges rely upon the dollar quantity of buy. For instance, a flat rate of $zero.50 is charged for purchases between $a hundred to $2 hundred. Thereafter, the fee is a percentage of the general dollar amount. For instance, a fee of two% of the whole quantity is charged for crypto purchases among $100 to $two hundred.

One downside of buying cryptocurrencies via PayPal is that you can't switch crypto outside the price processor's platform. Therefore, it isn't always feasible to switch cryptocurrencies from PayPal's pockets to an outside crypto wallet or your private wallet.

The other downside of using PayPal is that very few exchanges and online investors allow the charge processor to purchase payment. EToro is many of the few online investors who use PayPal to buy Bitcoin on its platform.

How to Buy Bitcoin with Credit Card

The technique to purchase Bitcoin with credit playing cards is just like getting the cryptocurrency with debit cards or thru computerized clearing house (ACH) transfers. You will want to go into your credit card details with the trade or online buying and selling firm and authorize the transaction. In trendy, however, it isn't always a terrific concept to purchase Bitcoin with credit cards. There are multiple motives for this.

First, not all exchanges permit Bitcoin purchases using credit cards because of associated processing expenses and the chance of fraud. Their selection to accomplish that may fit out inside the quality hobbies of customers. This is because credit card processing can tack extra fees onto such transactions. Thus, similarly to paying transaction charges, you will emerge as processing expenses that the alternate may also bypass onto you.

The 2nd motive is that credit card purchases can be high priced. Credit card issuers treat Bitcoin purchases as coins advances and charge hefty charges and interest quotes on such advances. For example, American Express and Chase both count purchases of cryptocurrencies as coins boost transactions. Thus, if you purchase $100 well worth of Bitcoin using an American Express card, you will pay $10 (current cash boost fee for such transactions) plus an annual percentage charge of 25%.

An oblique technique of buying Bitcoin using a credit card is to get a Bitcoin Rewards creditcard. Such playing cards characteristic like your normal rewards creditcard; besides, they offer rewards in the shape of Bitcoin. So, they make investments cash again earned from purchases into Bitcoin. An instance of a Bitcoin Rewards card is the BlockFi Bitcoin Rewards Credit Card.

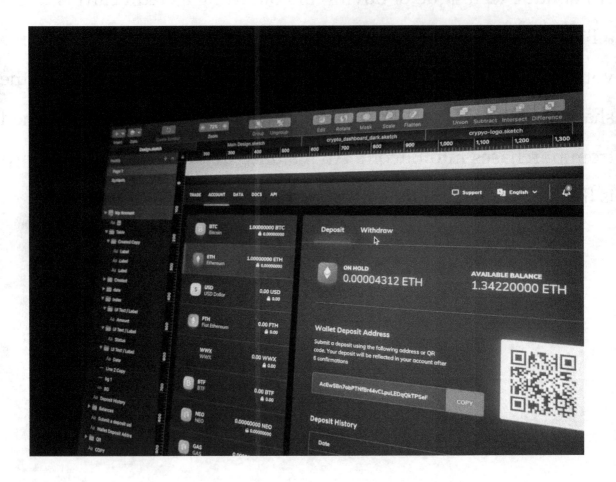

Beware, however, that the annual price on these playing cards may be steep, and there can be extra expenses associated with the conversion of fiat currencies into crypto.

Alternate Ways of Buying Bitcoin

While exchanges like Coinbase or Binance remain some of the most popular ways of purchasing Bitcoin, it is not the only method. Below are some additional processes Bitcoin owners utilize.

Bitcoin ATMs

Bitcoin ATMs act like in-person Bitcoin exchanges. Individuals can insert cash into the machine and use it to purchase Bitcoin that is then transferred to a secure digital wallet. Bitcoin ATMs have become increasingly popular in recent years; Coin ATM Radar can help to track down the closest machines.

P2P Exchanges

Unlike decentralized exchanges, which match up buyers and sellers anonymously and facilitate all aspects of the transaction, there are some peer-to-peer (P2P) exchange services that provide a more direct connection between users. Local Bitcoins is an example of such an exchange. After creating an account, users can post requests to buy or sell Bitcoin, including information about payment methods and price. Users then browse through listings of buy and sell offers, choosing those trade partners with whom they wish to transact.

Local Bitcoins facilitates some of the aspects of the trade. While P2P exchanges do not offer the same anonymity as decentralized exchanges, they allow users the opportunity to shop around for the best deal. Many of these exchanges also provide rating systems so that users have a way to evaluate potential trade partners before transacting.

How to Sell Bitcoin

You can sell Bitcoin at the same venues that you purchased the cryptocurrency, such as cryptocurrency exchanges and peer-to-peer platforms. Typically, the process to sell Bitcoin on these platforms is similar to the process used to purchase the cryptocurrency.

For example, you may only be required to click a button and specify an order type (i.e., whether the cryptocurrency should be sold instantly at available prices or whether it should be sold to limit losses) to conduct the sale. Depending on the market composition and demand at the venue, the offering price for Bitcoin may vary. For example, exchanges in South Korea traded Bitcoin at a Kimchi premium during the run up in its prices back in 2018.

Cryptocurrency exchanges charge a percentage of the crypto sale amount as fees. For example, Coinbase charges 1.49% of the overall transaction amount as fees.

Exchanges generally have daily and monthly withdrawal limits. Therefore, cash from a large sale may not be immediately available to the trader. There are no limits on the amount of cryptocurrency you can sell, however.

Chapter3. Before You Begin

There are numerous matters that every aspiring Bitcoin investor desires. A cryptocurrency change account, private identity documents in case you are using a Know Your Customer (KYC) platform, a comfy connection to the Internet, and a method of charge. Likewise, it is recommended that you have your own private wallet outside of the trading account. Valid strategies of payment using this path consist of financial institution accounts, debit playing cards, and credit playing cards. It is likewise viable to get Bitcoin at specialized ATMs and via P2P exchanges. However, be aware that Bitcoin ATMs have been increasingly requiring authorities-issued IDs as of early 2020.

Privacy and protection are vital issues for Bitcoin traders. Even though there are no physical Bitcoins, it is also a bad idea to gloat approximately huge holdings. Anyone who profits the personal key to a public address at the Bitcoin blockchain can authorize transactions. Private keys must be kept in mystery; criminals might also attempt to steal them if they analyze large holdings. Be conscious that anybody can see the balance of a public deal you use. That makes it a good idea to maintain vast investments at public addresses that aren't immediately linked to ones that are used for transactions.

Anyone can view a history of transactions made at the blockchain, even you. While transactions are publicly recorded at the blockchain, figuring out user information isn't always. Most effective, a person's public key appears next to a transaction — making transactions exclusive however not nameless on the Bitcoin blockchain. In an experience, Bitcoin transactions are greater transparent and traceable than coins, but the cryptocurrency can also be used anonymously.

Following are some steps you need to follow if you want to invest in cryptocurrency:

Step One: Choose an Exchange

Signing up for a cryptocurrency trade will permit you to shop for, sell, and maintain cryptocurrency. It is generally an exceptional exercise to apply a change that lets its customers additionally withdrawal their crypto to their very own non-public online wallet for more secure preservation. This feature might not depend on the ones trying to change Bitcoin or other cryptocurrencies.

There are many styles of cryptocurrency exchanges. Because the Bitcoin ethos is about decentralization and man or woman sovereignty, some exchanges permit customers to remain anonymous and do not require users to go into private information. Such exchanges perform autonomously and, generally, decentralized, which means that they no longer have a primary factor of manipulation.

While such structures may be used for nefarious sports, they're extensively utilized to offer offerings for the arena's unbanked population. For certain classes of human beings – refugees or those dwelling in international locations with little to no infrastructure for authorities' credit or banking – anonymous exchanges can help convey them into the mainstream economy.

Right now, but, the maximum popular exchanges now not decentralized and do require KYC. In the United States, these exchanges include Coinbase, Kraken, Gemini, and Binance U.S., to name some. Each of those exchanges has grown appreciably inside the variety of capabilities they offer.

Coinbase, Kraken, and Gemini offer Bitcoin and a growing wide variety of altcoins. These 3 are probably the perfect on-ramp to crypto in the entire enterprise. Binance caters to a more superior dealer, imparting greater critical trading functionality and a better style of altcoins to choose from.

A vital thing to note whilst creating a cryptocurrency change account is to apply secure net practices. This consists of the usage of -aspect authentication and using a precise and lengthy password, together with a variety of lowercase letters, capitalized letters, special characters, and numbers.

Step Two: Connect Your Exchange to a Payment Option

Once you have chosen an exchange, you now want to collect your non-public documents. Depending on the exchange, these may consist of snapshots of a driving force's license, social security variety, in addition to statistics approximately your business enterprise and supply of funds. The records you could need can depend upon your location and the laws inside it. The system is largely the same as putting in place a standard brokerage account.

After the trade has ensured your identity and legitimacy, you can now join a payment choice. At most exchanges, you may connect your financial institution account without delay, or you could join a debit or credit card. While you may use a credit card to buy cryptocurrency, it's miles usually something that should be avoided because of the volatility that cryptocurrencies can revel in.

While Bitcoin is legal inside the United States, some banks no longer take too kindly to the idea and might query or even forestall deposits to crypto-associated web sites or exchanges. It is a great idea to test to make sure that your financial institution deposits at your chosen alternate.

There are various costs for deposits thru a financial institution account, debit, or credit card. Coinbase is a stable exchange for beginners and has a 1.49% charge for financial institution money owed, with a 3.99% rate for debit and credit playing cards. It is essential to analyze the charges associated with every fee choice to assist in pick out and trade or pick out which price choice works great for you.

Exchanges additionally rate fees in step with the transaction. This rate can both be a flat fee (if the trading quantity is low) or a per cent of buying and selling quantity. Credit cards incur a processing rate similarly to the transaction costs.

Step Three: Place an Order

Once you have selected trade and connected a charged alternative, you may now buy Bitcoin and other cryptocurrencies. In latest years, cryptocurrency exchanges have slowly turn out to be more mainstream. They have grown notably in terms of liquidity and their breadth of capabilities. The operational modifications at cryptocurrency exchanges parallel the exchange notion for cryptocurrencies. An industry that became as soon as the notion of as a rip-off or one with questionable practices is slowly morphing right into a valid one that has drawn interest from all huge players in the economic offerings industry.

Now, cryptocurrency exchanges have gotten to some extent where they have almost identical functions as their stock brokerage counterparts. Once you have located an exchange and linked a charging method, you are geared up to move.

Crypto exchanges these days provide some order types and methods to invest. Almost all crypto exchanges offer each marketplace and limit orders, and some also provide stop-loss orders. Of the exchanges stated above, Kraken gives the most order kinds. Kraken lets in for market, restriction, prevent-loss, prevent-restrict, take-earnings, and take-profit limit orders1

.

Aside from diffusion of order types, exchanges also provide approaches to set up habitual investments allowing clients to dollar fee average into their investments of desire. Coinbase, for instance, we could users set habitual purchases for every day, week, or month.

Step Four: Safe Storage

Bitcoin and cryptocurrency wallets are a place to shop virtual property extra securely. Having your crypto out of the trade doors and your personal wallet guarantees that only you have manipulated the personal key to your funds. It additionally gives you the ability to shop funds far away from an exchange and avoid the threat of your change getting hacked and losing your funds.

Some wallets have extra capabilities than others. Some are Bitcoin best, and some provide the potential to shop numerous types of altcoins. Some wallets also offer the capability to change one token for any other.

When it involves deciding on a Bitcoin wallet, you have some options. The first element you will need to understand about crypto wallets is hot wallets (online wallets) and cold wallets (paper or hardware wallets).

Hot Wallets

Online wallets also are called "hot" wallets. Hot wallets are wallets that run on internet-related devices like computer systems, phones, or capsules. This can create vulnerability due to the fact these wallets generate the private keys on your coins on those net-related devices. While a hot pockets may be very convenient in the way you're capable of access and make transactions along with your belongings quickly, storing your non-public key on a web-linked tool makes it greater vulnerable to a hack.

This can also sound far-fetched, but individuals who are not the usage of sufficient protection whilst using those hot wallets may have their price range stolen. This isn't always an rare prevalence and it can take place in some of approaches. As an instance, boasting on a public discussion board like Reddit about how a good deal Bitcoin you keep while you are the usage of little to no safety and storing it in a hot pockets would not be smart. That said, these wallets may be made to be relaxed so long as precautions are taken. Strong passwords, two-component authentication, and safe internet surfing have to be considered minimum requirements.

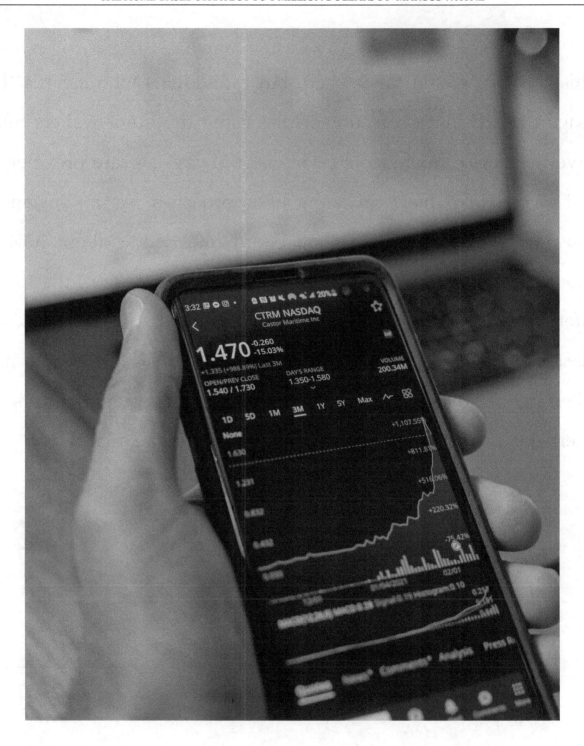

These wallets are nice used for small quantities of cryptocurrency or cryptocurrency that you are actively buying and selling on an exchange. You should liken a hot pockets to a bank account. Conventional financial wisdom might say to preserve handiest spending money in a bank account at the same time as the majority of your cash is in savings debts or different funding bills. The identical could be said for hot wallets. Hot wallets embody cell, computer, net, and exchange account custody wallets.

As stated previously, change wallets are custodial accounts provided by way of the alternate. The consumer of this pockets kind isn't always the holder of the personal key to the cryptocurrency that is held in this wallet. If an event were to arise where the change is hacked or your account becomes compromised, your budget could be lost. The phrase "now not your key, no longer your coin" is closely-repeated within cryptocurrency boards and groups.

Cold Wallets

The most effective description of a cold wallet is a pockets that is not related to the internet and consequently stands at a much lesser risk of being compromised. These wallets can also be referred to as offline wallets or hardware wallets.

These wallets keep a person's private key on some thing that is not linked to the internet and may come with software program that works in parallel in order that the user can view their portfolio with out putting their personal key at chance.

Perhaps the most secure manner to keep cryptocurrency offline is through a paper pockets. A paper wallet is a wallet that you can generate off of certain websites. It then produces each public and personal keys that you print out on a bit of paper. The capacity to get admission to cryptocurrency in these addresses is simplest viable if you have that piece of paper with the private key. Many people laminate those paper wallets and shop them in protection deposit packing containers at their financial institution or even in a safe of their home. These wallets are meant for excessive safety and long-time period investments because you can not quick sell or alternate Bitcoin saved this manner.

A more usually used type of cold wallet is a hardware pockets. A hardware pockets is commonly a USB power device that stores a person's non-public keys securely offline. Such wallets have serious benefits over hot wallets as they're unaffected by viruses that might be on one's pc. With hardware wallets, personal keys in no way are available contact together with your network-related computer or doubtlessly prone software. These gadgets are also commonly open supply, allowing the network to decide its protection thru code audits rather than aorganisation declaring that it is safe to apply.

Cold wallets are the most cozy way to shop your Bitcoin or other cryptocurrencies. For the maximum component, but, they require a piece greater understanding to installation.

A proper way to installation your wallets is to have three matters: an alternate account to shop for and sell, a hot wallet to keep small to medium quantities of crypto you desire to change or promote, and a cold hardware pockets to keep large holdings for long-term periods.

Best cryptocurrencies on the market to invest in

Cryptocurrencies are almost always designed to be free from government manipulation and control, although as they have grown more popular this foundational aspect of the industry has come under fire. The currencies modeled after Bitcoin are collectively called altcoins, and in some cases "shitcoins," and have often tried to present themselves as modified or improved versions of Bitcoin. While some of these currencies may have some impressive features that Bitcoin does not, matching the level of security that Bitcoin's networks achieves has largely yet to be seen by an altcoin.

Below, we'll examine some of the most important digital currencies other than Bitcoin. First, though, a caveat: it is impossible for a list like this to be entirely comprehensive. One reason for this is the fact that there are more than 4,000 cryptocurrencies in existence as of January 2021. While many of these cryptos have little to no following or trading volume, some enjoy immense popularity among dedicated communities of backers and investors.

Beyond that, the field of cryptocurrencies is always expanding, and the next great digital token may be released tomorrow. While Bitcoin is widely seen as a pioneer in the world of cryptocurrencies, analysts adopt many approaches for evaluating tokens other than BTC. It's common, for instance, for analysts to attribute a great deal of importance to the ranking of coins relative to one another in terms of market cap. We've factored this into our consideration, but there are other reasons why a digital token may be included in the list, as well.

1. Bitcoin (BTC)

2.

The closest thing you'll get to a blue-chip cryptocurrency, <u>Bitcoin</u> has dominated the market since the first bitcoins were mined in January 2009 – but that doesn't mean it has always been smooth sailing. Bitcoin prices hit a high of around $20,000 in December 2017 before collapsing in 2018, reaching a bottom at $3,234 by the end of that year. Since then, however, Bitcoin has enjoyed a comeback as prices surged to more than $40,000 in January 2021 for a market cap of more than $1 trillion – meaning bitcoins accounted for more than 69% of the cryptocurrency market. Bitcoin has its fair share of volatility, as prices have pulled back since hitting this high, but being the biggest name in crypto gives it a worldwide acceptance that lesser-known rivals don't have, arguably making it the best cryptocurrency to buy for investors new to the asset class.

1. Bitcoin Cash (BCH)

2.

Bitcoin Cash (BCH) holds an important place in the history of altcoins because it is one of the earliest and most successful hard forks of the original Bitcoin. In the cryptocurrency world, a fork takes place as the result of debates and arguments between developers and miners. Due to the decentralized nature of digital currencies, wholesale changes to the code underlying the token or coin at hand must be made due to general consensus; the mechanism for this process varies according to the particular cryptocurrency.

When different factions can't come to an agreement, sometimes the digital currency is split, with the original chain remaining true to its original code and the new chain beginning life as a new version of the prior coin, complete with changes to its code.

BCH began its life in August of 2017 as a result of one of these splits. The debate that led to the creation of BCH had to do with the issue of scalability; the Bitcoin network has a limit on the size of blocks: one megabyte (MB). BCH increases the block size from one MB to eight MB, with the idea being that larger blocks can hold more transactions within them, and therefore the transaction speed would be increased. It also makes other changes, including the removal of the Segregated Witness protocol which impacts block space. As of January 2021, BCH had a market cap of $8.9 billion and a value per token of $513.45.

1. Litecoin (LTC)
2.

Litecoin, launched in 2011, was among the first cryptocurrencies to follow in the footsteps of Bitcoin and has often been referred to as "silver to Bitcoin's gold." It was created by Charlie Lee, an MIT graduate and former Google engineer. Litecoin is based on an open-source global payment network that is not controlled by any central authority and uses "scrypt" as a proof of work, which can be decoded with the help of CPUs of consumer-grade. Although Litecoin is like Bitcoin in many ways, it has a faster block generation rate and hence offers a faster transaction confirmation time. Other than developers, there are a growing number of merchants who accept Litecoin. As of January 2021, Litecoin had a market cap of $10.1 billion and a per token value of $153.88, making it the sixth-largest cryptocurrency in the world.

1. Ethereum (ETH)
2.

The first Bitcoin alternative on our list, <u>Ethereum</u>, is a decentralized software platform that enables <u>Smart Contracts</u> and Decentralized Applications (DApps) to be built and run without any downtime, fraud, control, or interference from a third party. The goal behind Ethereum is to create a decentralized suite of financial products that anyone in the world can have free access to, regardless of nationality, ethnicity, or faith. This aspect makes the implications for those in some countries more compelling, as those without state infrastructure and state identifications can get access to bank accounts, loans, insurance, or a variety of other financial products.

The applications on Ethereum are run on its platform-specific cryptographic token, ether. Ether is like a vehicle for moving around on the Ethereum platform and is sought by mostly developers looking to develop and run applications inside Ethereum, or now, by investors looking to make purchases of other digital currencies using ether. Ether, launched in 2015, is currently the second-largest digital currency by market cap after Bitcoin, although it lags behind the dominant cryptocurrency by a significant margin. As of January 2021, ether's market cap is roughly 19% of Bitcoin's size.

In 2014, Ethereum launched a pre-sale for ether which received an overwhelming response; this helped to usher in the age of the initial coin offering (ICO). According to Ethereum, it can be used to "codify, decentralize, secure and trade just about anything." Following the attack on the DAO in 2016, Ethereum was split into Ethereum (ETH) and Ethereum Classic (ETC). As of January 2021, Ethereum (ETH) had a market cap of $138.3 billion and a per token value of $1,218.59.

In 2021 Ethereum plans to change its consensus algorithm from proof-of-work to proof-of-stake. This move will allow Ethereum's network to run itself with far less energy as well as improved transaction speed. Proof-of-stake allows network participants to "stake" their ether to the network. This process helps to secure the network and process the transactions that occur. Those who do this are rewarded ether similar to an interest account. This is an alternative to Bitcoin's proof-of-work mechanism where miners are rewarded more Bitcoin for processing transactions.

1. Binance Coin (BNB)
2.

Like Ethereum, Binance Coin is much more than a cryptocurrency – as a matter of fact, Binance Coin was originally hosted on Ethereum until the Binance decentralized exchange, or DEX, went online in 2017. The Binance DEX is a platform much like Ethereum, albeit with a different mission. The Binance DEX is a decentralized platform where users can not only buy and sell binance coins but also use BNB to convert other cryptocurrencies from one to another. This has made the Binance DEX the biggest cryptocurrency exchange on the planet by volume and has helped fuel the popularity of the digital asset. Most importantly, the Binance DEX offers a discount to users who pay transaction fees on the exchange with BNB – a smart strategy that keeps users on the platform and helps sustain Binance Coin's growth.

1. Tron (TRX)
2.

The past year brought extreme upheaval within the entertainment industry, leaving it ripe for disruption. This is exactly the sort of opportunity the founders of Tron must have been hoping for when they built a decentralized, blockchain-based platform for sharing content. Whereas many of the biggest entertainment companies in the world profit from gathering and selling data about their users, using Tron leaves no such footprints behind. While it protects users, Tron also allows creators to monetize their content directly via Tronix, Tron's form of cryptocurrency. The platform has gained fame and notoriety in equal measure over the last few years due to the antics of Tron Foundation founder Justin Sun, but no matter how you feel about him, it's undeniable that Tron is an ambitious idea – and while it isn't going to overthrow <u>Netflix</u> (ticker: <u>NFLX</u>) tomorrow, it is an excellent speculative investment.

1. Chainlink (LINK)

2.

Chainlink is a decentralized oracle network that bridges the gap between smart contracts, like the ones on Ethereum, and data outside of it. Blockchains themselves do not have the ability to connect to outside applications in a trusted manner. Chainlink's decentralized oracles allow smart contracts to communicate with outside data so that the contracts can be executed based on data that Ethereum itself cannot connect to.

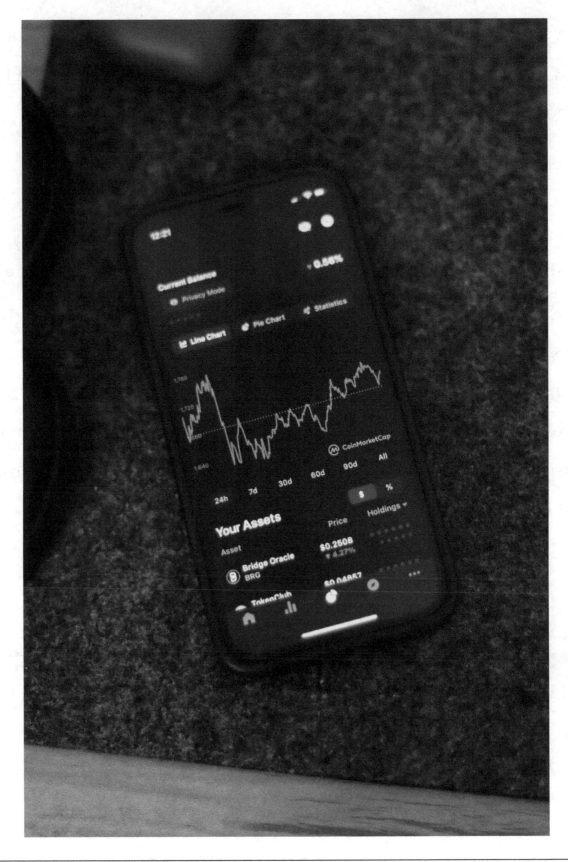

Chainlink's blog details a number of use cases for its system. One of the many use cases that are explained would be to monitor water supplies for pollution or illegal syphoning going on in certain cities. Sensors could be set up to monitor corporate consumption, water tables, and the levels of local bodies of water. A Chainlink oracle could track this data and feed it directly into a smart contract. The smart contract could be set up to execute fines, release flood warnings to cities, or invoice companies using too much of a city's water with the incoming data from the oracle.

Chainlink was developed by Sergey Nazarov along with Steve Ellis. As of January 2021, Chainlink's market capitalization is $8.6 billion, and one LINK is valued at $21.53.

1. USD Coin
2.

The stablecoin, which hit the markets in September 2018, is managed by a consortium called CENTRE, launched by peer-to-peer company Circle and crypto exchange Coinbase. Their aim, according to their website, is to "bring stability to crypto". It was trading at $1 with a market cap of $9.12bn as of 9:38am GMT on 9 March.

1. Cardano

2.

Cardano is an "Ouroboros proof-of-stake" cryptocurrency that was created with a research-based approach by engineers, mathematicians, and cryptography experts. The project was co-founded by Charles Hoskinson, one of the five initial founding members of Ethereum. After having some disagreements with the direction Ethereum was taking, he left and later helped to create Cardano.

The team behind Cardano created its blockchain through extensive experimentation and peer-reviewed research. The researchers behind the project have written over 90 papers on blockchain technology across a range of topics. This research is the backbone of Cardano.

Due to this rigorous process, Cardano seems to stand out among its proof-of-stake peers as well as other large cryptocurrencies. Cardano has also been dubbed the "Ethereum killer" as its blockchain is said to be capable of more. That said, Cardano is still in its early stages. While it has beaten Ethereum to the proof-of-stake consensus model it still has a long way to go in terms of decentralized financial applications.

Cardano aims to be the financial operating system of the world by establishing decentralized financial products similarly to Ethereum as well as providing solutions for chain interoperability, voter fraud, and legal contract tracing, among other things. As of January 2021, Cardano has a market capitalization of $9.8 billion and one ADA trades for $0.31.

1. Tether (USDT)
2.

Tether was one of the first and most popular of a group of so-called <u>stablecoins</u>, cryptocurrencies that aim to peg their market value to a currency or other external reference point in order to reduce volatility. Because most digital currencies, even major ones like Bitcoin, have experienced frequent periods of dramatic volatility, Tether and other stablecoins attempt to smooth out price fluctuations in order to attract users who may otherwise be cautious. Tether's price is tied directly to the price of the US dollar. The system allows users to more easily make transfers from other cryptocurrencies back to US dollars in a more timely manner than actually converting to normal currency.

Launched in 2014, Tether describes itself as "a blockchain-enabled platform designed to facilitate the use of fiat currencies in a digital manner." Effectively, this cryptocurrency allows individuals to utilize a blockchain network and related technologies to transact in traditional currencies while minimizing the volatility and complexity often associated with digital currencies. In January of 2021, Tether was the third-largest cryptocurrency by market cap, with a total market cap of $24.4 billion and a per-token value of $1.00.

1. Monero (XMR)

2.

<u>Monero</u> is a secure, private, and untraceable currency. This open-source cryptocurrency was launched in April 2014 and soon garnered great interest among the cryptography community and enthusiasts. The development of this cryptocurrency is completely donation based and community driven. Monero has been launched with a strong focus on decentralization and scalability, and it enables complete privacy by using a special technique called "ring signatures."

With this technique, there appears a group of cryptographic signatures including at least one real participant, but since they all appear valid; the real one cannot be isolated. Because of exceptional security mechanisms like this, Monero has developed something of an unsavory reputation—it has been linked to criminal operations around the world. While this is a prime candidate for making criminal transactions anonymously, the privacy inherent in Monero is also helpful to dissidents of oppressive regimes around the world. As of January 2021, Monero had a market cap of $2.8 billion and a per-token value of $158.37.

1. Stellar
2.

Stellar is an open blockchain network designed to provide enterprise solutions by connecting financial institutions for the purpose of large transactions. Huge transactions between banks and investment firms that typically would take several days, a number of intermediaries, and cost a good deal of money, can now be done nearly instantaneously with no intermediaries and cost little to nothing for those making the transaction.

While Stellar has positioned itself as an enterprise blockchain for institutional transactions, it is still an open blockchain that can be used by anyone. The system allows for cross-border transactions between any currencies. Stellar's native currency is Lumens (XLM). The network requires users to hold Lumens to be able to transact on the network.

Stellar was founded by Jed McCaleb, a founding member of Ripple Labs and developer of the Ripple protocol. He eventually left his role with Ripple and went on to co-found the Stellar Development Foundation. Stellar Lumens have a market capitalization of $6.1 billion and are valued at $0.27 as of January 2021.

1. Ripple (XRP)

2.

XRP is a digital asset built for payments. It is the native digital asset on the XRP Ledger — an open-source, permissionless and decentralized blockchain technology that can settle transactions in 3-5 seconds.XRP can be sent directly without needing a central intermediary, making it a convenient instrument in bridging two different currencies quickly and efficiently.

Ripple diverges from much of its cryptocurrency competitors in a number of ways. Ripple is an invention of Ripple Labs, and the Ripple token is being used in high-speed and low-cost money transfers worldwide.

Ripple Labs has announced a number of partnerships with leading money transfer services, with more financial market partnerships expected in the future.

Unlike many cryptocurrencies that trade on hopes and dreams, Ripple is being used in the real world today, showing signs of future adoption within the financial market community. Ripple rise in value over 36,000% in 2017, but similar gains may not be likely going forward

1. EOS (EOS)
2.

EOS is the native cryptocurrency for the EOS.IO blockchain platform with smart contract capabilities. The company Block.one created EOS.IO in September 2017 and it now has over 100 dapps with thousands of daily active users. It enables decentralized apps, or dapps, to be created by software developers. The platform is more scalable than many other blockchain networks, with the ability to process one million transactions per second without any fees. Its dapp development capability makes

EOS similar to <u>Ethereum</u> with the notable distinction that transaction confirmations are done through a different type of consensus system. Block producers are chosen by the EOS ecosystem through a voting mechanism known as delegated-proof-of-stake (DPoS). In order to vote, users must stake tokens for three days without selling them, putting them at risk of losing money should the price of the token drop during that time. There is no maximum supply limit of EOS tokens. The delegated proof-of-stake model uses inflation, capped at 5% annually, to fund transactions and pay block users. Many competitors, including Ethereum, have a transaction fee for transferring coins or tokens from one wallet address to another. EOS concluded its year-long ICO in May of this year, raising a total of $4 billion. The longer-duration ICO was done in an attempt to create an orderly market for EOS without the dramatic run-up and sudden crash common to cryptocurrencies when launched.

YTD performance for EOS is flat, with less volatility than has been seen with some competitors. Enthusiasm for the project remains high, and EOS is one of the most actively traded cryptocurrencies on exchanges.

1. Polkadot (DOT)
2.

Polkadot is a unique proof-of-stake cryptocurrency that is aimed at delivering interoperability between other blockchains. Its protocol is designed to connect permissioned and permissionless blockchains as well as oracles to allow systems to work together under one roof.

Polkadot's core component is its relay chain that allows the interoperability of varying networks. It also allows for "parachains," or parallel blockchains with their own native tokens for specific use cases.

Where this system differs from Ethereum is that rather than creating just decentralized applications on Polkadot, developers can create their own blockchain while also using the security that Polkadot's chain already has. With Ethereum, developers can create new blockchains but they need to create their own security measures which can leave new and smaller projects open to attack, as the larger a blockchain the more security it has. This concept in Polkadot is known as shared security.

Polkadot was created by Gavin Wood, another member of the core founders of the Ethereum project who had differing opinions on the project's future. As of January 2021, Polkadot has a market capitalization of $11.2 billion and one DOT trades for $12.54.

Chapter4. Are cryptocurrencies a good investment?

Cryptocurrencies may go up in value, but many investors see them as mere speculations, not real investments. The reason? Just like real currencies, cryptocurrencies generate no cash flow, so for you to profit, someone has to pay more for the currency than you did.

That's what's called "the greater fool" theory of investment. Contrast that to a well-managed business, which increases its value over time by growing the profitability and cash flow of the operation.

As NerdWallet writers have noted, cryptocurrencies such as Bitcoin may not be that safe, and some notable voices in the investment community have advised would-be investors to steer clear of them. Of particular note, legendary investor Warren Buffett compared Bitcoin to paper checks: "It's a very effective way of transmitting money and you can do it anonymously and all that.

A check is a way of transmitting money too. Are checks worth a whole lot of money? Just because they can transmit money?"

For those who see cryptocurrencies such as Bitcoin as the currency of the future, it should be noted that a currency needs stability so that merchants and consumers can determine what a fair price is for goods. Bitcoin and other cryptocurrencies have been anything but stable through much of their history. For example, while Bitcoin traded at close to $20,000 in December 2017, its value then dropped to as low as about $3,200 a year later. By December 2020, it was trading at record levels again.

This price volatility creates a conundrum. If bitcoins might be worth a lot more in the future, people are less likely to spend and circulate them today, making them less viable as a currency. Why spend a bitcoin when it could be worth three times the value next year?

Legal Risks for Cryptocurrency Investors

Along with the explosion of interest in digital currency and all of its implications for both new and traditional businesses, there is a growing need for clarity regarding the legal implications of these new technologies and currencies. As governments around the world, regulatory agencies, central banks, and other financial institutions are working to understand the nature and meaning of digital currencies, individual investors can make a great deal of money investing in this new space. On the other hand, <u>investors assume certain legal risks when they buy and sell cryptocurrencies</u>.

While digital currency might be easy to confuse for conventional electronic money, it is not the same; similarly, it is unlike conventional cash currencies because it cannot be physically owned and transferred between parties. Much of the murkiness of the legal standing of digital currency is due to the fact that the space has only recently become popular as compared with more traditional currency and payment systems. Below, we'll explore some of the emerging legal implications associated with investing in cryptocurrencies.

Cryptocurrencies as Property

One of the most critical legal considerations for any cryptocurrency investor has to do with the way that central authorities view cryptocurrency holdings. In the U.S., the IRS has defined cryptocurrencies as property, rather than as currencies proper. This means that individual investors are beholden to <u>capital gains tax</u> laws when it comes to reporting their cryptocurrency expenses and profits on their annual tax returns, regardless of where they purchased digital coins.

This aspect of the cryptocurrency space adds layers of confusion and complexity for U.S. taxpayers, but the difficulty does not end there. Indeed, it remains unclear whether digital currency investors who have purchased their holdings on foreign exchanges must face additional reporting measures come tax time. <u>According to a report by CNBC</u>, "anyone with more than $10,000 abroad usually needs to fill out the Report of Foreign Bank and Financial Accounts (FBAR)...with the Treasury Department each year. Another law--the Foreign Account Tax Compliance Act, or FATCA--requires certain U.S. taxpayers to describe their overseas accounts on Form 8938, when they file their taxes with the IRS."

Former federal tax prosecutor Kevin F. Sweeney offered a hint as to how foreign cryptocurrency exchanges could complicate tax matters for U.S. digital currency investors: "there probably is an FBAR requirement, but I wouldn't go as far as to say there always is one," he explained, adding that the lack of guidance from the IRS has created a "black hole" of uncertainty for investors and tax professionals alike. "It would seem awfully unfair if they would expect taxpayers to know that--and to then issue penalties for taxpayers who didn't do that--when practitioners can't even 100% figure out if there's an FBAR requirement," Sweeney added.

All of this suggests that digital currency investors should take special precautions to follow the advice of tax professionals when it comes to reporting cryptocurrency profits and losses. Because the rules are constantly changing, what may have been legally permissible last year or even months ago may now be cause for legal concern.

Decentralized Status

One of the great draws of many digital currencies is also a potential risk factor for the individual investor. Bitcoin (BTC) has paved the way for other cryptocurrencies in that it is <u>decentralized</u>, meaning that it has no physical presence and is not backed by a central authority. While governments around the world have stepped in to assert their regulatory power in various ways, BTC and other digital currencies like it remain unattached to any jurisdiction or institution. On one hand, this frees investors from being beholden to those institutions. On the other hand, however, this status could result in legal complications. The value of digital currencies is dependent entirely upon the value that other owners and investors ascribe to them; this is true across all currencies, digital or fiat. Without a central authority backing the value of a digital currency, investors may be left in the lurch should complications with transactions or ownership arise.

Another potential risk associated with cryptocurrencies as a result of their decentralized status has to do with the particulars of transactions. In most other transactions, currency with a physical presence changes hands. In the case of <u>electronic money,</u> a trusted financial institution is involved in creating and settling deposits and debt claims. Neither of these concepts applies to cryptocurrency transactions. Because of this fundamental difference, legal confusion between parties in various types of digital currency transactions is a real possibility. Once again, because of the decentralized state of these currencies, the path of legal recourse in these situations can be difficult to assess.

Business Registrations and Licensing

A growing number of businesses are taking advantage of digital currencies as a form of payment. As in other financial areas, businesses may be required to register and obtain licensure for particular jurisdictions and activities. Owing to the complex and evolving legal status of digital currencies, this area is significantly less clear for businesses operating in the crypto market. Companies which only accept cryptocurrencies, for example, may not need to register or obtain licenses at all. On the other hand, they may be required to submit to special considerations depending upon their jurisdiction. The onus of responsibility falls on business owners and managers to insure that they are following proper legal procedure for their operations at both the local and state levels. At the federal level, for example, financial institutions must maintain certain activities related to protections against <u>money laundering</u> and fraud, transmission of funds, and more. Considerations like these also apply to businesses dealing with digital currencies.

Fraud and Money Laundering

There is a widespread belief that cryptocurrencies provide criminal organizations with a new means of committing fraud, money laundering, and a host of other financial crimes. This may not directly impact most cryptocurrency investors who do not intend to use this new technology to commit such crimes. However, investors who find themselves in the unfortunate position of being a victim of financial crime do not likely have the same legal options as traditional victims of fraud.

This issue also relates to the decentralized status of digital currencies. When a cryptocurrency exchange is hacked and customers' holdings are stolen, for instance, there is frequently no standard practice for recovering the missing funds. <u>Digital currency investors thus take on a certain amount of risk by purchasing and holding cryptocurrency assets</u>. It is for this reason that developers and startups related to digital currency have focused such a great deal of attention on creating secure means of holding digital coins and tokens. Still, while new types of wallets are being released all the time, and while cryptocurrency exchanges are always improving their security measures, investors have so far not been able to fully eliminate the legal risks associated with owning cryptocurrencies, and it's likely that they never will.

Bookkeeping and QuickBooks Made Easy

A Comprehensive Guide of 87 Useful Tricks to Hack QuickBooks and Organize Bookkeeping as a Silicon Valley Company

By

Andy Magnet

Table of Contents

Introduction

This book is your basic guide to bookkeeping and QuickBooks. If you are a bookkeeper and want to upgrade your skillset and learn more about the QuickBooks software, this book is just for you. You will find a comprehensive detail of all the considerations, the advantages, and the ways you can become a QuickBooks bookkeeper. If you are a beginner and managing finances interests you, you can equally benefit from this book.

In the following chapters, you will find a detailed explanation of bookkeeping and why proper bookkeeping is necessary to keep businesses afloat. With people starting their businesses by the minute, the need for accurate bookkeeping is ever in demand. Small business owners invest in good financial handling software and outsourcing their account management to bookkeepers as affording an accountant is sometimes not possible for a small business owner.

You might question that bookkeeping is not as lucrative but do not pay head to that. Yes, conventional bookkeeping is becoming outdated, but still, there is demand. Most small business owners in the US use the software QuickBooks for their financial recording. Though some business owners know how to use it and keep updated, most of them will require help with crunching numbers and outsource professional bookkeepers to do the job.

QuickBooks was launched in the year 2003 by the company Intuit. After its launch, the company has launched various versions of the software to cater to different business owners' requirements. QuickBooks usage dominates the small business market by 80%. The company provides desktop-based and cloud-based versions of the software. From 2014 onwards there is a shift in trend. Before 2014, the business owners preferred the desktop model, but after the year 2014, more and more business owners are shifting to the cloud-based versions.

A whole chapter is dedicated to explaining the QuickBooks software. We discuss in detail the entire software. The services it provides and how a small business owner can benefit from it. There is a step-by-step guide to set up and install QuickBooks into your computer or other devices. After installation, guidelines are given to setup your account and add the vendor and customer accounts. A detailed explanation about how to enter employee details and how some versions can also manage automated payroll tasks. Reading about all this will make you understand the software's entire system and objective and realize how easy it is to operate. Technology has made even the most difficult and complicated tasks simpler for us. Now, it is our job to use technology for our benefit.

After you have understood the basic functioning of the software, you might want to invest in one. But this is not as easy as just purchasing one online. There are different packages of software available for different individuals. There are four basic packages available:

- QuickBooks Online

- QuickBooks Self-Employed

- QuickBooks Desktop

- QuickBooks App

Choosing the correct package that suits your requirements is also an important and difficult decision. In this book, we give you an overview of all the available packages and their specific features. All this information will hopefully make your decision easy.

In the US, the small to mid-size business market is denominated by QuickBooks users, and the owners are always on the lookout for professional QuickBooks bookkeepers for the job. You do not have to do it full time; you can manage all the accounts as a side hustle because QuickBooks software makes everything easy. You have to setup your accounting needs in the software, and most of the work is done by the software. However, it is n0t as easy as it sounds. The software is user-friendly, but you still require basic accounting knowledge and correct usage of the program. You might consider becoming a certified QuickBooks bookkeeper.

In this book, we have also discussed how in 2021, QuickBooks bookkeepers who work online make good money. There is a whole chapter in which we discuss working part-time as a QuickBooks bookkeeper is becoming a high-paying job. The average income of a QuickBooks professional in the US is discussed along with the US's best cities where you can practice QuickBooks bookkeeping. The considerations you should keep in mind while moving base to become a bookkeeper. California is the best place to be because the money QuickBooks bookkeepers are making there is approximately $10000 more than the US average per year.

There is an entire chapter dedicated to the ways you can become a certified QuickBooks bookkeeper. Sometimes a person knows what he/she wants but is unable to do anything because of the lack of guidance. This book gives you just that, proper step-by-step guidance on how to qualify yourself to become a QuickBooks bookkeeper. It does take time and effort, but you have numerous possibilities and options once you are qualified. To become a bookkeeper, you will need a certification. There are commonly three types of certifications you can choose from:

- QuickBooks Online Certification: Basic

- QuickBooks Desktop Certification: Basic

- QuickBooks Desktop Certification: Advance

The certifications are not just a one-time feat. You must keep your certifications up to date. You will require recertification each year by taking the certification exam. These tests are expensive but worth it.

Finally, we discuss the tricks and hacks you can use to use QuickBooks efficiently and effectively. These trips and hacks make your work easier and quicker. You will have to put in fewer hours. It is always wise to use trips and hacks and make the most benefit of the latest technologies. Sometimes doing online courses and certifications enable you to learn these tricks and hacks. Therefore, it is always recommended to keep your knowledge latest and keep improving your skills. The process of learning never stops. You keep learning throughout life. In present times learning has become a necessity rather than a luxury. In the ever-changing world, you will be left behind if you do not keep your skillset updated.

We hope you are going to find this book informative and helpful for your future professional endeavors. If bookkeeping is your calling, you should pursue it. It is one of the most in-demand services in the small business and mid-size business sector.

Chapter 1. Bookkeeping

In this chapter, we will focus on the basics. We will discuss the concept of bookkeeping and how it is the one-stop solution to all your accounting needs. Before anything else, we will try to understand what bookkeeping is and its importance.

Bookkeeping is an essential part of financial management. Small business owners sometimes try to manage the bookkeeping themselves, which becomes a reason for their businesses to fail. People do not realize that bookkeeping is a full-time job. You cannot manage a business and run numbers simultaneously. For this purpose, it is always wise to hire professionals for your accounting and bookkeeping.

What is Bookkeeping?

You must have heard about the term accounting. Bookkeeping is just that; it is related to managing the accounts. This term is used for business. The management of the complete finances of a business is termed bookkeeping.

To be more specific, we say that bookkeeping involves recording all the financing situations of a business. Bookkeeping is about keeping a record of all financial transactions daily, the influx and efflux of cash, the Payroll, profits, loss, investments, return on investments, and all the decisions related to the business's finance aspect. Bookkeeping helps the business owners keep track of all the information regarding the financial transactions.

After learning about what bookkeeping is, one wonders how a business owner can do all that by themselves? Not all business owners are literate about managing their finances. So, how can a business owner manage their accounts and finances? The simple answer to this question is a bookkeeper.

Who is A bookkeeper?

Bookkeepers are professionals who are responsible for managing all the finances of a company. They keep the owners aware of their present financial situation, record all related financial data and the total transactions made.

Correct bookkeeping is important for the business owners as well as prospected investors as well. Bookkeeping information is beneficial for the government and financial institutions as well. It will give a clear overview of the economic impacts of that certain business. Big companies and individual investors tend to research before they invest their money somewhere. The best and most reliable source of this information can be found in the company books. Looking at the books, the investor will decide whether he/she wants to invest in a certain company or project. In this way, bookkeeping is important for the owners because it is like his business introduction to the investment world. The better and more accurate the bookkeeping, the more chances of investment.

(A typical Bookkeeper)

Importance of Bookkeeping

When people start a new business, they tend to neglect the importance of good bookkeeping. Finance must be taken charge from day one and cannot be neglected for a single day. Now, what does bookkeeping do? It gives the company a tangible indicator of its performance and current situation. With this information's help, it becomes easier for the owner to make proper decisions financially, revenue generated, the profits, the loss, the income goals, etc. Each transaction must be recorded; the cash influx, efflux, credits, assets, liabilities all need to be recorded.

Bookkeeping is essential to keep the business afloat. Bigger companies usually hire accountants for the financial department, but it is not always possible for small business owners. So, small business owners mostly rely on hiring a bookkeeper. There whole accounting companies from where you can outsource a bookkeeper. It is cheaper than employing a full-time accountant, and a bookkeeper can easily manage a small business account. Anyone who starts a new business should never ignore the importance of keeping a record of every dime they spent and earn. Everything should be recorded.

Type of Accounting Method

Each business model follows one of the two accounting methods.

- Cash Basis of Accounting

- Accrual Basis of Accounting

To implement the bookkeeping function properly, the business owner should decide which accounting method they will follow. There are two basic models for accounting which are mentioned above. Now, what is the difference between these two? We will try to explain:

Cash Basis of Accounting:

In this type of accounting, a transaction is only recorded when a payment or cash is received or spent.

For example, if you buy fifty units of a product and the payment will be done after two weeks. No transaction will be recorded. It will only be recorded after two weeks when the payment is made.This type of accounting model is now considered outdated in present times.

Accrual Basis of Accounting:

In accrual accounting, the expenses and revenue are put down when the transaction is made rather than when the payment is made.

We use the same example of buying 50 units of a product and payment must be made after two weeks. The record will be entered as soon as the receipt is received and will be recorded as payables. This is the more modern model for accounting and is widely accepted.

What do the bookkeepers do?

Now that you have a basic idea of who a bookkeeper is let us move to the set of responsibilities and jobs the Bookkeeper carries out. Listed are the tasks carried out by bookkeepers that make it convenient for the business owner to systematically run the business and provide a clear picture of its financial position. The responsibilities of bookkeepers include:

- Recording transactions every day.

- Sending invoices to clients.

- Keep track of payments.

- Prepare and maintain the payable ledger.

- Manage the cash flow.

- Compile and maintain all accounts.

Record the Transactions Each Day

One of the jobs of the Bookkeeper is to enter the transactions each day. These include bank transactions. Nowadays, most companies use software to manage accounts. Some software has a function to generate automated bank feeds, which makes the task easier. You must keep a check on the cash, and precious data entry time is saved.

Sending Invoices to Clients

Another responsibility of the Bookkeeper is to make receipts and invoices on purchases and send them to the clients.

Keep Track of Payments

Once the invoice is sent out, keeping a record of the payments received is also the Bookkeeper's responsibility. To keep a follow-up to receive pending payments is also the responsibility of the Bookkeeper. This is also known as being responsible for the receivable ledger.

Being Responsible for the Payable Ledger

Up to a certain amount determined by the business owner, the Bookkeeper makes the payments made on the owner's behalf. The Bookkeeper keeps records of all the payments made by the business. These include the payments to the suppliers, the extra cash available, and the other business expenses. The Bookkeeper records all this information and checks it every day.

Responsible for Managing the Cash Flow

One of the most important business rules is that a certain amount of cash is always available. The responsibility of the Bookkeeper is to always maintain the balance. This can be done by keeping a record of the day-to-day expenses and revenues. There should always be cash available for the day-to-day expenses. If the Bookkeeper suspects that the balance might be disrupted, he/she can offer advice to the owner by telling them ways to control the outflow and increase the inflow. These devices are almost always short-term fixes.

Compile All Accounts

The most important job of the Bookkeeper is to maintain the account books. The account records should all be up to date. These include all the ledgers. This is necessary for further investments and business decisions. The owner or prospect investor looks at these accounts and makes decisions according to the financial situations mentioned in the books.

How can a Bookkeeper be Beneficial for Business?

When you have a smaller business setup, it makes sense to manage your account yourself. But when the business expands, it is always a good idea to hire someone to take care of the bookkeeping. In this way, you can concentrate on expanding the business, and your Bookkeeper can take care of your day-to-day expenses. Many people do not hire a bookkeeper to save money but lose a lot of precious time in managing their account that they could be using to innovate and expand their business. Bookkeeping is a time-consuming job, and it should be left to the ones who are professionally trained to do so. They might as well do the job better and take less time. Following are listed a few benefits of hiring a bookkeeper:

Let you Focus on Your Business Strategy

As explained earlier, bookkeeping is a time-consuming task and demands attention to detail. Hiring a bookkeeper will save you all that time, and you will have plenty of time to focus on your business.

The Accounting Cost can be Saved.

If you have a small business, it is a better idea to hire a bookkeeper. If you hire an accountant, it will cost you more money and will become a liability. All the recording and accounts can be easily managed by a bookkeeper as well, and it will cost you a lot less money.

Double Check Your Cashflow

As a business owner, it is wise to always keep your eyes on the cashflow. But sometimes, you can get caught up, and in that situation, your Bookkeeper is there to tell you when you need to manage your cash flow. The Bookkeeper can warn your earlier, and you will still have time to manage the situation.

Be Informed of Current Financial Situation:

As the Bookkeeper is working on a day-to-day basis, he/she will be aware of all the business's financial situations. If you require any help and advice in this department, you can advise your Bookkeeper to have the complete information and explain the clear picture to you.

The Financial Data is Organized

In case you get hold of good software like QuickBooks, the Bookkeeper will work on the same software. The data is kept organized and transparent using the software because the margin for mistakes is highly reduced. The accountant can analyze the same data if you wish to get advice regarding business expansion and investment.

All in all, bookkeeping is particularly useful for business owners and investors alike. If you are not a businessperson and are interested in managing accounts for other small businesses, bookkeeping could be a good profession for you. The possibilities are limitless.

Chapter 2. QuickBooks Explained

With a basic knowledge of bookkeeping and what it means for small businesses, we can now discuss bookkeeping solutions. 2021 is all about solutions. Bookkeeping is a difficult task. It can be made easy with the help of accounting software. In this chapter, we are going to discuss software known as QuickBooks.

2.1. What is QuickBooks?

If you are a small business owner and you aim to reach the next level, you might want to start keeping track of your finances. Most people control their finances when they start with a business, but it becomes difficult once the business gains pace. If you wish to expand your business, you will have to become more proactive, take hold of your finances, plan your next financial moves, keep an eye on day-to-day transactions, and organize a cash inflow and outflow system. You should set up a payroll. All the administrative work should be organized. Reading all this must have given you a headache. You were thinking about making some money; how are you going to manage all the financial stuff?

It would be best if you were thankful for your stars that you live in the 21st Century and there is software available for everything. In this chapter, we are discussing accounting software that works like magic. The software is known as QuickBooks. QuickBooks is the perfect tool for your financial necessities.

2.1.1. QuickBooks

It is accounting software that has features to organize the financial aspects of small businesses. The functions of QuickBooks include:

- Recording everyday transactions

- Track and record revenue and expense.

- Report generation for planning

- Prepare bills.

- Preparation of Payroll

The software is targeted towards small to medium-sized business setups. The QuickBooks software has features that make it possible for you to manage report generation, sales, cash flow, billing, revenue, taxes, reporting and expenses. The best part about the software is that there are inbuilt templates for reports that you can easily set and customize according to your specifications. It is easy to fill in data to an already prepared template compared to create by yourself. You can take control of your finances. It is a user-friendly software, but it has a learning curve, and you must have some basic accounting knowledge to operate and use this software. To use the software effectively, you must learn and have an in-depth knowledge of the software's essential functions.

2.1.2. The History of QuickBooks

In 1983, two inventors Scott Cook, and Tom Proulx, created the company Intuit. QuickBooks is a product of this company and was first launched in 2003 and targeted to small businesses. Over the years, better and more functional versions of the software have been launched. It remains one of the most widely used financial software for small businesses in the US. Different versions of the software are available in the international markets as well.

2.2. QuickBooks Features

QuickBooks is amazing software with multiple features and functions. Here is a list of a few features of the software.

2.2.1. user Friendly

This software is super user-friendly. It is easy to use and navigate. All the financial features needed for a small to medium business are present in this one program. You do not have to record your data in different locations. This single software manages all your data.

2.2.2. Data Migration

This is a wonderful feature. If you want to transfer any data from QuickBooks to the spreadsheet, the transition is smooth. When there is a requirement to present the data on a spreadsheet, you can easily transfer all the software from the software without manually copying it.

2.2.3 Smooth Navigation

To use this software is easy because the navigation is simple. Everything is displayed clearly, and working is smooth. The program interface is clear and simple. However, you will have to learn and get used to the software before you can use it. You need to learn and understand all the financial terms and data entry methods to using this software effectively.

2.2.4. Smooth Transactions

The bank transactions are systematically recorded. Each entry you make is recorded. You can even set up regular transactions like salary payments, commissions, and bills repeated each month or every two weeks. These transactions will be automatically recorded.

2.2.5. Invoices

You can set up the invoices to be generated. The software can even generate invoices from your smartphone or tablet if they are installed with the software. You are not dependent on the computer system or laptop to generate business invoices. This feature is truly per the present requirement where everything can be achieved with a click of a button anytime, anywhere.

2.2.6. Calculate Tax

The feature of tax calculation is included in the software. To do taxes is always a tricky business. With the QuickBooks software, you can easily calculate the taxes quickly, efficiently, and accurately.

There is an automated feature in the software that will present you with projections. The software can generate all kinds of projections, including profits, expenses, sales etc. Getting the projections makes it easy to make financial decisions.

2.3. Set-up QuickBooks

To use QuickBooks, you must have basic accounting knowledge and your own business. To use this software, you must be organized and willing to manage your finances seriously and as a daily feature. Some people install QuickBooks, put in the money, and forget it for months. Some purchase it and never even learn how to use it. QuickBooks does not work in that manner. You must be willing to learn and be consistent. Consistency is the key.

Let us discuss step-by-step guidelines for using QuickBooks.

2.3.1. Start

The first step will be to install the software properly. For installation, you must decide how you are going to use it. When you start the program, you will have two options:

- Network

- Custom Options

You will choose the Custom settings if you use the software on only one computer and use the same computer for installations.

In case more than one computer will use the software, chose the Network setting.

After that, choose the location or folder in your PC where you wish the software to be installed. Add your details, and then set up your company file. After that, click on the QuickBooks icon on the desktop.

2.3.2. setup

As soon as you click on the QuickBooks program, you will see an Easy Setup Wizard to help you set up your company file. By following the simple instructions, you can set up your company file. If you are new to this kind of software, you will be favorable to take help from the wizard. It will make the setup smooth and easy.

2.3.3. Vendor Setup

The next step will be setting up the accounts for your vendors. You will click the Vendor Center in the toolbar placed at the top. Next, select the New Vendor option, and create a vendor account. To add a new transaction, click the New Transaction and fill in the details. You can even bring in details from MS Excel and MS Word.

Add all the vendors similarly if you have more than one.

2.3.4. Setup Employee Accounts

To set up the employee accounts, click the Employee Center. Then click the New Employee button and then add the related information. After the information, you click the button for New Transaction. Add the salary details and any other transaction related to that specific employee. For salary, you must add the date and time for each month. For that, you will click Enter Time and then add the specific time and frequency of salary. Some employers pay per month, and some pay by the week. Put in the information accordingly.

2.3.5. Set Up Customer Account

Like the vendor and employee accounts, add the customer accounts. First, you go to the customer center, then Add Customer and Job. Here you can add it as an income source. Now add the related transaction by clicking New Transaction. Here you will add the information for payments and generation of invoices. There is a link for Excel as well as Word. You can bring the information from Excel and use Word to prepare letters for the customer.

2.3.6. Setup Report Generation

Next, you will go to the Report Center. All the information added by you can be viewed here. You can also customize the kind of report you want to generate. Reports for-profits, payments and expenses can be generated separately.

Add all the employees the same way if you have more than one.

2.4. Using QuickBooks

After the set up let us try to understand the day-to-day working of the QuickBooks software. What should we expect from the software? How can we manage our finances? What is the essential feature of the software? All these questions will be answered in the following part of this book. Together we will try to understand how the QuickBooks software works.

2.4.1. Chart of Accounts

So, what can you find on the chart of accounts? It will display the company's income, liability, expense accounts, assets, and equity to assign day-to-day transactions. This is what you will find:

- All the financial information about the company. It has the balance sheets, dividend, savings, receivables, and expenses. All this can be seen in the Chart of Accounts as a list.

- All the accounts related to the business, along with the account balances and account numbers. The details of the account holder will also be shared, like the full names and contact numbers. All these accounts will appear when you click the List Menu in the QuickBooks chart of accounts.

2.4.2. Other Lists

These include the list of vendors you deal with. All your regular customers and customer accounts are listed. All the items you deal with and their inventory is listed.

How this is favorable for the QuickBooks user:

- You can manage everything in one place. You do not have to manage multiple lists and settings. All information is compiled in one place. Either it is the product inventory or the vendor; all can be managed in one place.

- When you have all the information in a single space, you can move back and forth with all the lists, account details and information. You can simultaneously manage all your financial situations together. Everything is easy to navigate and extremely user-friendly.

- Another feature is the easy addition ad deletion of details. It is simple to add new accounts, and it is equally simple to delete accounts. Anytime you want to change the existing settings, it is easily done.

- Apart from adding ad deleting details, you can also edit details. Correction and updating details are easy in this software.

2.4.3. The Reports

Report templates are already included in the software so that you can customize them according to your needs. Add the details of your vendors, customers, and items. You must add dates and times as well.

Once you start adding details accordingly and you update daily transactions and activities. The reports will be forming themselves. Anytime you feel like having an overview of your business, you can pull out reports with just one click, and the reports will be generated. These reports will help you make important financial and investment decisions.

2.4.4. payroll

QuickBooks makes it easy to manage payrolls. With the software, you add the information, and the program will itself arrange the payroll process. The software can itself manage the accounts of the employees who have tax exemption. You can customize the settings for other incentives and deductions. If you turn on the setting, the software automatically sends emails, deposits, and receipts.

More than one person can manage the payrolls in this software, the one who has purchased the software has to allow the other users on the network by assigning permission.

2.5. QuickBooks Versions

QuickBooks is available in different types and versions. Each has a different package and fee. The versions are discussed in detail in the following chapters. Here we will list down the various versions of QuickBooks software:

- QuickBooks Online

- QuickBooks Self Employed

- QuickBooks App

- QuickBooks Desktop Products

    o QuickBooks Pro

    o QuickBooks for Mac

    o QuickBooks Enterprise

    o QuickBooks Premier

Chapter 3. Choosing the Best Version of QuickBooks

With the knowledge you have gained in the previous chapters, you know that QuickBooks is a financial solutions software. It was launched 25 years ago, and it has been the top choice for financial management since 2003. If you look at the company profits, they will show you an upward trend for the last 11 years straight. In addition to that, QuickBooks is used by 80% of small business owners in the US. This information enough should convince you to invest in the software.

Once you have decided to purchase the QuickBooks software, you are faced with yet another dilemma. Which version is for you? As discussed in the previous chapter, various versions of QuickBooks are available.

The QuickBooks family has a product for everyone. Here is a quick assessment of what you may want to purchase.

- If you are self-employed, run your company alone, and are looking to invest in a cloud-based accounting system, you should invest in QuickBooks for Self-Employed.

- If you own a small business and are interested in a cloud-based accounting system, you should invest in QuickBooks Online.

- If you are a small to medium-sized business owner, you must invest in QuickBooks Desktop.

- If you are already using QuickBooks and wish to update to another version, invest in QuickBooks Apps.

One of the deciding factors in any investment is the price range and affordability. This is the approximate price of the QuickBooks Packages available, making it easy for you to decide which product is best for you and is easy on the pocket.

Version	Usage	Price
QuickBooks Online	For businesspersons who want flexible financial access. This is suitable for small to mid-size business owners.	$25 up to $150/month
QuickBooks for Desktop	Suitable for small to medium size business owners in any sector	$399.99 with a one-time payment to $1,213 for one year
QuickBooks for Self-Employed	This is suitable for individual property agents, independent vendors, and Uber workers.	$15/month

QuickBooks Mac	This is for small to mid-size businesspersons who have their business setup on MAC	$399.99 paid once

(Prices of Different Versions of QuickBooks)

3.1. QuickBooks for Self-Employed

QuickBooks Self Employed is the newest addition to the QuickBooks software versions. This is cloud-based software for financial services. It is specially designed for self-employed business owners and freelance service providers. It is ideal for independent workers like Lyft and Uber drivers. Property agents can also use it.

As this is a cloud-based program, you can access it with any computer or device with the given login.

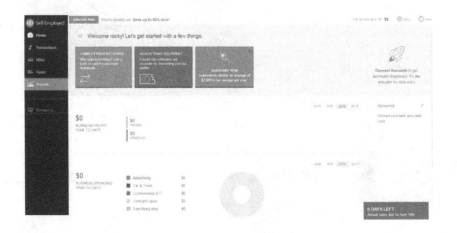

(QuickBooks Self Employed Interface)

(Display of Reports on QuickBooks Self Employed)

Using this program, you can send data to TurboTax and track personal and business expenses from a single bank account. It also calculates the Quarterly Tax and reminds you of payment.

You will find three types of packages available for QuickBooks for Self-Employed:

3.1.1. QuickBooks Self Employed Package

Investing in this package gives you the following features:

- Users can easily connect to their bank account through QuickBooks Self -Employed

- The users can also connect to their credit cards.

- Users can track the expenses and income from the same account but can be separated into personal and business groups.

- The software calculates taxes quarterly.

3.1.2. QuickBooks for Self-Employed Tax Bundle

This offers all the services provided by the simple package with an addition:

- Users can connect to Intuit Turbo Box that enables them to pay taxes online each quarter.

3.1.3. QuickBooks for Self-Employed Live Tax Bundle

Provides all the services as the packages mentioned above with an addition that:

- Users can consult a CPA all year round.

- The users can get the services of a CPA to review taxes.

3.1.4. Benefit

It can track traveling and Mileage. You can enter trips with dates, reasons, and distance traveled. The system will automatically calculate deductions.

3.1.5. Drawback

Does not provide a service to generate invoices and online payments.

3.2. QuickBooks Online

QuickBooks Online is also a cloud-based financial solutions software. This had become exceedingly popular after 2014 when it was observed that more business owners preferred the online version over the desktop version. After that, the number of subscribers to the QuickBooks online version has been more than 1 million subscribers. This also tells us about the shift of business owners to a cloud-based system and shows their confidence in solely cloud-based software.

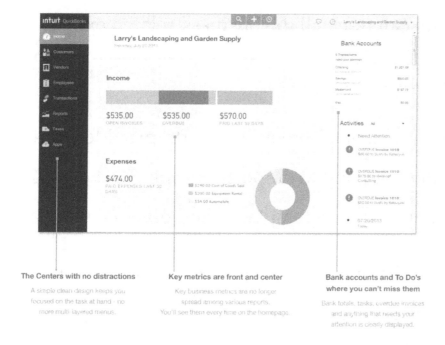

(QuickBooks Online Interface)

3.2.1. Common Features

The common features of QuickBooks Online are:

- Payable and Receivable Accounts:

The program can successfully manage expenses as well as income.

- Invoices and Bills:

It offers recurring or single-time invoices and can pay bills online.

- Management of Expenses:

The software can track all the business-related expenses.

- Reporting:

There are templates of prebuilt reports provided in the software, including the sales and tax reports. Simple Start gives 20 templates, Essentials gives 40 such templates, and gives 60 templates.

The QuickBooks online package does not need to be installed and comes in four packages:

3.2.2. QuickBooks Online Simple Start

The features provided in this package are:

- There is a single-user license.

- You can import your data from the QuickBooks Desktop version or MS Excel.

- You are entitled to consult two accounting professionals (bookkeepers and accountants)

3.2.3. QuickBooks Online Essentials

This version has all the abilities of the above version and, in addition to those capabilities, also has the following capabilities:

- The user is entitled to have 3 user licenses.

- The owner can set up user permissions to determine who is entitled to use the software.

3.2.4. QuickBooks Online Plus

All the capabilities of the Essentials version plus the following added qualities:

- Can setup 5 user licenses.

- The ability to track inventory.

- Users can create and send orders of purchase.

3.2.5. QuickBooks Online Advanced

This includes all the capabilities of the Plus version andthe following capabilities:

- Can set up 25 user licenses.

- The ability for automated bill payment.

- The user can setup customized permissions.

3.2.6. Benefits

It is available for iOS, Windows, and Android devices. It can be connected to PayPal and Shopify for transactions.

3.2.7. Drawbacks

All the functions available in the QuickBooks Desktop are not available on QuickBooks Online. This version does not allow the addition of more than one company.

3.3. QuickBooks Desktop

The QuickBooks Desktop is the most elaborated software version among all three of the versions. Most business owners prefer cloud-based financial services, but if you prefer desktop-oriented software, the QuickBooks Desktop version is for you. This version further has six more variations suitable for different types of small businesses. The six types are briefly explained as follows:

3.3.1. QuickBooks Desktop Pro:

This is good for most small businesses that are not involved in product manufacture.

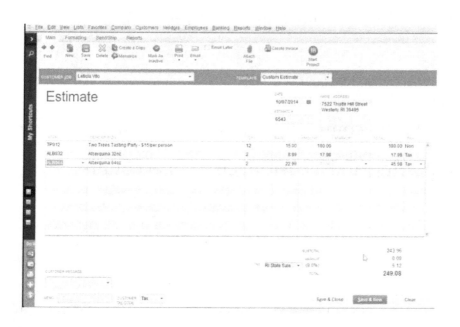

(QuickBooks Desktop Pro)

3.3.2. QuickBooks Desktop Premier:

This version is ideal for businesses involved in manufacturing, retail, and related to charity and non-profit organizations.

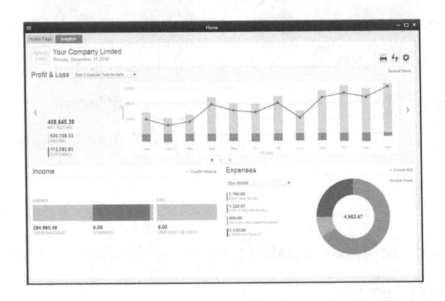

(Homepage of QuickBooks Desktop Premier)

3.3.3. QuickBooks Desktop Enterprise:

This is for large companies and enterprises. This version has industry reporting and a custom chart of accounts.

New! Improved sales order management and inventory picking
Now you can prioritize urgent orders and fulfill them across multiple warehouses. Your employees can have more control and see inventory availability right on their mobile devices. Plus a faster picking process that works across locations will empower workers and delight customers with faster fulfillment.

(QuickBooks Desktop Enterprise sales management)

3.3.4. QuickBooks Desktop Plus and QuickBooks Desktop Pro

The QuickBooks Desktop Plus and QuickBooks Desktop pro versions are sold as a yearly subscription rather than a one-time purchase. With these versions, your QuickBooks version is updated yearly, you are entitled to customer support, and your company data will be backed up.

3.3.5. QuickBooks for Mac

This is the only version compatible with Mac. It is like the QuickBooks Desktop Pro version. This is useful for most of the small businesses which are not involved in manufacturing.

3.4. QuickBooks Apps

QuickBooks Apps are applications that can be used in combination with the QuickBooks software to enhance their features. These are also known as add-on applications. These add-ons can be purchased from the QuickBooks website. Some of the QuickBooks Apps are as follows:

3.4.1. QuickBooks Payments

This can be used as an add-on for the QuickBooks desktop to add some payment functions. This app enables the business to accept payments online as well as through credit cards. This also enables emailing of invoices.

3.4.2. QuickBooks Point of Sale

This is a cloud-based application. It enables the businesses to accept credit cards, track inventory and ring up sales through a point-of-sale dashboard.

3.4.3. QuickBooks Payroll

This app enables businesses to provide salaries to up to 50 employees by cash deposit or check. Two types of versions are available:

- Self-Service Solutions

- Full-Service Solutions

The app can calculate the state, federal, and local taxes automatically.

3.5. Find the Best Version for You

QuickBooks has been a prominent player in the American market as a financial solution provider. The possibilities are numerous with this software. If you are a new business owner or plan to expand your business, QuickBooks will have a suitable version for you. But how to choose one which best suits your requirements? Here is a list of actions you can take before purchasing QuickBooks software. These activities will clear your dilemma, and the choice can be made easily:

3.5.1. Read Reviews

The best way to get a clear idea about a product is by reading reviews of people who have already used it. See which product is continually rated better. Read about the kind of services the software provides. Sometimes you get more knowledge about a product or service from reading someone's review. Always go through people's reviews and consider the products that most people are buying. Their performance must be the reason for their higher sales.

3.5.2. Take an Online Survey

When you are doing your research online, you may come across some online surveys which ask a few basic questions about your business and earnings. When you have entered your answers, the automated program will suggest the best software for you.

3.5.3. Talk to an Expert.

If you are still confused about which software to buy, try talking to an expert. A professional will be in a better position will suggest you according to your needs.

Chapter 4. The Best Way to Make Money In 2021

The year is all about small businesses and freelance work. In uncertain times everyone is pushing for a side hustle. We often have a misconception that the difficult part is setting up a business; other things follow once that part is covered. We cannot be more wrong in that approach. Though getting an idea, arranging for the finances, resources, place, and the raw material is tough and difficult to obtain, keeping the business afloat once launched is the trickier part. Most businesses come to an end, not because there is a lack of work, but because they could not manage the finances. Not all are indeed good at numbers and finance, and often, help is required.

People have now understood the importance of managing finances and are eager to outsource business financing. Here enters the role of bookkeepers and financial professionals. With the small business boom, there is also a huge demand for financial management. Our focus is on QuickBooks Bookkeeping and how it is the best way to earn money in 2021. In the following chapter, we will see how much a bookkeeper earns in the US. What services you can provide as a QuickBooks Bookkeeper, and which cities are the best for practicing QuickBooks bookkeeping.

4.1. Salary of Part-Time QuickBooks Bookkeepers

We hear that QuickBooks is a good way to earn money. It is a good side hustle. Be a part-time QuickBooks bookkeeper. No one tells us how much you can make and how much time should be spent to earn a certain amount.

Here we will give you a clear picture of the earnings. A breakdown by weekly, monthly, and yearly earnings.

According to the latest surveys up to 2021, in the United States of America, a QuickBooks bookkeeper's average salary is $50,618 a year. This comes to be around $4,220 per month, around $1000 a week, and about $24 an hour. This sounds very decent for a part-time job. Especially in recent times when we are surrounded by uncertainty, QuickBooks Bookkeeping is a good side hustle.

The figure of $50,618 is the average; it has been reported that you can earn as high as $95,000, and the earnings can even be as low as

$29,000. If you want to look at its percentile wise it will look something like this:

- 90th Percentile earnings $93,500 yearly

- 75th Percentile earnings $ 58,500 yearly

- 25th Percentile earnings $ 36,000 yearly

As the survey is based on all kinds of bookkeepers, from entry-level ones to more professional ones, you see a huge income difference. This also suggests that the more experienced and professional abilities you acquire, the higher you will earn.

The following charts must explain the salaries of part-time QuickBooks bookkeepers in a better way.

- The Yearly Average Income of QuickBooks Bookkeepers

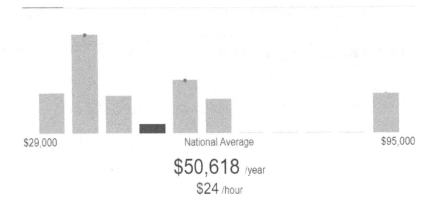

$29,000   National Average $95,000
$50,618 /year
$24 /hour

- ## The Average Monthly Income of QuickBooks Bookkeepers

- ## The Average Weekly Income of QuickBooks Bookkeepers

- ## The Hourly Average Income of QuickBooks Bookkeepers

The following table will give you a better understanding of the earning possibilities that come with QuickBooks bookkeeping. These are the results of a recent survey. Thus, they also indicate the present trends as well.

	Annual Salary	Monthly Pay	Weekly Pay	Hourly Wage
Top Earners	$93,500	$7,791	$1,798	$45
75th Percentile	$58,500	$4,875	$1,125	$28
Average	$50,618	$4,218	$973	$24
25th Percentile	$36,000	$3,000	$692	$17

4.2. The Top 10 Highest Paying Cities for Bookkeepers in the USA

The survey also indicated that the pay varies from location to location. Here we have compiled the top ten cities in the US where QuickBooks Bookkeepers' salaries are higher than the national average.

The state that offers the highest salaries to the QuickBooks Bookkeepers is, without any doubt, California. Companies in California employ the highest paying QuickBooks bookkeepers. The top salaries are recorded from San Francisco, CA. San

Francisco's salaries are around $13,636 higher than the national average. That counts for a whopping 26.9% higher average salary than the average. The second highest is Fremont, CA. The third position is held by San Jose, CA, with a $9,337 higher average salary than the national average of $50,618. Following close behind in Oakland, CA, with an $8,668 higher average. After this is Tanana, AK, with an average yearly salary of $ 59,078, number six is Wasilla, AK, with a higher average of $8459 than the national average. Hayward, CA, has an average income of $58,044 for QuickBooks Bookkeepers. At number eight is Sunnyvale, CA, with an average income higher by $7,268 than the national average. The average salary for this part-time job in Jackson, WY, is $57,870. The last of the tip than in Norwalk, CT.

The table will give you a better understanding of the top ten cities for QuickBooks Bookkeeping.

City	Annual Salary	Monthly Pay	Weekly Pay	Hourly Wage
San Francisco, CA	$64,254	$5,355	$1,236	$30.89
Fremont, CA	$61,596	$5,133	$1,185	$29.61
San Jose, CA	$59,956	$4,996	$1,153	$28.82
Oakland, CA	$59,286	$4,940	$1,140	$28.50
Tanaina, AK	$59,078	$4,923	$1,136	$28.40
Wasilla, AK	$59,077	$4,923	$1,136	$28.40
Hayward, CA	$58,044	$4,837	$1,116	$27.91
Sunnyvale, CA	$57,886	$4,824	$1,113	$27.83
Jackson, WY	$57,870	$4,823	$1,113	$27.82
Norwalk, CT	$57,752	$4,813	$1,111	$27.77

Having mentioned all these cities does not mean that the prospects of getting jobs are higher in these places. This is just an overview of the average income you can earn in these states. Other factors should also be considered when you decide to work in a specific location. For example, you see many six cities from the state of California. You might be tempted to search for work there. But according to research, the job market for QuickBooks Bookkeepers is not active in California. The companies might be paying higher, but the job opportunities are less. It is always smarter to work in a place where the prospects of being employed are better. However, you might be earning more if you locate in one of these locations. It all depends upon the service you provide and the requirements of the employer. It would help if you did your survey before deciding to change your location.

Another important consideration when thinking about making a location change as a QuickBooks bookkeeper is the cost of living. San Francisco may be paying the highest, but the basic cost of living is high. You might be earning more but even spending more on necessities like housing, insurance, and food. This might not prove to be a smart move. For a QuickBooks bookkeeper, an important factor in choosing a location might be the salary and a place with a lower cost of living.

4.3. Best Paying QuickBooks Bookkeeping Jobs in the USA

This is true for any field of practice that your job prospects and earnings increase if you specialize in a specific field. This part will discuss the five types of specialized QuickBooks Bookkeepers who earn higher than the typical part-time QuickBooks bookkeepers. All the jobs discuss earn around $7,683 to $14,935 more than the national average. This makes the values about 14.5% to 29.5% more than a regular QuickBooksbookkeeper's salary. So, it is highly recommended that you try to specialize in a certain domain to improve your higher earnings chances. The five jobs we will be discussing are:

1. CPA Firm Bookkeeper

2. QuickBooks Remote Bookkeeper

3. Telecommute Bookkeeper

4. At home Bookkeeper

5. QuickBooks Consultant

4.3.1. CPA Firm Bookkeeper

The Bookkeeper associated with a CPA firm earns around $65,553 annually. This translates to a $5,463 paycheck each month, roughly $1,261 a week. In this case, you will be charging approximately $31.52 an hour. If you consider it seriously, this is quite a decent earning.

4.3.2. QuickBooks Remote Bookkeeper

This job fetches you a whopping $64,952 annual earning. This is more than $14,300 than the national average. You will be earning $5,413 per month, which is decent.

4.3.3. Telecommute Bookkeeper

According to the survey, the Telecommute Bookkeeper earns $60 795 per year. This is $10,000 higher than the national average. This brings you a decent paycheck of $5,000 per month and weekly earnings of $1,000 plus. Working as a telecommute bookkeeper, you will be charging approximately $30 by the hour.

4.3.4. At Home Bookkeeper

The best thing about this type of bookkeeping is that you can practice it from the comfort of your house, and you will be earning good money. You will be making savings on the commute time, fuel expenses, and outside food expenses, if you practice work from home. Continuing from home, you will still be earning $8,000 more than the national average. You will be earning around $5,000 per month from the comfort of your home.

4.3.5. QuickBooks Consultant

As a QuickBooks consultant, you can earn $57,986 per year. The good part about this is that you can work part-time and take home a paycheck of around $5,000 each month.

This table will give you a better understanding of the benefits of specializing and the financial prospects related to it.

Job Title	Annual Salary	Monthly Pay	Weekly Pay	Hourly Wage
CPA Firm Bookkeeper	$65,553	$5,463	$1,261	$31.52
Quickbooks Remote	$64,952	$5,413	$1,249	$31.23
Telecommute Bookkeeper	$60,795	$5,066	$1,169	$29.23
Work From Home Bookkeeper	$58,536	$4,878	$1,126	$28.14
Quickbooks Consultant	$57,986	$4,832	$1,115	$27.88

Chapter 5. Becoming a QuickBooks Bookkeeper

Now that you have a thorough understanding of bookkeeping and QuickBooks, it must be clear that in present times the knowledge of QuickBooks is essential if you want to work in the US small business community. Sometimes learning the software is not enough. To get the job, you require to show some qualifications and expertise as well. Unfortunately, we are still living in the workplace where showing your qualifications and certificates is essential to acquire a job. But when we talk about QuickBooks, there is no harm in doing a certification. Doing a certification will open many opportunities for you. No one wants to hire an unqualified person. With this Certification, you will be considered qualified for the job. The Certification might teach you the software's basics, but the actual learning is always done practically. Nevertheless, gaining this Certification is beneficial even if it gives you a head start.

Sometimes you have this clear picture in your mind regarding what you want to do but you have no access to proper guidance. Many people want to work as bookkeepers and want to learn further to upgrade their skill set but there is no one to guide them. The information around us is so much that sometimes we are overwhelmed by the excess of information rather than its lack. Sometimes all we need is a plain simple instruction in the right direction. This chapter does just that. It will push you one step further in the right direction.

In this chapter, we will discuss how you can gain this Certification, how much it cost, how long it takes to become certified, the difficulty level of this Certification, the types of certifications available for QuickBooks; all will be discussed in this chapter. In this chapter, we will discuss:

- The type of investment required for Certification.

- Different courses available

- Information about QuickBooks Certification.

- The course fees.

- The duration of the course

5.1. The Type of Investment Required for Certification

Getting a certification is a big investment. Not only are you investing your money, but you also invest your time and money in such courses as well. In present times, the world is ever-changing and keeping up with the fast-moving times has become mandatory. Otherwise, you will be left behind. Similarly, if you are a bookkeeper,you must upgrade your skillset. You might be employed right now, but what if the employer changes technology and you are no more required to work for him/her, and they hire a person with better qualifications. For such times it is important to be well prepared and keep up with times. Your aim should be to become an asset to the company rather than a liability.

5.2. The Different Courses Offered

There are three types of courses offered for QuickBooks Certification. Two of them are for the QuickBooks Desktop, and one is for QuickBooks online. Nowadays, most people prefer a cloud-based financial management system, so it would be wise to take the Certification for the online version. The different types of certifications offered are:

- QuickBooks Online Edition: Basic

- QuickBooks Desktop Edition: Basic

- QuickBooks Desktop Edition: Advanced

5.3. Information About QuickBooks Certification

If you are working as an employee, getting a QuickBooks certificate will reassure your employer of your abilities with the software and convince them that you are an asset to their company. Certification will enhance your credibility. This will equip you with the expertise to deal with any situation that involves QuickBooks. You will be in a better position as a QuickBooks certified employee to tackle tricky situations involving QuickBooks.

When you pass the exam, you will gain the following skills, and your certificate will be proof of your abilities:

- Easily use the main measures of QuickBooks and manage business accounts on the software.

- You can manage all the accounting functions like Payroll, transactions, invoices, and sales smoothly with QuickBooks software.

- Can solve and manage complex scenarios that come up while using QuickBooks.

One thing you should keep in mind, the certifications are not cheap, they cost high prices. But you should consider investing in this Certification as a step towards your better career. You will get profits from this investment very soon.

5.4. Why Should You Invest

It is a known fact that QuickBooks Certifications do not come cheap. If you are an employer, you might feel that this is a lot of investment, and the courses are time-consuming. If you have many employees, the cost might be an issue for sure. If you are a freelance bookkeeper, the fee might be a big investment. But consider this a useful investment. This is one of the investments you should make. Some business owners consider it an initial investment, and the profits and dividends are gained when the work is done more efficiently and faster.

A lot of groups are offering QuickBooks certification courses. If you are an employer, you can look for bundle package discounts and monthly packages. If you are a freelance service provider, you should look for packages that offer monthly installments as one-time payments are sometimes difficult to pay at once.

You should always look for online courses. Nowadays,many online courses are available, and you can take them from the comfort of your home or office. This can save you the commute expenses and the time which is wasted with the commute. Always look for certifications with live tutoring. These sessions are more interactive, there are live questions and answers sessions, and you learn more this way.

You should be convinced not to take up a QuickBooks certification. If you are still not convinced, maybe this is not for you. But if you want to further your career in bookkeeping, this Certification is essential.

5.5. The Certification Fee

Most bookkeepers follow the method that they do their training from a tutor and then take the certification exam. Two groups conduct the Certification:

- Intuit, through their ProAdvisor Program

- NBA (National Bookkeepers Association)

Intuit is the maker of QuickBooks, and they conduct the test for free. However, they cover their cost by making you purchase the mandatory membership, which is hundreds of dollars. You will have to become a member to get access to the test.

NBA conducts the other Certification. This is a much affordable option. If you decide to take the test through them, the fee is $150 for the ones who are taking the test for the first time. This fee includes a practice test and the actual test. At successful completion, you get a certificate. The certification must be updated every year. The fee for each subsequent year is around $75.

5.6. The Length of Courses

There is no specific length for courses. The courses and workshops are carried out by professionals who specialize in QuickBooks software. The Certification is only a 2-to-4-hour program. If you are already familiar with the software, you might just book your test and pass. But for someone, the learning might take from weeks to months. All this depends upon few factors:

- Do you have basic knowledge about the software?

In this case, if you have basic knowledge and take the test straight away, the chances are that you might not be able to gain Certification. It would be best if you had more than basic knowledge to pass the Certification. You should not take these exams lightly. Since these exams are expensive, you should prepare your best before taking the exam to get greater chances of passing.

- The Certification you might wish to do.

So, there are different certifications offered. In the Desktop version certifications, there is a basic certificate and an advanced certificate. As the name indicates, the advanced certification will be harder and thus require more expertise.

- When you decide to take the test

You must be responsible when you decide the date to take the test. Do not take the test before you are fully prepared. If you decide the test date before proper preparation, the chances are that you might not be able to pass.

Mostly, the tests can be completed in one sitting. The level of the exams is according to the Certification you wish to do. It is recommended to get the basic Certification before you try to obtain an advanced certification.

Chapter 6. Hacks and Tricks for QuickBooks

With every software, you should know about the tricks and tips to make your work more efficient and streamlined. The same is the case with QuickBooks. You can use the experience of others to better your work. You must have heard the term; time is money, and these tips and tricks save your time. And by saving time, they save your money. In present times we are blessed with technology, and we should try to benefit from t as much as possible. The lives we lead in present times are quite stressful, and the work-life balance is frankly off-balance. In such a situation, it is wise to take as much help as possible. That help can be from technology, or you can even benefit from others' experiences and mistakes. Here we will discuss some hacks and tricks the professionals from the field have agreed upon and shared with everyone to benefit from. Here is a list of a few tricks and hacks to make your work quicker and easier.

The trend of 2021 is focused more on cloud-based QuickBooks software. In this chapter, we will discuss the tips and tricks we can apply in QuickBooks Online to gain better results. We have compiled a list of six hacks that you might find helpful:

- Cash receipts should be created.

- Use attachments.

- Use keyboard shortcuts.

- Automate the emails.

- Use QuickBooks Online to track the time.

- Always use the bank rules

6.1. Cash Receipts Should be Created.

It is always a good idea to organize your working space. The same is the case with finances. If you have your cash receipts created and recorded, you will easily overview all money received at any time. With QuickBooks Online, you can enter the details in the sales center and review the records anytime you want. This is a feature of QuickBooks online, which is easy to use and convenient for financial tracking.

- Usage

How you will create cash receipts is simple, go to the sales transactions and create a file med cash receipts. Next, go to the filter list and go to 'Money Received' and enter the date appropriately.

(Cash Receipt Usage)

6.2. Use Attachments

This is a hack that is overlooked a lot of the time, and most people ignore using it. The hack is to attach all related forms and documents to the vendor accounts to be managed at once. For example, you can attach a W-9 to the vendor's account.

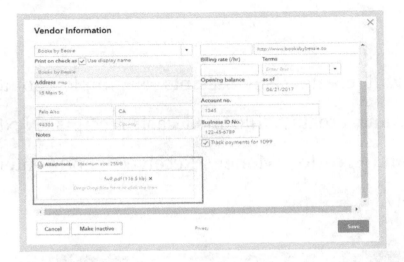

(Using Attachments)

So, when you use attachments, you can also attach the bank accounts' files and the credit card details and statements. When all the documents are attached and compiled in one place, they will be easy to review. Another pro tip will be to use naming conventions. This will make the work more streamlined and easier to track. According to experts, not using attachments wastes time you could be spending on other activities. There is no need to work so hard if you have applications in your software that make your work easier and smoother to operate. If you are using a mobile version of QuickBooks online, you can even take a screenshot of any receipt and attach it to the folder. In the same way, you can even attach the invoices and enter the yearly or monthly estimates. If you have the add-on of QuickBooks Payments, you can even receive payments.

6.3. Use Keyboard Shortcuts

This is also a huge time saver. When you are working on multiple things, clicking from one program to another makes everything confusing. The same is the case with QuickBooks. When you are managing multiple entities, you need to work fast, and shortcuts are a lifesaver. Following is a summary of all the important shortcuts found within QuickBooks.

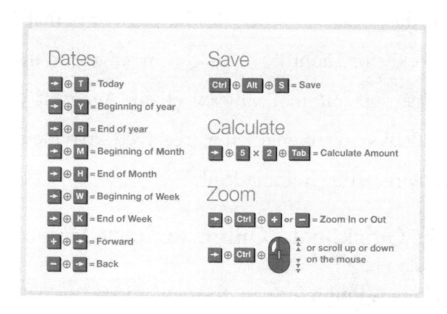

(QuickBooks shortcuts)

6.4. Automate the emails.

For all the regular payments and receiving, automation is the way to go. You should automate your emails for sales, financial statements, and invoices. You must be thinking about how to go about this? It is easy; you will first set different reports scheduled to email on a specific date. For example, you can set a schedule that emails you your financial statement monthly. You can even get an email for the collection report, and the sales report every week. This will help you keep track of the open invoices.

Apart from this, you can schedule the payments that have to be sent out weekly or monthly. You can arrange for the recurring invoices to be sent automatically by email. Again, if you use the app QuickBooks payments, the received payments can be automatically recorded automatically.

6.5. Use the QuickBooks Online to Track Time

If time tracking is tough for you, the newer versions of QuickBooks Online will help you. In the older versions of the program, you had to import the T reports to QuickBooks. In the newer versions, you can create the T sheets within QuickBooks online. These are the integrated T sheets. This means that any change, addition, or deletion would apply automatically to the T sheet, and it will be updated by itself. You will not have to manually update the information. This process is carried out in a seamless manner. You can create several employee T sheets and even approve several T sheets simultaneously.

6.6. Always use the Bank Rules

This is a simple and logical hack. The bank rules are already made, and time tested. If you implement them and set your regular payments to the utilities, vendors, suppliers, etc., on bank rules, the task will become easier. This can save a lot of time for you as well. At the end of the month, all you will need to do is an overview of all the payments carried out in a smooth and streamlined fashion.

These hacks and tips may seem simple but implementing them can save you hours and hours' worth of labor. There will be far fewer things on your mind. It is a one-time setup, and it will be automated from then on. You will easily manage the payments, receiving, employee timesheets, Payroll, and everything else with ease, and you will become less stressed.

Chapter 7. QuickBooks Usage in Small Businesses

Many small businesses use QuickBooks to manage their finances. The software takes care of their bill payments, monitors their cash flow, and manages invoices. QuickBooks is a good software to generated automated monthly financial reports as well as yearly financial reports. Some business owners manage their accounts themselves and are pro users of the software, but most business owners employ professionals to manage their accounts. QuickBooks certified bookkeepers are employed by small to mid-size business owners to manage their accounts.

Small business owners use QuickBooks for several functions and use. Following are the functions for which the small business owners use QuickBooks:

- Make and track invoices.

- Monitor expenses and other bills.

- Generate business and financial statements.

- Manage payroll.

- Do the inventory.

- Simplify taxes.

- Online payments.

- Record Receipts.

- Manage mileage.

7.1. Make and Track Invoices

The software has the option to create invoices, and you can easily print them or directly send them to your customers. Each invoice generated by the software will be automatically recorded in the system. In this way, you can track all the amount that has already been paid, and the receivables will also be displayed.

7.2. Monitor Expenses and Other Bills

You have an option to link the QuickBooks software to your accounts and credit cards. This will enable the program to record all payments and bills automatically and keep a record. It will be available for your view whenever you require.

You can enter other bills you receive in the system and take care of the payables. This will help you keep track of your expenses and payables. The software will make sure you do not miss your payments. If you attach the QuickBooks payment app, the payments can even be managed automatically.

7.3. Generate Business Financial Statements

The software can generate financial statements that will give you an overview of your business performance. The kind of statements you can generate with the QuickBooks software are:

- Cashflow Statement

- Profit and Loss Statement

- Balance Sheets

7.4. Manage Payroll

The software can manage the Payroll and working hours of each employee automatically. You must create a separate account for each employee, enter each employee's information, and schedule the salary, deductions, schedules, and hours. All can be managed automatically by the software. If you use the software, you can easily manage:

- Payment to the employees can be made by checks or cash.

- The taxes can be deducted automatically, and the tax-exempt employee payments are also managed.

- The software fills tax forms automatically

- The payroll taxes can be managed automatically.

7.5. Do the Inventory.

The software manages the inventory. It records the quantities and keeps track of the total cost of inventory. The software will indicate when the inventory is getting low, and there is a need to replenish. This all is not done automatically, you will have to enter the amounts manually, but they will be managed and calculated automatically.

7.6. Simplify Taxes

Taxes is one of the most difficult parts of the business. Most people are fearful of taxes, and in the end, their taxes are piled up. QuickBooks takes care of your taxes. The Tax becomes difficult because your financial statements are not in order. QuickBooks makes the financial statements simplified, and you can easily print them out and let a tax preparer assess the statements and use the required information.

7.7. Online Payments

The QuickBooks Payments app enables you to accept payments directly from your customers. This app is integrated into the software, so all the payments are recorded in the system automatically.

7.8. Record Receipts

The QuickBooks app makes it possible for the business owner to upload all the payment and expense receipts to the software, and they can be easily scanned and recorded in the system.

7.9. Manage Mileage

If you use your vehicle for business purposes, a tax deduction is applied. But to receive the tax deduction, you will have to prove your traveling. You get a deduction of 57.5 cents per mile. To record the miles, you can link QuickBooks Online to your vehicle's GPS, and it will easily record your miles, date, and time

Conclusion

If you have read the whole book, many of your doubts must have been cleared regarding bookkeeping and QuickBooks. This is an amazing opportunity for you to avail yourself if you want to take up bookkeeping as a profession. It is always a better idea to keep up with the current trends and technology because it ensures better job and working opportunities. Therefore, we have mentioned QuickBooks. Being a QuickBooks certified bookkeeper gives you an edge in business. This is because most small to mid-size businesses have installed the QuickBooks software for their financial management. There are different versions of QuickBooks available:

- QuickBooks Self-Employed

- QuickBooks Online

- QuickBooks Desktop

- QuickBooks Apps

QuickBooks is user-friendly and is compatible with other programs like MS Word and MS excel. Different versions are available that are compatible with iOS, android, windows, and Mac operating systems.

It will be a good idea to specialize in cloud-based QuickBooks software because, as of 2014, more and more business owners are interested in keeping their records on the cloud-based package offered by QuickBooks. If you are planning to get your Certification any time soon, the cloud-based product should be your focus. There is a basic course offered in QuickBooks Online; you should consider that.

Another consideration when thinking about QuickBooks bookkeeping seriously is what type of Bookkeeper you are going to be. According to a survey, these five types of part-time QuickBooks bookkeepers are making the highest number of average incomes:

- CPA Firm Bookkeeper

- QuickBooks Remote Bookkeeper

- Telecommute Bookkeeper

- At home Bookkeeper

- QuickBooks Consultant

The next most important point to think about is your location. At different locations in America, bookkeepers make different yearly incomes. The QuickBooks bookkeepers make the highest yearly earnings in San Francisco, California. But before quickly packing your bags towards the sunny state, keep in mind the expenses as well. Before shifting your location, always consider the basic expenses and how you will be managing them. It may be possible that you are earning less in one city, but the cost of living is cheaper, and in another city, you might be making more money, but the expenses are equally higher. In the latter case, you end up losing more money. So, always take a well-thought-out and informed decision.

In all, if you are someone good with numbers and have a consistent work ethic, you can very manage to be a QuickBooks bookkeeper. You can even work as a freelance service provider. Providing services is also generally a risk-free approach. The only investment you make is the training you do and the courses you take. After that, all is gain. In this way, you can set your schedule and take up as much work as you can manage. In present times where the future has become unpredictable, freelancing is the way to go.